DISCA

BUCKNELL REVIEW

Reconfiguring the Renaissance: Essays in Critical Materialism

STATEMENT OF POLICY

BUCKNELL REVIEW is a scholarly interdisciplinary journal. Each issue is devoted to a major theme or movement in the humanities or sciences, or to two or three closely related topics. The editors invite heterodox, orthodox, and speculative ideas and welcome manuscripts from any enterprising scholar in the humanities and sciences.

This journal is a member of the Conference of Editors of Learned Journals

BUCKNELL REVIEW
A Scholarly Journal of Letters, Arts, and Sciences

Editor
PAULINE FLETCHER

Associate Editor
DOROTHY L. BAUMWOLL

Assistant Editor
STEVEN W. STYERS

Editorial Board
PATRICK BRADY
WILLIAM E. CAIN
JAMES M. HEATH
STEVEN MAILLOUX
JOHN WHEATCROFT

Contributors should send manuscripts with a self-addressed stamped envelope to the Editor, Bucknell University, Lewisburg, Pennsylvania, 17837.

BUCKNELL REVIEW

Reconfiguring the Renaissance: Essays in Critical Materialism

Edited by
JONATHAN CREWE

LEWISBURG
BUCKNELL UNIVERSITY PRESS
LONDON AND TORONTO: ASSOCIATED UNIVERSITY PRESSES

© 1992 by Associated University Presses, Inc.

Associated University Presses
440 Forsgate Drive
Cranbury, NJ 08512

Associated University Presses
25 Sicilian Avenue
London WC1A 2QH, England

Associated University Presses
P.O. Box 39, Clarkson Pstl. Stn.
Mississauga, Ontario,
L5J 3X9 Canada

The paper used in this publication meets the
requirements of the American National Standard for
Permanence of Paper for Printed Library Materials Z39.48-1984.

(Volume XXXV, Number 2)

ISBN 0-8387-5223-3
Library of Congress Catalog Card Number 91-55211

PRINTED IN THE UNITED STATES OF AMERICA

Contents

Notes on Contributors

Introduction	JONATHAN CREWE	9
Psychoanalysis and the Subject in/of/for the Renaissance	ELIZABETH J. BELLAMY	19
Resisting the Marketplace: The Language of Labor in Benvenuto Cellini's *Vita*	JANE TYLUS	34
Elizabethan Music as a Cultural Mode	T. G. BISHOP	51
The Commodity of Names: "Falstaff" and "Oldcastle" in *1 Henry IV*	JONATHAN GOLDBERG	76
Spenser's Saluage Petrarchanism: *Pensées Sauvages* in *The Faerie Queene*	JONATHAN CREWE	89
Making History Straight: Collecting and Recording in Sixteenth-Century Italy	STEPHANIE JED	104
Translating Montaigne's Crypts: Melancholic Relations and the Sites of Altarbiography	TIMOTHY MURRAY	121
Saints and Lovers: Mary Magdalene and the Ovidian Evangel	DEBORA KULLER SHUGER	150

Recent Issues of BUCKNELL RIVIEW

The Arts, Society, Literature
Text, Interpretation, Theory
Perspective: Art, Literature, Participation
Self, Sign, and Symbol
Criticism, History, and Intertextuality
New Interpretations of American Literature
The Senses of Stanley Cavell
John Cage at Seventy-Five
Comedias del Siglo de Oro and Shakespeare
Mappings of the Biblical Terrain: The Bible as Text
The Philosophy of John William Miller
Culture and Education in Victorian England
Classics and Cinema

Notes on Contributors

ELIZABETH J. BELLAMY is associate professor of Renaissance and Critical Theory at the University of Alabama, Birmingham. She has published in *South Atlantic Quarterly, Journal of English Literary History, Comparative Literature Studies,* and *Renaissance Papers* and is completing a book on psychoanalysis and epic history.

T. G. BISHOP is assistant professor of English at Case Western Reserve University, where he teaches Renaissance literature. He has published work on Commonwealth literature and is at present writing about Shakespeare.

JONATHAN CREWE currently teaches Renaissance literature and critical theory at Dartmouth College. In addition to numerous essays, his publications include *Unredeemed Rhetoric: Thomas Nashe and the Scandal of Authorship, Hidden Designs: The Critical Profession and Renaissance Literature,* and *Trials of Authorship: Anterior Forms and Poetic Reconstruction from Wyatt to Shakespeare.*

JONATHAN GOLDBERG is the Sir William Osler Professor of English literature at The Johns Hopkins University. His most recent publications include *Writing Matter: From the Hands of the English Renaissance* and an edition of Milton co-edited with Stephen Orgel.

STEPHANIE JED teaches Italian and comparative literature at the University of California, San Diego. Her publications include *Chaste Thinking: The Rape of Lucretia and the Birth of Humanism* (1989). She is currently interested in issues of literacy, gender, and interethnic contact in the sixteenth-century "Old" and "New" Worlds.

TIMOTHY MURRAY is associate professor of English at Cornell University. He is the author of *Theatrical Legitimation: Allegories of Genius in Seventeenth-Century England and France, Subliminal Libraries: Writing the Death Drive of Vision,* and the editor of *Poststructural Performance: The Stakes of Theatre in Contemporary French Thought.* He was the editor of *Theatre Journal* from 1984 to 1987.

DEBORA KULLER SHUGER is associate professor of English at the University of California, Los Angeles. Her recent work includes *Sacred Rhetoric: The Christian Grand Style in the English Renaissance* and *Habits of Thought in the English Renaissance: Religion, Politics, and the Dominant Culture.*

JANE TYLUS is assistant professor of comparative literature at the University of Wisconsin, Madison. She has recently completed a manuscript entitled *Writing and Vulnerability in the Late Renaissance* and is presently studying seventeenth-century treatments of the rape of the Sabine women.

Introduction

BOTH the title of this volume and the selection of essays in it derive in part from an NEH-sponsored symposium, held at the University of Tulsa in 1990, under the title "Reconfiguring the Renaissance: Leading Approaches and New Directions." This rubric was chosen for two reasons. First, simply to allow new work to be presented and discussed. Nothing more was necessarily being aimed for than the creation of an opportunity for professional exchange. The second reason was, however, to raise the *question* of "leading approaches and new directions" in Renaissance studies. What could now (or still) be identified as leading approaches? To what extent could leading recognized approaches now (or still) count as new directions? Could new historicism or cultural materialism, for example, still be regarded as innovative? Could new directions meaningfully be represented by emergent neoconservative critiques primarily opposed to, or openly reacting against, the politically emancipatory or progressive agendas of, for example, deconstruction, feminism, gay studies, and postcolonial studies? Then again, would an unheralded new direction take everyone by surprise and lead to a realignment of critical positions? In short, the rubric of the symposium was intended to prompt reflection on the current state of affairs in a field in which for well over a decade the production of trend-setting criticism had been taken almost for granted.

Although this introduction is written in the questioning spirit of the symposium, it isn't intended as a summary of the proceedings, nor does it try to answer all the questions listed above. Nor, in fact, does it imply that what transpired at the symposium broadly represents the current state of Renaissance scholarship and criticism. While nothing was ruled out in advance, the interests represented turned out mainly to be those of an emergent "second generation" of theoretically informed and politically conscious Renaissance interpreters, this being the group to which the advertised topics of the symposium had primarily appealed. Yet even the interests of this "second generation" are not fully represented in this volume, since some of the symposium papers—on gay studies topics, for example, and on the careers of English Renaissance women—were not available for inclusion.

Subject to these disclaimers, the subtitle "Essays in Critical Materialism" identifies an interpretive practice discernible at the symposium and, as I will suggest, in this volume, that I hesitate to bring under the leading approaches/new directions rubric. It is a practice with reference to which that rubric might be misplaced, since it is not, and never has been, a practice wholly subject to the shifts of modern professional criticism. The term "critical materialism" is meant to identify a fairly diverse, widespread attempt to read (resourcefully continue reading) Renaissance texts in recognizably materialist ways, but without any fixed, prior assumption about the obligatory terms or necessary outcome of such reading. In other words, a manifest interest in the category or discourse(s) of materiality is enough to bring any essay in the volume under the proposed description; perhaps the majority of the essays uncontentiously *do* fit that description.

It is in this broad and somewhat eclectic sense, then, that the subtitle "essays in critical materialism" is to be understood. Yet the subtitle does intentionally recall the "cultural materialism" practiced in recent Renaissance interpretation.[1] This cultural materialism, informed by the work of Louis Althusser and Antonio Gramsci (Raymond Williams and E. P. Thompson requiring more than just honorable mention as well), undertakes to account for cultural phenomena—including literary texts—in historicomaterialist terms rather than universalizing humanistic ones.[2] To put it another way, *culture* rather than just political society or the state emerges as the primary object of an elucidatory critique. The work of anthropologists and cultural historians is accordingly subsumed in this critique. Subversive or anticanonical reading strategies are pursued with the double purpose of undoing ideology and promoting more authentic cultural interpretation, from both of which the possibility of cultural reconstruction may arise. Identifying something like a malign conjunction between modern ideology and Renaissance false consciousness, cultural materialism attempts to recover the material element *in* the discourse of the Renaissance while producing a contemporary discourse *of* the Renaissance in which the ideological structures of "universal" humanism are undone. The term *critical* materialism is intended, however, to mark at least a shade of difference in the work published here. Trying to avoid the impasses of the cultural materialist critique of ideology and/or hegemony, as well as the recurrent problem of containment and subversion in that critique, these essays (perhaps rightly so called) undertake explorations at once tentative and preoccupied with the logic of materialist interpretation. A strong interest in political and other economies, hence in further revisionary application of a "classical" Marxist paradigm, is also evident.

Unfortunately, the last statement needs to be elaborated at once. It could be understood to mean that another phase of *marxisant* interpretation is in the offing, or merely that "neo-Marxism" unaccountably persists in the literary academy. Taken either way, the statement is almost bound to provoke questions of the kind recently asked of me by a high-ranking academic philosopher: "Why is it only in literature departments that [a now totally discredited] Marxism survives? Haven't they noticed what has been going on in the world lately?"

These rhetorical questions do of course echo widely dispersed public assertions that Marxism has ended up on "the rubbish heap of history" where it belongs. Further, that with the "winning" of the Cold War—i.e., at the now-transpired end of history or of ideology—Adam Smith has triumphed over Marx, his longtime rival. Implicitly, the real is now to be identified solely with, or as, the competitive operation of the so-called free market—in which operation, however, strife arising from competitive "unfairness" is not unforeseen, any more than is racist, nationalist, and other vicious reencoding of the competitive struggle.

Under these perhaps too readily welcomed circumstances, any critical discourse that features Marx will predictably be stigmatized by some as an obsolete "neo-Marxism of the literary academy." It can then peremptorily be called on to justify its anachronistic existence. This can't be a matter of political indifference to anyone interested in the further development of materialist critiques, or in the future of a materialist pedagogy, yet it is also not a matter that necessarily engages intellectually rigorous attention.[3]

Critical materialism as I am trying to define it remains strongly conscious of, and committed to, its own intellectual antecedents. These antecedents are by no means exclusively Marxist but include philosophical discourses of the material (of materiality) enunciated at least since the Renaissance. Indeed, the importance of such Renaissance figures as Leonardo, Montaigne, and Bacon in the historical Western effort to "think the material" is part of what keeps the Renaissance field open to subsequent efforts along the same lines.[4] Furthermore, insofar as our conception of the Renaissance remains Burckhardtian, it is irreducibly the conception of an epoch in Western material culture, and not in the first instance of what has been called "the historical Renaissance."[5]

By this I mean that Burckhardt's material reconstruction of what he calls the *civilization* of the Renaissance in Italy invokes a category larger than that of the chronological period of the Italian Renaissance.

Not just historical antecedents but recent rigorous attempts to "think the material" further inform the critical materialism to which I refer. The materiality of language, of writing and textuality, and of the body are among the now-familiar topics of this exceptionally productive, gender-inflected, undertaking.[6] It goes almost without saying that this "material" discourse presupposes the achievements of poststructuralism, especially insofar as they have contributed to the undoing of materialistic positivisms. Furthermore, poststructuralist critiques of oppositional and categorical thinking, which is also to say of dialectical thinking in a somewhat mechanical sense, leave no one the possibility of treating "the ideal" and "the material" as secure containers with a self-declaring content (or lack of content). Particularly important in this context is Derrida's specific upping of stakes for the thinking of the material while forestalling any naive oppositional or positivistic understanding of what such thinking would be like. For the Derrida of *Grammatology* above all, "the material" is tantamount to the still virtually unthought in/of Western philosophy, as well as being the horizon toward which any discourse of the material must remain oriented. Any critical materialism worthy of the name will have internalized this fastidious claim, at least as a caveat, and will thus aim to be a *self*-critical materialism as much as anything else.[7]

It is partly within these broader contexts that Marx continues to be read at present. Attempts by commentators as diverse as Richard Rorty and Michel Foucault to restrict Marx's legitimate impact or modeling capacity to a particular moment in the nineteenth century may be understandable, given their respective undertakings, and may legitimately repudiate long-standing tendencies in Marxism to dehistoricize Marx.[8] Yet from the standpoint of critical materialism these efforts at containment are virtually irrelevant. It is models rather than transhistorical explanations that are being sought in critical materialism.

What counts in critical materialism, apart from the dazzling economic heuristics of *Grundrisse,* is Marx's exemplary "critique of political economy" (identified as such in the regularly ignored subtitle of *Capital*). Of course, the debatable particulars of this critique matter, as does the context of its historical appearance, yet it also matters that Marx establishes both the terms and the potential, unrestricted in advance, of such a critique. What can be made of those terms, and what that potential encompasses, continues to be investigated in what I am calling critical materialism. So do basic yet still-baffling questions regarding production, consumption, work, money, value, exchange, and equivalence. Or rather, economies in and of *representation,* with reference to which all these questions arise, are the principal focus of critical materialism. The notion of an economy prior to representation, or not subject to it, is largely moot from the critical-materialist standpoint I am invoking, while the term "critical" here insists that textual interpretation cannot be circumvented by any appeal to supposedly unmediated economic or other data. (If this critical-materialist interpretation is a phenomenon "of the literary academy," that is partly because of the exegetical obligation to be discharged there, but not necessarily elsewhere.) The degree of interest displayed at the symposium in Jean-Joseph Goux's *Symbolic Economies,* recently published in English translation, gave evidence of a continuing interest in questions that would be almost unaskable without reference to Marx. Since this text embodies work going back at least two decades, interest in it is hardly a matter of trend spotting but rather an indication of sustained and sustainable commitment.[9]

If interest in Goux's text implies a certain renewed consciousness of Marxist fundamentals, it does not exclusively imply that, any more than it means that a fundamentalist Marxism (or deterministic economism) has been waiting for the demise of "old," discredited Marxisms in the political world before being reborn. It is an interest strongly conditioned by the ways in which the term "economy" has been used in various poststructuralist contexts, above all psychoanalytic ones, and in the work of Jean Baudrillard.[10] If the paradox is allowable, the critical materialist interest in Marxist fundamentals is philosophically antifoundationalist; it does not, in other words, entail any return to the economic as absolute "ground."

This point can briefly be elaborated with reference to Goux's work. While the conceptualization of an "economy" effected by Marx is important to this work, the economic is not thereby given the status of the real ("base") in relation to which psychic or representational orders can be only figurative or derivative ("superstructural"). For Goux, the economy that is the object of Marx's critique is symbolic all the way through, it being definitively a system (in which money functions as the "universal equivalent") of symbolic rather than "real" exchange. Nothing produced or exchanged in that system has (use) value pure and simple; nothing in it belongs simply to the order of the real. (Which helps, of course, to explain efforts to resist or refuse exchange in that economy, or to posit an "original" use value.) For Goux, this economy serves as a strong interpretive model for other, putatively homologous, symbolic economies—not secondary *orders*—of psychic or cultural life. Conversely, recognition of those symbolic economies facilitates an antifoundationalist reading of Marx.

The apparent congeniality of Goux's work to symposium participants is part of what leads me to suggest that "critical materialism" may be a term capable of describing a shared, still-developing, critical practice. Even this tentative identification may, however, promise a greater degree of programmatic consistency in this volume than will appear, since the methodological debts of certain essays to psychoanalysis or deconstruction, for example, may seem to outweigh any strictly "materialist" ones. What I think *can* safely be said is that all the essays in the volume reveal the extent to which "material" considerations now pervade Renaissance interpretation. (The essay by Debora Shuger might be taken to suggest that this permeation is now the *enabling* precondition for interpretation even of the religious aspect of Renaissance culture.) This permeation, and what it allows in the way of a steadily expanding interpretive practice, relatively independent of shifting polemics in the profession, is not necessarily made apparent by the leading approaches/new directions formula.

The sequence of the essays that follow isn't wholly random. Roughly speaking, the essays that appear early in the volume are the ones that most programmatically review (sometimes in the "second generation" terms to which I referred) existing critical options in the Renaissance field. Fairly brief and sharply focused, these essays might well be presented under the title "positions." The essays later in the volume tend to be the more broadly speculative or exploratory ones. This distinction is, however, only a modest working one.

In the first essay, Elizabeth Bellamy rereads the story of Martin Guerre that Stephen Greenblatt made into a central parable of Renaissance "selfhood." Objecting to Greenblatt's delegitimation of psychoanalysis and hence of the discourse of the unconscious in broad historicocultural interpretation, Bellamy argues that a historicocultural "unconscious," comprising the affective residue of archaic modes of production, is strongly operative in the story of Martin Guerre. For Bellamy, the subject of *history* is neurotic, not merely the Viennese bourgeois subject regarded as being so by those who seek, like Greenblatt, to limit Freud's applicability.

In a discussion of Benvenuto Cellini's *Vita*, Jane Tylus raises questions about Renaissance productive mode and ideology akin to the ones raised by Bellamy. She argues that the rhetorical work being done in Cellini's *Vita* is primarily that of resistance to the psychic and material economy of the marketplace. Insofar as scholars have typically regarded Renaissance artists as abetting rather than resisting the apparent early modern transition to a market economy, Cellini brings this interpretive stereotype into question.

T. G. Bishop's "Elizabethan Music as a Cultural Mode" attempts to bring music into the sphere of new historicist and/or cultural materialist interpretation from which it has hitherto been almost totally banished. Taking William Byrd's music as a case in point, Bishop argues on one hand for the intelligibility of Elizabethan music in those interpretive terms, while on the other he identifies serious limitations in the interpretive practice that has made music "inaudible." Refunctioning a musical term as a critical one, he argues for a modal approach to cultural interpretation in which "diverse fields of synchronic activity," and complex relations between them, can gain proper recognition.

Jonathan Goldberg's primarily deconstructive discussion of the editing of *Henry IV, Part 1*, in the new Oxford Shakespeare cannot readily be billed as an essay in critical materialism. Since, however, the questions raised in his essay are related to the ones raised in *Writing Matter: From the Hand of the English Renaissance* (Stanford, 1990), its inclusion in this volume isn't particularly anomalous. In this essay, Goldberg questions the determining power given, implicitly under the aegis of first-generation new historicism, to (reified) historical context in Renaissance interpretation. Taking up Gary Taylor's much-publicized substitution of "Oldcastle" for "Falstaff," Goldberg contests Taylor's recourse to immediate historical *reference* as a principle of editorial adjudication.[11] Such recourse determines that, where alternatives exist, the preferred reading will be the one that evidently identifies or refers to historical persons or situations roughly contemporary with the text. Goldberg not only challenges this working assumption, but the belief in definitive historical interpretation it implies.

My own essay on Spenser implicitly poses the question, the terms of which are made available by Derrida, of a general economy of Renaissance Petrachanism. In other words, the essay implicitly asks whether the dissemination of Petrarchanism during the Renaissance should be read as an index of a particular, restricted economy or whether, on the contrary, its dissemination is to be read as one phenomenon of an emergent general economy. The essay concludes by suggesting that Petrarchan dissemination can be correlated with the emergence of a general economy of "excess" consumption, the transition to which it at once represents and helps to effect.

Stephanie Jed's essay plays on various senses of the phrase "making history straight." In her archivally informed study of the political reality being constructed in sixteenth-century Italy, not primarily by major humanists but by state bureaucrats, reporters, and correspondents, Jed argues that this "straightening out" generally entails the establishment of a single imperialistic construction of events in which all forms of threatening alterity are suppressed. It also entails the establishment of a specifically male, heterosexual construction of events in which homosexual motivations and/or instances of female "disruption" are suppressed. These constructions, being produced along the networks of state correspondence and reporting, are ones that will eventually be enshrined as primary "materials" in archives and collections, to be recovered in turn by historical scholars, generally male ones invested in the same constructions. It is this process that Jed subjects to an elucidatory critique.

In an essay that enacts its own transition from the "positional" to the speculative, Timothy Murray proclaims the moral bankruptcy and/or exhaustion of current Renaissance interpretation. He argues that the curiously suspended terminal condition of such "melancholy" interpretation (produced under the sign of death) can be investigated with reference to Montaigne's philosophizing as "learning how to die," but can also be recuperated through feminized application of Nicolas Abraham and Maria Torok's psychoanalytic discourse of incorporation.[12] In effect, he and Bellamy present contrasting views of how psychoanalytic paradigms as material ones can inform our reading both of Renaissance texts and our relationship to the Renaissance as an object of study.

In a learned and challenging essay ranging across a wide variety of texts and historical moments, Debora Shuger traces an exegetical tradition in which the carnality of Magdalene is not so much "redeemed" by Christian spirituality as constitutively subsumed in its symbolic economy. In other words, while challenging many trite antinomies of the carnal and the spiritual, Shuger explores the constitutive presence of women's sexuality and "passion" in at least one historically important strand of Christian representation. At the same time, she spells out in no uncertain terms the implications of her view for current Renaissance interpretation, whether religious, feminist, or new historicist.

My warm thanks and appreciation, finally, to the editors and publishers of *Bucknell Review* for making this collection possible, and in particular to Professor Pauline Fletcher of Bucknell University.

JONATHAN CREWE

Notes

1. For an overview, including express and implied assessment of cultural materialism in Renaissance studies, see Walter Cohen, "Political Criticism of Shakespeare," *Shakespeare Reproduced: The Text in History and Ideology*, ed. Jean Howard and Marion O'Connor (New York: Methuen, 1987), 18–36.

2. Extensive crisscrossing between the categories of culture, history, and politics has contributed to the somewhat eclectic character of recent Renaissance interpretation. So has crisscrossing between the putatively separate discourses of cultural materialism and new historicism. From the standpoint of this volume, so much the better.

3. It is fair to mention that Richard Rorty's liberal pragmatism has facilitated a material discourse in which the free market becomes the ground rather than the object of a cultural critique. It appears to me, however, that this critique has so far had little impact on Renaissance studies; whether it can do so, given the preliberal era under consideration in Renaissance studies, remains to be seen.

4. This hardly needs announcing as a mere fact; the point is that genuinely interesting "subsequent efforts" continue to be made. Noteworthy ones concerning Leonardo, whose work currently supplies powerful interpretive leverage, include those of Jacqueline Rose, "Sexuality in the Field of Vision," *Sexuality in the Field of Vision* (London: Verso Books, 1986), 225–33; Sander L. Gilman, "The Rediscovery of the Body: Leonardo's First Image of Human Sexuality and Disease," *Disease and Representation: Images of Illness from Madness to AIDS* (Ithaca: Cornell University Press, 1988), 50–62; Elaine Scarry, "Donne: 'But yet the body is his booke,'" *Literature and the Body: Essays on Populations and Persons*. Selected Papers from the English Institute, 1986, New Series, no. 12, ed. Elaine Scarry (Baltimore: Johns Hopkins University Press, 1988), 70–105.

5. I borrow this phrase from *The Historical Renaissance: New Essays on Tudor and Stuart Literature and Culture*, ed. Heather Dubrow and Richard Strier (Chicago: University of Chicago Press, 1988).

6. Two very notable contributions to the material discourse of writing have recently been made by contributors to this volume. These are Jonathan Goldberg, *Writing Matter: From the Hand of the English Renaissance* (Stanford: Stanford University Press, 1990) and Stephanie Jed, *Chaste Thinking: The Rape of Lucretia and the Birth of Humanism* (Bloomington: Indiana University Press, 1989).

7. An effective denial or overlong *deferral* of "material thinking" can be regarded as the unfortunate counterpart to this fastidiousness. Even or especially "vulgar" beginnings during the Renaissance will not be ignored by critical materialists.

8. For example, Richard Rorty, "On Truth, Freedom and Politics," *Critical Inquiry* 16, no. 3 (Spring 1990):634, and Michel Foucault, *The Order of Things: An Archaeology of the Human Sciences* (New York: Vintage Books, 1973), 260–63.

9. Jean-Joseph Goux, *Symbolic Economies: After Marx and Freud*, trans. Jennifer Curtiss Gage (Ithaca: Cornell University Press, 1990).

10. Jean Baudrillard, *For a Political Economy of the Sign*, trans. Charles Levin (New York: Telos Press, 1981).

11. Gary Taylor, commentary on *1 Henry IV* in *William Shakespeare: A Textual Companion*, ed. Stanley Wells et al. (Oxford: Clarendon Press, 1987), 330–31.

12. Nicolas Abraham and Maria Torok, *The Wolf Man's Magic Word: A Cryptonomy*, trans. Nicholas Rand (Minneapolis: University of Minnesota Press, 1986).

Psychoanalysis and the Subject in/of/for the Renaissance

Elizabeth J. Bellamy

University of Alabama, Birmingham

WHEN Freud quotes briefly from Jacob Burckhardt in his essay "The Moses of Michelangelo,"[1] we might use the act as an occasion to ponder the larger question, What would constitute a meaningful convergence of psychoanalysis and the Renaissance? Freud's fascination with the Renaissance is, of course, revealed in his by now virtually canonical discussions of Shakespeare, but before getting to the specifics of my argument, I propose that we turn some very brief attention to some of the specific implications of Freud's use of Burckhardt.[2] Certainly what is most intriguing is its embodiment of a symbolic convergence of two powerful epistemic moments in the history of ideas: the "Renaissance" as the humanist "discovery" of modern individualism, and psychoanalysis as the "discovery" that the individual is always subverted by an unconscious. If Burckhardt's *The Civilization of the Renaissance in Italy* (1860) was instrumental in inaugurating what Kerrigan and Braden have referred to as an "inherited idea of the Renaissance" that has contributed to our understanding of the development of modern consciousness,[3] then Freud was responsible for demonstrating how this self-recognition is always compromised through repression. The point of this observation is not to suggest psychoanalysis as a corrective for the assumptions of Renaissance humanism, but rather to search for some ways in which we can begin to conceive of how these two *epistemes* can mutually enrich one another. The two terms, one a period concept within political, cultural, and intellectual history, and the other a quasi-scientific (and often biologistic) theory of (un)consciousness, are not homologous, but as monumental "epistemic moments" they do share some interesting insights into the "fate" of the psyche.

Both the Renaissance and psychoanalysis are, it goes without saying, much larger than the figures of either Burckhardt or

Freud. Moreover, neither Freud nor Burckhardt problematized their respective models of consciousness by placing them in the perspective of the sociocultural. Neither Burckhardt nor Freud experienced any privileged insight into how their *epistemes* suppressed the truth of their bourgeois origins by divorcing the subject of inquiry from a complex matrix of socioeconomic and class factors—factors that have contributed to generalizations of psychoanalysis as less a "master discourse" than, in the words of V. N. Volosinov, "an abiding and profound expression of certain crucial aspects of European bourgeois reality."[4] The insight of the new historicism, then, takes on signal importance here, particularly its mandate that the Renaissance (and the Renaissance "subject") must be contextualized within the sociocultural. At the same time, however, I would like to argue that psychoanalysis *can* serve as a useful interpretive tool for Renaissance studies, but only if we, ironically, *de*-contextualize it from unfair generalizations that it is (like Burckhardt's humanistic "Renaissance") merely a bourgeois praxis that is of little value in elucidating the role of the subject in history.

Certainly any study of the Renaissance subject either in literature or in history must at least address itself to the successes of the new historicist project. As I mentioned earlier, under the influence of the new historicism, the Renaissance has for some time now been under scrutiny to redefine itself as less a cultural (or period) concept than as a complex and problematized network of sociocultural codes, institutions, and practices. Accordingly, one of the results of the new historicism has been to place the concept of a Renaissance subject under siege. The unity of the Renaissance subject is no longer assumed by new historicism, but is rather dispersed in the overdeterminations of ideological appropriations of the subject. In Louis Montrose's conception, to cite only one influential example, Elizabeth Tudor, the central subject of Spenser's *The Faerie Queene,* was less a historical person than "the whole field of cultural meanings personified in her"—in short, the site of a "collective discourse."[5] For new historicism, then, the "subject" is of significance only insofar as he/she can be perceived as *sub-jected* to—embedded in—a network of cultural configurations and relations of power.

The primary challenge I wish to address is, Where can we situate psychoanalysis, as the formalized study of the ego, in these new historicist repositionings of the subject? Why should and how can psychoanalysis be recuperated as a useful methodological tool in the field of Renaissance studies, where the cry is, "Always historicize!"? The new historicism, though continuing to obscure its own methodology,[6] remains firmly opposed to psychoanalysis as a meaningful contributor to locating the place of the subject in/for/of the Renaissance. As the new historicism attempts to strengthen its hold over reconfiguring the Renaissance (and, in particular, the Renaissance subject), psychoanalysis, implicitly or explicitly, finds itself marginalized. Stephen Greenblatt's essay "Psychoanalysis and Renaissance Culture" is to date the most explicit attempt to expunge psychoanalysis from the narrative of new historicism as *the* emergent critical discipline of the discourse of the Renaissance subject. Greenblatt theorizes psychoanalysis out of Renaissance studies through a focus on, for him, the exemplary Renaissance subjectivity of Martin Guerre as "peripheral"—as "the *product* of relations, material objects, and judgments [in the legal struggle to determine his "real" identity] . . . rather than the *producer* of these relations, objects, and judgments."[7] Greenblatt's argument constitutes the paradigmatic new historicist one whereby psychic experience disappears in the gaps of the subject's dispersal in the discursive formations of ideology.

I would argue that the new historicism, prematurely foreclosing on the unconscious, has allowed itself to be influenced by the recent objections to psychoanalysis that underwrite so much of current critical theory and, in the process, has recapitulated some of the same oversimplifications that plague these objections. Greenblatt's charge that psychoanalysis is "marginal"—and that it "can redeem its belatedness only when it historicizes its own procedures" (221)—can perhaps best be viewed as a micro-level reenactment of some of the current (non)receptions of psychoanalysis within the larger spectrum of post-Marxist culture critique. Here, psychoanalysis (in either its clinical or hermeneutic forms) has for some time now been dismissed as a bourgeois praxis—perhaps, indeed, the last gasp of bourgeois, or even ironically Renaissance (or Burckhardtian) humanism—perpetuating obsolete emphases on the importance of the psychic history of the ego as an "object" of study. The de rigueur charge is that psychoanalysis does not sufficiently problematize the status of the subject—and the frequent conclusion seems to be that, as the conventional notion of an "actual" subject goes, so goes psychoanalytic criticism.

I would like to turn now to a detailed consideration of Greenblatt's essay. A close analysis of this essay is essential for my argument that psychoanalysis can be used to problematize the very sociocultural codes that presumably render it belated. And through my analysis of his essay, it should become apparent that the unconscious must be factored into any discussion of the intersection of the subject and history.

Following a detailed summary of the historical record of the strange case of Martin Guerre, in which Arnaud du Tilh, attempting to "usurp" his look-alike's identity, is sentenced as an imposter in a court of law, Greenblatt focuses on what must be determined as minimally inherent in the declaration of "selfhood." He argues that "what is at stake in this case is not psychic experience at all but rather a communal judgment that must, in extraordinary cases, be clarified and secured by legal authority" (215). The effect of declaring Martin Guerre to, in fact, *be* Martin Guerre is not so much to establish him as a subject complete with his own inalienable psychic history, but is rather a legal determination that has been shaped by a community consensus of what defines, in Greenblatt's words, "a complex system of possessions, kinship bonds, contractual relationships, customary rights, and ethical obligations" (216). The "selfhood" of the subject is constituted not within psychic experience, but within a matrix of sociocultural discourses, institutions, and practices, underwritten and validated by legal authority. "The move," continues Greenblatt, "is not from distinct physical traits to the complex life experience generated within, but outward to the community's determination that this particular body possesses by right a particular identity" (216). On this basis, then, Greenblatt concludes that psychoanalysis is belated—that it is "from this perspective, less the privileged explanatory key than the distant and distorted consequence of this cultural nexus" (216). Selfhood is not, as psychoanalysis would have it, "the very form of the human condition" (216), but a belated act of self-fashioning made possible only after cultural and legal authority has defined the concept of "self."

Greenblatt envisions psychoanalysis as requiring the stable origin of a self as "a given upon which to construct interpretations" (217)—that psychoanalysis and its desire for mastery are disabled when the subject is perceived as crisscrossed within a field of sociocultural codes and logics. But Greenblatt's argumentative move seems dependent on a peremptory foreclosure of the role of the unconscious in constituting the subject.[8] "The Return of Martin Guerre" might be subtitled, after Lacan, "The Subversion of the Subject and the Dialectic of Desire," because the more far-reaching issue at stake in this bizarre story of a purloined identity may be not the (legal or communal) constitution of the subject, but rather the *subversion* of the subject by the strange transferences that make up what we could term the mimetics of imposture—a subversion occurring long before legal authority intervenes to enunciate the subject. Greenblatt argues that Arnaud du Tilh "can manipulate appearances . . . but he cannot seize the other man's inner life" (216). But a standard Lacanian axiom that can be readily invoked in any story of the uncanny double (whether in history or in literature) is that a subject is not simply a subject for another subject, but rather the subject represents itself as a subject *for the other*—and that other is itself never a subject, but only another signifier. Or, put even more succinctly by Lacan, the signifier represents the subject for another signifier.

Exactly how is it possible that Arnaud du Tilh can step in and *become* (imitate, assume the identity of) Martin Guerre? The question is so basic to the action of the story that its psychic complexities are easy to overlook. An analysis of such a mimetic gesture of imposture is facilitated by a presupposition that the "subject" Martin Guerre exists only as a collection of easily appropriated signifiers for Arnaud (the "signifying subject" as husband, son, nephew, father, heir to property, etc.), who, having earlier insinuated himself into his double's psychohistory, chooses to represent himself *as* Martin for the benefit of the Other (of the wife, Bertrande, of the uncle, Pierre, and even of Jean de Coras, the judge in the case who was actually poised to rule in Arnaud's favor just prior to Martin's unexpected return). One of the more resonant speculations concerning this strange story is the strong possibility that Martin's wife, Bertrande, knows that Arnaud is not her husband. This is by no means to make the absurd claim that Martin no longer exists; but her acceptance of this more tender and loving version of Martin as her surrogate husband enacts Bertrande's own fantasy of the Other and is crucial to sustaining the allegory of Arnaud's representation of himself in his fantasy of being Martin—crucial to sustaining the allegory of signifiers representing the "subject" (Martin/Arnaud) for the Other.

In such a scheme, "Arnaud du Tilh" is a signifier that represents Martin Guerre for another signifying subject—in this case, Bertrande. Arnaud's mimetics of imposture is enabled by a psychic allegory of intersubjective exchange that effaces Martin Guerre, the "subject," at the point at which Arnaud abandons his uninterpellated life on the margins of society in favor of a "Martin Guerre" that is perhaps best conceptualized as a network of signifying positions (husband to Bertrande, nephew to Pierre, prosperous heir of property, etc.)—a network ensuring that the subject is merely an "effect" of the Other to which it seeks to represent itself. It is worthwhile to note here that, according to

Natalie Zemon Davis, it is not known exactly *when* Arnaud began preparing for his usurping role as Martin.[9] Here we are confronted with a case of how the order of the signifier will often elude historical detective work. The ambiguous psychic moment when Arnaud takes on the "desire" of Martin (the Other) as his own desire quite simply escapes historical documentation.

But the perhaps even more significant "other" story of the strange case of Martin Guerre is what happens when legal authority intervenes in this psychic field of signification to determine the integrity of the subject—the determination of what Greenblatt refers to as "a primal, creatural individuation" (214), necessitated by the reappearance of the "other" Martin Guerre.[10] The sliding of the signifiers that make up the subject would seem to come to a halt in the lengthy trial in the court of law at Artigat, where the sentence finally passed by Jean de Coras, as recorded in the register of the Parlement, is that Arnaud is guilty of "imposture and false supposition of name and person and of adultery."[11] But a key question here is, What validates the final authority of a legal speech act when it must intervene in psychic matters? As the judge in the case, Jean de Coras has the power to proclaim identity as a function of, in Greenblatt's words, "customary rights and ethical obligations," but that is not to say that this arbitrary declaration has power or authority over the signifier. To what extent can de Coras's court legislate against the "false suppositions" of the subject representing itself as a subject for the Other? To what extent can it "discipline and punish" the dialectic of desire that constitutes every subject's encounter with the Other in the order of the signifier?

The heart of the dilemma here is that the sociocultural and contractual field that Jean de Coras's court draws from to make a legal determination concerning who is allowed to *be* Martin Guerre (i.e., husband, son, nephew, heir to property) is precisely the psychic field of the Other that Arnaud appropriates for the successful representation of himself as Martin. When the Law becomes implicated in the "arresting" of the psychic Other as the place of the signifier, it begins to lose its metaphysical grounding as the final arbiter of identity. One could say that Arnaud "knows" that his claim to be Martin resides in the unarrested and sliding chain of signifiers that constitutes his "dialectic of desire" to *be* Martin. In short, he seeks no higher authority beyond the Other to ground his act of imposture. But the court at Artigat falls into the paradoxical trap of claiming that it *is* the "Other" for the Other, that it *is* the metaphysical grounding for the signifier. In effect, Jean de Coras validates the subjecthood of Martin Guerre through a matrix of social codes that shifts so freely (that is so psychically interchangeable) that it can also sustain the subjecthood of an uninterpellated man so marginalized that, as the signifier "Arnaud du Tilh," alias "Pansette," a "man of bad life from Sajas,"[12] he can scarcely be mapped by the communally agreed upon patrimonial coordinates of possessions, bonds, rights, and obligations. Or, to put it more simply, Arnaud has so insinuated himself into the psychohistory of Martin that he can without difficulty proclaim a rightful interpellation into the patrimonial codes of obligation that were unsuccessful in binding the latter to his legal identity.

In this context, it is appropriate to consider Lacan's critique of metalanguage from his essay "The Subversion of the Subject" and its implications for Jean de Coras's sentencing of Arnaud.

> Let us set out from the conception of the Other as the locus of the signifier. Any statement of authority has no other guarantee than its very enunciation, and it is pointless for it to seek it in another signifier, which could not appear outside this locus in any way. Which is what I mean when I say that no metalanguage can be spoken, or, more aphoristically, that there is no Other of the Other. And when the Legislator (he who claims to lay down the Law) presents himself to fill the gap, he does so as an imposter.[13]

Lacan's exposure of the metalinguistic impulse as an "imposter" has an uncanny resonance for Arnaud's trial of imposture. Jean de Coras rules against Arnaud, assuming the role of a legal *sujet supposé savoir* by using conventionally agreed upon cultural codes to "arrest" the signifiers of subjecthood. But if de Coras's legal enunciation concerning Martin's right to his own identity is directly dependent on bonds, rights, and obligations that are vulnerable to the psychic allegory of the Other—if de Coras tries to "speak" (metalinguistically) as the (legal) Other of the (psychic) Other—then, to echo Lacan, he can do so only "as an imposter" himself. Jean de Coras, then, attempting to pass legal sentence on Arnaud's imposture, doubles back mimetically as an imposter of the very Other he seeks to delegitimize through legal enunciation. And the consequence is that Martin Guerre must "authorize" his freedom from imposture by a law that is itself an imposter. The authority of the legal utterance is questioned by Samuel Weber, who argues, "How, in general, can authority itself *take place,* if this place, as site of the Signifier, is not one that can ever be simply, or fully 'taken'?"[14] Weber's metaphors of positionality—his characterizations of the struggle for authority to find a place for itself—are crucial here, for they get us to the heart of what's wrong with what amounts to Greenblatt's "placing" of psychoanalysis. Greenblatt's argument is that the legally determined codes of the sociocultural take (prior) place over psychoanalysis (over what Weber might refer to here as "the site of the Signifier"), which comes into being only as a belated effect of the establishing of subjecthood by the law. But it can just as readily be demonstrated that the law, seeking to establish (arbitrary) authority over the insistence of the signifier, must intervene to dis-"place" psychoanalysis from the (always) already occupied site of the signifier.

My point here is not to prioritize psychoanalysis as a discipline that renders the law belated, for such an argument merely puts psychoanalysis back in the undesirable place of striving, as it is often accused of doing, to be a master discourse.[15] But the easy reversibility of the places of psychoanalysis and the law in the story of Martin Guerre should lead us to suspect that the real issue at stake is how we are to interpret the always shifting signifier of psychoanalysis. When we invoke psychoanalysis to refute or support an argument, I would call for a heightened awareness of what we mean by "psychoanalysis." I would argue that the enabling strategy of Greenblatt's argument that psychoanalysis is belated is his marked tendency to interpret psychoanalysis as an orthodox Freudian endeavor—to view it in its almost monolithic incarnation as a kind of ideological state apparatus that can assume clinical operation only after the bourgeois subject has been defined (and, hence, Greenblatt's allusion to Freud's celebrated and virtually canonical Rat Man case to illustrate how psychoanalysis defines selfhood [214]).

Greenblatt's summarizing interpretation of the moral of the return of Martin Guerre as the securing of "proprietary rights to a name and a place in an increasingly mobile social world" (221) is surely well perceived, as is his articulation of the emerging conditions under which the (bourgeois) subject sees itself as "continuous" (and, implicitly, beginning to take shape for the analyst as a future case history that can respond to psychotherapy). But as part of his argumentative move to make psychoanalysis belated, Greenblatt places it solely as a bourgeois praxis, reducing its theoretical resonances and hermeneutic possibilities to, in effect, a disciplinary moment in the history of the bourgeois subject—a history, for Greenblatt, beginning at some point in the Renaissance and, perhaps, culminating somewhere in the bourgeois ills of Freud's clients, "hystericalized," writes Michael Schneider, "by the decline of the Austro-Hungarian monarchy."[16] Even as he (justifiably) calls for psychoanalysis to historicize itself, Greenblatt overhistoricizes psychoanalysis as an *episteme* conceived at a particular (bourgeois, capitalist) point in the history of ideas, thus placing it as a belated effect of sociocultural codes already in place.[17] While continuing our awareness of the clinical will to power of Freudian analysis and its complicities with the Oedipal competitions that have been so instrumental in shaping the suspect ethics of bourgeois capitalism, we must also realize that "psychoanalysis" is as much a shifting signifier as the sociocultural codes that made the "Freudian moment" possible—a signifier that must elude its reduction to merely a bourgeois ideological state apparatus.

Let us, for the moment, broaden the scope of our discussion from Greenblatt in particular to the goals of the new historicism in general for the purposes of determining where we can place psychoanalysis as immanent in ideology critique. In its elucidation of the complex dispersals of the subject within ideology, the new historicism has been careful to avoid making the subject disappear from history entirely—to avoid making compensatory and oversimplifying claims that the subject is merely the collective sum of its sociocultural "parts." Even as it successfully attacks the notion of the unified bourgeois subject, the new historicism (at least the new historicism that is not so inclined to accept a deterministic pervasiveness throughout society of power and domination) has always attempted to address the complexities of the interdependence of subject and structure, and has, for that matter, shown how the individual subject-as-poet can create, "fashion," and even to some extent control ideology.[18]

But these processes remain entirely on the level of consciousness. In its call for (re)articulating the interdependence of subject and structure, the new historicism has come up squarely against the vexed and, by now, rather tired question of the tug-of-war between the individual and the social that has plagued ideology critique since the Frankfurt School. I would argue that at the point at which some hard questions must be asked of the exact nature of these rearticulations, the new historicism and its assembling and reassembling of the subject within sociocultural formations flatten out and threaten to lose their innovative edge. At what historical junctures (economic, political, social, cultural) is this interdependence between subject and structure most likely to occur? What are the conditions under which sociocultural structures are most likely to succeed in interpellating an individual subjectivity? Why can we reasonably conclude that not every subject is fully interpellated into the sociocultural? More particularly, why *does* a Martin Guerre seek to de-interpellate himself from legal and cultural codes, only to invoke the power of those codes over another site of de-interpellated subjectivity? What becomes of new historicist articulations of the intersection between subject and structure when we consider that the story of *The Return of Martin Guerre*, which, as we have seen, Greenblatt uses as a proof-text for his specifications of the conditions for the emergence of a bourgeois consciousness as an aftereffect of cultural codes, is also an account of an individual subject's refusal to "see" himself interpellated in the discourses of social bonds. In this direct abutting of subject and structure, what is the precise explanatory key that can make sense of *why* Martin leaves, only eventually to force a sociocultural articulation of his identity?

My argument is that the sociocultural overdeterminations that problematize the point of intersection between the subject and history are *themselves* overdetermined by the eruptions of the unconscious at perhaps unpredictable points in the constantly shifting rearticulations that make up the discontinuities of subject positions. The new historicism forecloses on the unconscious just when it can help us in a further nuancing of the problematics of the subject within history. But it is possible to demonstrate that the unconscious works in history—that the unconscious is thoroughly implicated in historical specificity—and that a reconsideration of the operations of the unconscious can thereby offer us some new opportunities for rethinking the complex mediation between subject and history.

The larger metatheoretical issue at stake here is, of course, the highly elusive synthesis of Marx and Freud. It is useful at this point to refer to the work of Jean-Joseph Goux, whose concept of "symbolic economies" offers a synthesis of psyche and of socioeconomy that can pave the way for a meaningful use of psychoanalysis as an interpretive tool in historical materialism—and a synthesis that can be used to enrich, in particular, certain investigative areas of the new historicism.[19] If the Renaissance can be summarized as, among other things, the historical and socioeconomic site of the development of a nascent capitalism, then a link between psyche and economy can have some far-reaching implications for any study of the Renaissance subject.

In an almost anthropological sense, Goux argues that the psychic structure of the individual subject is constituted not just by discrete events in the individual's psychohistory, but also, more phylogenetically, by the stratified layers or historically progressive stages of modes of production and exchange. In Goux's conception of the interrelationship between (un)consciousness and modes of production, when we speak of a lack in the psychic structure, it is not just the Lacanian *manque-à-être* that has so often been the target (unfairly, as I will discuss later) of ideology critique as too limited to the mechanics of merely individual desire, but a real, unrepresented absence of earlier forms of social consciousness: "The unconsciousness is built upon the traces of historically *outdated* symbolizations, in that the current mode of production and the current forms of consciousness that correspond to it and to which the subject must accede effectively supplant and thus *repress* these traces" (75). Where these phylogenetic forms of social consciousness are absented *to* is the unconscious. For Freud, one of the essential operations of the unconscious is condensation, which is, not coincidentally, also an "economic" concept (i.e., involving the circulation of energy). Though Goux does not make this explicit, the stratified layers of repressed modes of production seem analogous to Freud's condensation, where a manifest element is properly seen as determined by latent meanings. When we speak of the intersection between subject and structure, one could argue that what has taken place is a condensation and displacement of earlier forms of consciousness shaped by outdated modes of production and economic signification that are now merely latent. For Goux, the present modes of production that make up the social consciousness of capitalism are predicated on the repression of earlier forms of consciousness. It is in this sense, then, that we may say, with some degree of specificity, that the (after)effects of the unconscious leave their observable, symptomatic traces within history.

What is at stake in Goux's psychoeconomic conception is that it is no mere bourgeois act of belatedness to refer to the subject within history as "neurotic." The subject is neurotic because something in the dominant socioeconomic mode is not being represented—hence the lack that "structures" an unconscious within history. And indeed, it is with Goux's "symbolic economies" in mind that we can now effect a return to *The Return of Martin Guerre* to see how neurosis not only is displaced within ideology, but also *itself displaces* ideology, leaving its residues of repressed traces. Through a focus on the "economy" of the unconscious, we can make a connection between two seemingly unrelated details in the story, Martin's eight-year impotence (presumably imposed by witchcraft but later mysteriously "cured") and the theft of his father's grain, which precipitates the crisis of his departure. A psychoeconomic reading of the theft of the seed begins to assume the complex contours of a parable. The father's Oedipal seed, signifying both bodily potency and the economic power of currency, can be identified as a site of overdetermination for the once impotent Martin, who is *himself* on the threshold of becoming an heir to and participant in the Oedipal structures of the Name-of-the-Father. Within the cycle of "phallic circulation" that dominates modes of production, both Martin's impotence and his theft (the refusal, we could say, of the subject to enter both gender and structure) can be interpreted as a "neurotic" act of protest against the father's de-eroticized seed and its merely symbolic function as an abstract representation of exchange value. Martin's theft could be seeking, in effect, to de-commodify the seed, perhaps, in some ritual sense, linking its original affective value as semen to his own lost bodily potency. We can properly understand Martin's unconscious here as operating according to earlier, more feudal modes of production, where the commodity (and its immediate use value) represents virtually a degree zero of signification, such that it signifies only itself and has not yet been riven by the alienating disjunction between money and commodity. The withholding of seed that once constituted Martin's impotence mimes the deferrals of exchange whereby seed no longer symbolizes fertility but rather a substitute currency (or a substitute for money as a universal equivalent of exchange).

What must be emphasized, though, is that the stolen seed is overdetermined in this play, both literal and metaphoric, of libidinal economy. As in dream interpretation, the point of a focus on the unconscious in this story is not to push for a deciphering of what the hypersignifying seed "really" means. There is no psychoanalytic or macroeconomic supercode that can explain precisely how and where Martin is interpreting the latent meaning of the seed as having purely affective value. The displacements, detours, and deferrals of signification that eventually enable the seed to exist as an autonomous agent of economic exchange are vestigially repressed in the distortions and condensations that characterize the operations of the unconscious—and they cannot be definitvely retraced. All that remains of these psychic detours are the symptoms of Martin's erratic and arbitrary behavior.

Thus, there will always be something in the unconscious that eludes full appropriation within and representation by ideology. Martin's theft of his father's seed enacts not just the "loss" of his own seed, but also the loss suffered by the seed as it becomes transformed into a medium of exchange—a lack (a lack of affective value) *unrepresented* by the nascent capitalism and, hence, difficult to reconstruct hermeneutically. For Greenblatt, the point of the story of Martin Guerre is that subjectivity is constituted by sociocultural codes. But in this story, "ideology" is not only the site of the constituting of the subject, it is also the site of repression within the subject. In this sense, then, the point of the story may be that there exists very little difference between the "neurotic" subject and the "ideological" subject. As Goux writes, "The neurotic subject, like the ideological subject, is *constituted* by the place it occupies in one of the modes of the process of symbolization" (83)—which is to say that the subject's positioning within social codes is itself inherently "neurotic." And this "place of occupation" that Goux refers to is the "place" of psychoanalysis itself—the "place" of repression. Because the ideology of a nascent capitalism is built on the stratigraphy of outdated modes of production, because ideology rests on the socioeconomic foundation that the neurotic lacks, we could say that ideology is itself "always already" neurotic. If, by the time of Freud's Vienna, capitalism and psychoanalysis (as one of its ideological state apparatuses) *do* go hand in hand, it is because, throughout its socioeconomic history, capitalism has become the overdetermined site of repressions too deep to be contained within ideology. The subject's repressions have, in some sense, surpassed ideology's containment of the historical succession of modes of production.

Notes

1. Freud quotes Burckhardt's description of Michelangelo's Moses from his *Der Cicerone:* "'His form is animated by the inscription of a mighty movement and the physical strength with which he is endowed causes us to await it with fear and trembling.'" *The Standard Edition of the Complete Psychological Works of Sigmund Freud*, ed. and trans. James Strachey (London: Hogarth Press, 1953–74), 13:216. Freud used Burckhardt's description to lend further evidence to his interpretation of Michelangelo's Moses as an embodiment of suppressed fury.

2. Freud also quotes from Burckhardt in his essay on another titan of the Renaissance, Leonardo, in his essay "Leonardo da Vinci and a Memory of His Childhood," *Complete Works*, 11:63.

3. William Kerrigan and Gordon Braden, *The Idea of the Renaissance* (Baltimore: Johns Hopkins University Press, 1989), xi.

4. V. N. Volosinov, *Freudianism: A Marxist Critique*, trans. I. R. Titunik, ed. Titunik and Neal H. Bruss (New York: Academic Press, 1976), 8.

5. Louis Montrose, "The Elizabethan Subject and the Renaissance Text," *Literary Theory/Renaissance Texts*, ed. Patricia Parker and David Quint (Baltimore: Johns Hopkins University Press, 1986), 303, 317.

6. For an account of the new historicist's characteristic "reticence to discuss the theory that informs his practice," see Jean E. Howard's excellent overview, "The New Historicism in Renaissance Studies," *English Literary Renaissance* 16, no. 1 (1986), esp. 35–43.

7. Stephen Greenblatt, "Psychoanalysis and Renaissance Culture," *Literary Theory/Renaissance Texts,* 216. Further page references will be cited in the text.

8. Here I should confess that Greenblatt's motives for his critique of psychoanalysis in this essay remain obscure to me. At times, he seems actually to be supporting the claims of psychoanalysis. Significant portions of his essay are given over to granting that "identity in Freud does not depend upon existential autonomy" (214); and there are times when it is as if his impulse is to show that he understands Freud's project better than Freud himself. Moreover, surely in Greenblatt's earlier landmark *Renaissance Self-Fashioning,* we are justified in viewing his concept of "self-fashioning" as a brilliantly rich merger between the Renaissance and psychoanalysis, a reflection that his interest in Renaissance "selves" remains at least as strong as his interest in the "larger networks of meaning" (4) that disperse these "selves." (Indeed, Greenblatt's account of Iago's "improvisations of power" over Othello rather uncannily resemble the erosions of Martin Guerre's identity through Arnaud du Tilh's improvisatory will.) Greenblatt's almost Oedipal ambivalence toward Freud is itself a major topic of interest and one that itself invites psychoanalytic speculation. In the meantime, his ambivalence makes for treacherous and oversimplifying ground when one makes the simple claim that he *is* "critiquing" psychoanalysis in his essay on Martin Guerre.

9. Natalie Zemon Davis, *The Return of Martin Guerre* (Cambridge: Harvard University Press, 1983), 40.

10. It is worth noting here that Martin's ill-tempered return seems more calculated to take revenge on his uncanny double than it does an admirable decision to reassume the burden of his abandoned responsibilities.

11. Davis, *The Return of Martin Guerre,* 86.

12. Ibid., 58.

13. Jacques Lacan, "The Subversion of the Subject and the Dialectic of Desire in the Freudian Unconscious," *Écrits: A Selection,* trans. Alan Sheridan (New York: Norton, 1977), 309–10.

14. Here, I am much indebted to Samuel Weber's essay "Psychoanalysis, Literary Criticism, and the Problem of Authority," *Psychoanalysis and . . . ,* ed. Richard Feldstein and Henry Sussman (New York: Routledge, 1990), 21–32. In his discussion of the current legal battle in Paris as to whether Lacan's Seminars constitute "works" by an author, Weber has constructed an intriguing critique of legal authority itself: "For what does it mean to 'assume' the authority of a law that necessarily remains without an author? Can we be sure that such a 'law' is itself legitimate? What if it were 'only' *powerful,* based on a more or less opaque force?" (23).

15. I want to emphasize, too, that it is certainly not my point to privilege a Lacanian "return to Freud" as somehow better than a "Freudian return" to the "return of Martin Guerre."

16. Michael Schneider, *Neurosis and Civilization: A Marxist/Freudian Synthesis,* trans. Michael Roloff (New York: Seabury Press, 1975), 70.

17. In their introduction to their recent collection of essays, *Psychoanalysis and . . . ,* Richard Feldstein and Henry Sussman call for a kind of postpsychoanalysis, a kind of "hybrid form of psychoanalysis [that] could become decontextualized from the mirror of clinical relations that has customarily supported its claims" (1). A "decontextualized" psychoanalysis would be one that is, we could affirm, the better off for having no "proper place"—for being "dis-placed" from the shadowy hegemony of bourgeois clinical practice. There is no question here that if psychoanalysis wishes to develop its "place" within post-Marxist culture critique, it will truly have to become a *post*psychoanalysis, giving up its place

in bourgeois therapy, and giving itself over to tracking the shifting rearticulations of the subject within the sociocultural. But what *is* the cultural space of a psychoanalysis that, despite its presumed role as a "master discourse," has always been as shifting and unstable as the subject it analyzes—in some sense, "always already" decontextualized, always multiply constituted within someone else's rhetorical domain?

18. Montrose argues that such a strategy of poetic fashioning is particularly evident in Spenser's many representations of Queen Elizabeth: "In the Spenserian text, and elsewhere, we can observe a mode of contestation at work within the Elizabethan subject's very gestures of submission to the official fictions" ("The Elizabethan Subject," 331).

19. Jean-Joseph Goux, *Symbolic Economies: After Marx and Freud,* trans. Jennifer Curtiss Gage (Ithaca: Cornell University Press, 1990). Further page references will be cited in the text.

Resisting the Marketplace: The Language of Labor in Benvenuto Cellini's *Vita*

Jane Tylus
University of Wisconsin, Madison

> We happened to stay at a place on this side of Chioggia, on the left as you go towards Ferrara. The innkeeper wanted to be paid in his own way before we went to bed, and when I said that in other places it was usual to pay in the morning, he answered, "But I want to be paid this evening, and in my own way." In reply to this I said that men who wanted to be paid to suit themselves had better make a world to suit themselves, since it was done differently in this world.[1]

SO begins yet another of Benvenuto Cellini's remarkable exploits. Partly because of the frightened companion, Tribulo, with whom Cellini is traveling en route from Ferrara to Florence, Cellini gives in to the innkeeper's demand and pays him the *scudi*, but he will not let the incident go unremembered. Before parting the next morning, he takes care to slash the four beds upstairs to shreds, "in such fashion that I knew I had done damage worth more than fifty *scudi*, far more than the innkeeper had been paid the night before." So does Cellini awaken his host to the "real world" in which he, perforce, must play a part, and the artist escapes, the trembling Tribulo at his side, without having to pay his own price in return.

Slashing four beds is clearly less heinous than the various thefts, rapes, and murders which fill Cellini's autobiography, but this particular action, like many of the others, attests less to Cellini's "enemies'" refusal to conduct their lives as others insist than to *Cellini*'s refusal to do so. What is especially relevant about the incident recounted above, however, is the fact that it is occasioned by a request for money: and by the representative of a world of commerce and exchange from which Cellini, like a later Don Quixote, would prefer to keep himself aloof. But Cellini's act of violence, uncannily echoed in Cervantes's text when Quixote assaults the innkeeper's bedclothes believing them to be demonically inspired monsters, also reveals the extent to which Cellini was unable to avoid the claims made on him by that world. Such entrapment prompts a relentless cycle of insult and revenge of which an admiring Goethe, praising the forcefulness of the Italian character, would remark, "the offended one, unless he takes his revenge instantly, falls into a kind of fever that plagues him like a physical disease until he has healed himself through the blood of his opponent."[2]

This comparatively minor incident in Cellini's *Vita*, published for the first time only in the eighteenth century and in an era which professed to see in the goldsmith's intense "individualism" a mirror for its own antipathies to authority, offers itself as an example of Cellini's ceaseless efforts to exist outside of a monetary economy "contaminated" by self-interest, alienated labor, and a failed correspondence between work and its value. This essay will focus on Cellini's attempt to autonomize artistic productivity in a period during which it was becoming possible for artists to rise above the lower-class status they had been granted in the past. Cellini's violence against the innkeeper is a symbolic violence directed against those who would "remove" him from a realm of gift exchange based on liberality and trust: an attack Cellini perpetrates verbally on his one-time patron Cosimo de' Medici in the pages of his autobiography when he declares that a stingy Cosimo who no longer supports his genius is little more than a "merchant." Constructed as a reaction to the perceived failure of a patronage system that does not nourish the artist, directed against the "usury," and "illegitimacy" of a market system in which the artist must compete against base rivals, the *Vita* provides striking testimony to an early modern crisis in conceptions of artistic *work*.

This discourse of economics in which we are still engaged—in puzzling over the relationship of artistic "work" to the "marketplace," or that of creative endeavors to grant-giving agencies—affects the dynamics of the community and the construction of gender in Cellini, but in a manner not always allowed for by either the practice of new historicism or the type of feminist study that has tended to dominate Renaissance scholarship. As an example of the latter, the work of Nancy Vickers comes most readily to mind. In several far-ranging articles on Shakespeare, Cellini, and Petrarch, Vickers has called attention to the creation of a "homosocial community" in which the always and already dangerous "feminine" is offered up for survey and appropriation to the male reader or patron. From the sonnet sequences to Laura written by Petrarch in the mid-fourteenth century, to the *Vita* of Cellini and the revisionary sonnets to Shakespeare's young man, one finds the creation and defense of an Oedipal community in which the mother is always silenced so that creativity can be placed in exclusively male hands. Thus Petrarch "fragments" his would-be mistress so that he may be protected from the insistent revelation of his own castration; Cellini manipulates the "mistress in the masterpiece" so as to win praise from his male "buddy," King Francis I; and Shakespeare's narrator, fearful of objectifying his beloved young man in the same manner in which Petrarch had commodified Laura, willfully silences and, in Vickers's reading, "feminizes" his own voice so as not to subject the beloved to the scrutiny of other men.[3] This influential and important feminist critique, emphasizing the solidarity of the homosocial community whose exclusivity is threatened but never overturned, is characteristic of scholars such as Vickers and Patricia Parker, who in turn have based much of their work on that of Eve Sedgewick and Laura Mulvey.[4] Many readings by new historicists, however, demonstrate the manner in which this community is undermined and unsuccessful. Jonathan Goldberg sees in *Macbeth* the "defeat of a hypermasculine world"; Louis Montrose finds "political impotence" in the works of Edmund Spenser and in Shakespeare's early plays; and Stephen Orgel discovers in *The Tempest* a "male fantasy of the mother" that must finally jeapordize Prospero's willful claims to power.[5] These predominantly male new historicists deny what Vickers and others perceive as the solidarity of the homosocial community, turning instead to its rifts, its gaps, its weaknesses before the likes of a Queen Elizabeth or a dark lady of the sonnets.

Despite this crucial difference, both critiques are marked by common concerns, perhaps the most troubling being fidelity to what has been a fairly traditional view of the historical trajectory of the so-called early modern period: an uncomplicated passage from feudalism to capitalism; the emergence of an individualism which grows into modern subjectivity.[6] In these passages, the Renaissance "artist" is understood to be notably complicit, even energetically encouraging. Cellini and Petrarch emerge triumphant from the Oedipal rivalries into which Vickers casts them; Greenblatt notes that in Shakespeare's *Henry VI*, "status relations are being transformed before our eyes into property relations"; in an essay on the "chorographies" of Drayton and William Brown, Richard Helgerson suggests the manner in which "nationalism and individualism are deeply implicated in one another;" finally, Louis Montrose claims that the experience of female fecundity is one for which men seek mercantile compensations: hence the emergent ideology of a capitalism that excludes women from the public marketplace.[7] But the artist deeply indebted to the patronage system, and thus to a symbolic economy that bears traces of the "gift exchange" Marcel Mauss analyzed at the beginning of this century,[8] met this supposedly painless and welcome transition with a great deal of resistance, as the powerfully conservative gestures of the *Vita* attest. As the picaresque genre to which Cellini's work has been said to belong[9] so brilliantly exposes, the producer is thrown out on his own, without family "nourishment." Like Lazarillo, Cellini is forced to enter the realm of competition and furious rivalry, a locus of materialism which the protective court had successfully masked. In thus registering the tensions produced by the slippage between the realm of patronage and that of the market, the *Vita* demonstrates that the homosocial community which Vickers sees as insulated from a hostile "outside" and the new historicists as vulnerable to that hostile outside, is not so much threatened from with*out* as from with*in*. By valorizing the *work* which assumes the value of the powerful, socially superior, Other—the patron who is often glossed in the role of a nurturer—Cellini's autobiography marginalizes the *workplace*. Thus while Pierre Bourdieu speaks of the "symbolic revolution [inaugurated only in the nineteenth century by the aesthetic autonomy of Flaubert], whereby artists emancipated themselves from bourgeois standards by refusing to acknowledge any master other than their art"—a revolution "which had the effect of making the market disappear"[10]—such an attempt at "emancipation" is already apparent in the highly transitional society of sixteenth-century Italy, in which the place of the artist was ambiguous at best.

"With Jupiter's protection and with a pledge of future grace, I go happily into exile" (Tuta Jove / ac tanto pignore / laeta fugor).[11] Such is the saying carved into the base of Cellini's most famous statue, commissioned by Cosimo de' Medici shortly after Cellini arrived in Florence in 1545: his Perseus, a bronze copy of which still stands in Florence's Piazza della Signoria, displaying the head of Medusa, as one of Cellini's admiring contemporaries wrote, for all the world to see. The words are uttered by Danae, the mother of Perseus, whom Cellini sculpted on the base just above the inscription, as she flees from her cruel father after having been impregnated by a Jupiter who came to earth in the form of a golden shower. Following this plenteous rainfall Danae is banished to a distant country, although it is with the promise of Jupiter's protection and her son's future vengeance ringing in her ears, a testament not only to the tyranny of earthly fathers but to the generosity and solicitude of heavenly fathers.

The political rationale for such a carving, displayed beneath the writhing body of a Medusa on which Perseus casually stands, was the desire of Cellini's final patron, Duke Cosimo de' Medici, to have a statue representing his Perseus-like heroism in rescuing Florence from the Medusa of past tyrants. Cosimo is thus the child exiled from the city and returned to become one of Florence's most powerful leaders. Such a program is implicit in Cosimo's desire to have a statue to offset Donatello's Judith about to sever the head of Holofernes, next to which Cellini's Perseus would be placed. Sculpted in the early quattrocento during Florence's final days as a republic, the Judith attested to the vitality of popular revolt against tyrants, which the Perseus, symbolic of ducal order, would ideally decenter.[12] But if Cosimo is the child Danae is carrying as she flees from the city, he is also the lover and guardian Jupiter who protected Florence from afar in the years when she was figuratively exiled from herself, suffering under Cosimo's despotic relative Alessandro. Finally, there may well be another allegory at work in the bronze statuette and inscription. Hardly an artist who carried out the desires of his patrons to the letter (Cellini made his Perseus a good third higher than it was supposed to have been, and the body of Medusa is mentioned nowhere in the original commission), Cellini may have meant the base to serve as a gloss on the patronage and protection of the ideal prince: a patronage that manifests itself in a shower of gold, unasked for but deserved; protection from indigence and the numerous civil and criminal charges which Cellini avidly recounts in his autobiography. "Impregnated" by the priceless value of Cosimo's gold, Cellini, like Danae, will give birth to priceless sons.[13]

Or, to cite Cellini's paraphrase (in the *Vita,* 2.46) of Francis I's words to him after a friendly disagreement between monarch and favorite artist, "e poi aggiunse che mi affogherebbe nell'oro" (the king added that he would drown me in gold). And it is in Cellini's *Vita,* if not in this fanciful recasting of Danae's flight from her father, that the tale of wealth and immunity is told again and again. As a personal tale, however, it was over by the time Cellini began his *Vita* in 1558, almost six years after completing the Perseus. Writing in Cosimo's Florence while under house arrest on charges of sodomy, complaining that the duke no longer gives him commissions, the goldsmith mourns the loss of a patronage system that sought a mirror for its immunity and generosity in the artist it suported.[14] More precisely, Cellini exposes the failings of a Cosimo who refused to guarantee Cellini's immunity at the risk of undermining his own. In so doing, he removes the duke from his pinnacle of power and reveals the larger institutional forces already at work in mid-sixteenth century Italy that would indeed, in time, compromise the politics of petty tyrants such as the Medici.

Such exposure occurs through a narrative that progresses from an ideal "golden" age of patronage to a corrupt modern one; and if the *Vita* is a tale of "three cities," Rome, Paris, and Florence,[15] it is also a tale of three styles of Renaissance patronage. In Rome of the 1520s, Cellini is welcomed by Pope Clement VII, who notoriously forgives the artist for various homicides he has committed within the holy city's walls by proclaiming that Cellini, like himself, is *above* the law. But if Cellini finds immunity for his person beneath the shadow of the pope, he is not immune from Clement's insistence that he complete his commissions in a specified period of time. Thus after several grueling months in the rat-infested jail of the Castel Sant'Angelo, Cellini makes his way to a more liberal patron, Francis I. It is in Paris—a city which, like its monarch, is a place "without equals"—that Cellini finds his most understanding audience, a king who addresses him as "mon ami" and offers him his own castello in which to fulfill his commissions at leisure. If the monarchs of Rome shielded Cellini temporarily from the weight of the law, Francis removes Cellini from the realm occupied by other "vulgar" artists, placing him beyond all possible rivals. Thanks to his own invaluable status, the king becomes capable, in Cellini's retrospective gloss, of conferring upon his "equal" Cellini a similarly immeasurable value. As long as the patron exists outside of a quantitative system of exchange, the work produced for the patron is removed from that realm as well: a fragile, illusory relationship at best, but one which suggests that the worth of *both* king and artist is beyond measure.

Within this symbolic economy that resists the commodification of the work of art,[16] the patron or would-be patron is frequently addressed not only by Cellini but by others throughout the Renaissance as the natural participant in an organic process of a work's coming to fruition. Thus in an obvious and perhaps ironic allusion to the rhetoric of the many dedications that circulated in

Renaissance England, Shakespeare writes to the earl of Southampton, a generous "patron" of the arts, at the beginning of *Venus and Adonis,* "if the first heir of my invention prove deformed, I shall be sorry it had so noble a godfather, and never after ear so barren a land, for fear it yield me still so bad a harvest." Moreover, at least one powerful patron in the early seventeenth century, King James I, often used the rhetoric of maternal bounty when speaking of his role as patron and king. In *The True Lawe of Free Monarchies,* he wrote that his first "fatherly duty" is that of "nourishing" his subjects; and in the *Basilikon Doron,* he claimed that he was a "loving nourish-father" to his people.[17] As Coppélia Kahn has noted, with James I, the *pater patriae*'s attempt to encompass the "generative" power of women—the magical power to give—conferred upon the royal patron greater majesty while often playing upon his subjects' logically heightened dependency.[18] Such "bountifulness" was mythologized in one of Ben Jonson's masques for James entitled *The Masque of Queenes,* in the figure of "Heroic Vertue," or Perseus, a parent figure who is claimed by Jonson to give birth to none other than Fame: "Sing then *good Fame,* that's out of *Vertue* borne, / For, Who doth fame neglect, doth vertue scorn."[19]

But if Francis became the ideal nourish-father through whom Cellini was raised to noble status, Cosimo de' Medici failed to fulfill the generous role Cellini had come to expect of royalty. In returning to his "motherland" of Florence in 1545, Cellini fully anticipated a greeting equivalent to that of the foreign King Francis. But despite Cosimo's initially enthusiastic welcome and his insistence that Cellini begin at once on the Perseus, the years following Cellini's arrival were plagued by the duke's parsimony and impatience, climaxing in the negotiations over Cellini's Perseus—for the materials of which Cellini had still not been reimbursed when he began the autobiography in 1558. When, upon the statue's belated completion, Cosimo sends his secretary to ask Cellini how much he wants for the Perseus, Cellini is rendered at first (uncharacteristically) speechless. He is then informed that unless he names a price he will be in danger of falling into complete disgrace with his Excellency—a response that provokes Cellini's heated retort that not even ten thousand crowns would be enough. Valuing the Perseus at a fixed price takes away from Cellini's pricelessness—and obviously from that of Cosimo, who has become little more than a merchant or middleman rather than the *maker* of value. Cellini's question for the duke when the two confront each other is, "Oh, how is it possible that anyone can estimate the price of my work, when there's not a single man in Florence who knows how to make it?" (2.97). The artist's uniqueness *should* find its mirror in the duke's uniqueness, but Cosimo's response is that he will simply name another, quite competent sculptor—Cellini's enemy Bandinelli—to fix a price (a "giusto prezzo") which the artist will then be paid. Such goings-on lead the exasperated artist to claim in his autobiography, "Not realizing that this lord behaved more like a merchant than a duke, it was as with a duke rather than a merchant that I mistakenly dealt with him."

With such a judgment, Cellini condemns Cosimo by relegating him to a position within rather than above an explicitly monetary economy and thus within a system in which "any possession is alienable and its worth unstable."[20] But by so displacing Cosimo from his role as duke and insisting on his bourgeois origins, Cellini also risks placing *himself* within a real rather than symbolic economy he had so carefully fostered throughout his previous dealings with patrons.[21] To this danger, the *Vita* becomes a response in its insistence on what might be called a labor theory of value: not only with its emphasis on "la vita travagliata," the laboring life Cellini has led, but with its meticulous account of the "fatiche" that have produced his artworks.

Given such emphasis, Cellini's *Vita* forms a striking contrast to other sixteenth-century narratives which seek to displace or to annul the role of physical labor. Castiglione's *Cortegiano*, with its ethic of *sprezzatura* or elitist disdain for visible effort, was one such influential example of the cinquecento. The courtier must labor to disguise his efforts to secure the good graces of a prince, and the *Cortegiano* ultimately glorifies the aesthetic object as an artifice that bears no traces of its work. These concerns of the "good courtier," the bureaucrat anxious to be absorbed into the ennobling atmosphere of Urbino, found their way into numerous writings of Italian artists shortly thereafter. They were equally anxious to proclaim the ennobling status of their art in an era in which it finally seemed possible to escape the reduction of the fine arts to merely mechanical praxis (Wittkower, chapter 2). In the ongoing debate as to whether painting or sculpture was nobler, the painter Bronzino, who fared much more successfully with Cosimo than did Cellini, wrote to Benedetto Varchi, "sculpture is an art that lacks dignity, because the more one exercises the body and the hands, the more one smacks of a mere mechanic, and consequently the less of nobility."[22] In contrast, Cellini would write in a letter to Varchi which formed part of a lively debate during the 1540s among leading Florentine artists:

> Sculpture is the mother of all the other arts where *disegno* plays a part . . . Painting is nothing other than a tree or man or anything else that views itself in a fountain. The difference between sculpture and painting is such, that the one is merely a shadow; the other is that which casts the shadow.[23]

The supreme sculptor—and thus the supreme laborer—is God, who "made the heavens and the earth, and made us worthy of his hands, without first designing them" (*Opere*, 893); the supreme painter the infernal Lucifer, who because he could not be God, "has made shadows in order to fool mens' souls." Sculpture originates in the creative actions of the father, "Dio," while it also takes primacy over all the other arts as their "mother." The sculptor himself becomes the true "nourish-father" on whom all the other lesser arts and artists depend.

In light of Cellini's defense of labor and, by the time of the *Vita*, his hostility toward Cosimo, it is possible to turn to the most memorable section of the autobiography—the casting of the Perseus—and to find there yet another dimension of the statue unanticipated in the original program: Perseus becomes the laboring and heroic "parent," Cellini, and Medusa the failed and dangerous patron whose gaze, far from conferring nourishment and bounty, engenders only a fatal sterility. The Perseus' fantastic birth from the fiery and explosive furnace described in suspenseful prose comes only after dozens of pages recounting the artist's careful and prolonged *fatiche* in designing a clay model, casting the decapitated figure of the Medusa, and building a furnace that can contain the large, twisted figure of Perseus. In the course of these labors, which take over seven years, Cosimo and his wife continually interrupt the artist to give him less important commissions and to interrogate him on his proceedings, exuding mistrust over Cellini's capacities to consummate such a great work. Finally, however, Cellini sets the stage of the dark backroom of the *bottega* on the day when the bronze statue of the Perseus, holding Medusa's head aloft, is to be cast and the difficult, perhaps impossible act of fusion performed. During this dramatic finale, the workshop catches fire, and an exhausted and overworked Cellini is forced to take to his bed with a bout of fever. When all hope that the metal will melt inside the clay seems to be lost, the inspired (and still feverish) artist commands that two hundred pewter bowls be thrown energetically into the furnace to feed the flame. With an awesome "thunderbolt" ("un lampo di fuoco grandissimo," 2.77) that suggests that the power of the divine has been guiding Cellini's massive enterprise all along, the furnace erupts and ejaculates a long stream of fire, as Cellini's assistants rejoice over the imminent fusion of the statue and praise their master for having "brought a corpse back to life" (2.77). The long, painstaking process of labor and the overcoming of tremendous *difficoltà* that climax in the threatened sterility of Cellini's "opera" enable Cellini to turn in the *Vita* from celebrating his own power to revive the dead to that of God, who with his "great powers brought himself back from the dead, and ascended in glory to the heavens!" (2.77).

If the miraculous resuscitation of the Perseus is depicted as the deserved completion of Cellini's seven years of labor and his victory over cynics such as Cosimo, there is little that is "natural" about the gestation or rebirth itself. Rather, the narrative that describes Cellini's labors is marked with others' observations of his transgressiveness, from Cosimo's initially skeptical remark that the rules of art won't permit the statue's completion[24] to the exaggerated report of Cosimo's majordomo to his prince that Cellini was not human but "an authentic and powerful devil, since he had done that which art was unable to do; and other great things which would have been too much even for a devil" (2.77). With these remarks, Cellini's fellow artists admiringly concurred, although without replicating the language of demonic force. One Latin couplet affixed to the Perseus when it was first unveiled remarks, "Once nature was the archetype of art. But since Cellini has cast the Perseus, now art has become the archetype of nature." And yet another writer commented that it was no longer Medusa's face but Cellini's Perseus which would turn onlookers to stone (Pope-Hennessy, 186). Thus has Cellini overtaken Medusa—the threatening powers that would deny his worth, the maternal principle of nourishment become a monstrosity in the hateful figure of Cosimo—and neutralized her, appropriating her powers as his own.[25]

To an extent, such transgressiveness, as Mircea Eliade has suggested, is part of the languge of metallurgy itself—a rite that undertakes to penetrate the bowels of the earth and to appropriate the natural process of ripening ore. Cellini's masculinization of labor, his taking upon himself the role of the father-mother in the creation of *his* Perseus, thus participates in what Eliade described as "venturing into a domain which by rights does not belong to man. . . . The artisan takes the place of the Earth-Mother, and it is his task to accelerate and perfect the growth of the ore. The furnaces are, as it were, a new matrix, an artificial uterus where the ore completes its gestation."[26] If the patron's help was not forthcoming, Cellini himself had to delve into the "source" of creation and appropriate it, through his infernal yet godlike labors, as his own. But this act of violent appropriation is far from being self-contained. The section on the Perseus in the *Vita* is rather designed to force the reader—like Cosimo—to marvel over the account of the statue's making. Indeed, it is not so much the object itself which prompts others to marvel, but the story of Cellini's labors. When Cellini travels to Pisa to tell the duke and duchess the tale of the Perseus in his own words, "it seemed to their Excellencies far more of a stupendous and marvellous experience to hear me tell of it in person. When I came to the foot of the Perseus which had not come out—just as I had predicted to his Excellency—he was filled with astonishment" (2.78; Bull, 349). Marvel, the petrifying reaction which Descartes would describe a century later as "a sudden surprise of the soul which causes it to consider with attention the objects which seem to it rare and extraordinary,"[27] is produced upon hearing Cellini narrate his "extraordinary" labors: labors which have transgressed into the realm of the gods. It is a marvel to which Cosimo is momentarily forced to be submissive, until, some time later, as he hides behind a curtain in his palace to watch the crowds gaze admiringly at the newly unveiled Perseus, he informs Cellini that he will make *him* the submissive subject of *meraviglia:* he asks his *cameriere* Sforza Almeni to find Cellini and tell him "that for my part I'm much more content than I'd expected; and tell him that I will content him in such a manner that I will astonish him" (2.92).

Thus at the heart of Cellini's narrative of labor and insistence on the arduous and often transgressive nature of *il fare,* is a rhetoric of violence and subjugation that is designed to force the rich and powerful into willing submission.[28] That such momentary subjugation might be overturned by the prince in a manner that would make Cellini marvel suggests that the production of awe is hardly limited to the artist alone. Rather, its effect is created in order to be reversed so that Cellini can finally become the submissive figure "subject" to a duke's or king's liberal gift of gold. But that such a reversal never occurred in the case of Cosimo, despite the latter's false promise as he stood spying onto the crowded Piazza della Signoria, suggests that the indifferent

Cosimo is immune to the force of Cellini's labors and *virtù,* with its powerfully gendered etymology. It suggests too that the labors of individual creation, dependent as they are on violence and transgression, are ultimately dependent on another's gaze, another's propensity to articulate the forceful rhetoric implicit in Cellini's acts of making: acts which can have no value in and of themselves. As Jean Baudrillard has suggested in his analysis of a Marxian economics that also privileges a labor theory of value, no labor can generate its own value in isolation. Only in the realm of the imaginary can labor and the mirror of production, to cite the title of Baudrillard's most influential study, assume a totalizing—but falsely totalizing—status.[29]

Cellini's attempt to validate the autonomy and inestimable worth of his labors produces, as it must in a society which increasingly values the marketplace on the one hand and the superficial *sprezzatura* of the aristocracy on the other, a narrative doomed to incompletion and obscurity. Cellini's defiance of market value, coupled with his unrelenting insistence on the worth of his labor, makes the *Vita,* like the Perseus, a fantastic narrative, although the nature of the fantasy changed considerably after Cellini's disappointment at the hands of the merchant of Florence. Yet while it is possible to read the *Vita* as an unsuccessful work of "compensatory narcissism"[30] in which what Cellini claims as his "own" is never fully his, it is important to add a necessary epilogue. For Cellini went on from the unfinished *Vita* to write a different kind of text, the *Trattati dell'oreficeria* and the *Trattato della scultura.* They are works, moreover, generated for a different reader than that "ideal" one of the *Vita,* which one critic has intriguingly hypothesized as none other than Cosimo himself.[31] For the *Trattati* represent Cellini's attempt to locate himself within a community that he had often earlier spurned: that of other artisans. If the *Vita* had functioned largely to place Cellini beyond the realm of his fellow artists—with the exception of a rare few, such as the great Michelangelo from whom Cellini claims to have learned everything he knew—the *Trattati* make Cellini's life of labors an exemplary one, from whose example others may also learn. While Cellini's work is still dependent on recognition from others—as is evident in a poignant moment where he expresses his hope that others will be moved to great disdain for his bad fortune and compassion for himself[32]—those others are less frequently monarchs or popes and more often the artisans who initiated Cellini into his trade. He speaks fondly of one elderly goldsmith with whom he worked in Rome and reprints the verses by fellow artists affixed to the base of the Perseus in an appendix to the *Trattato della scultura,* thereby placing himself more securely than before within a group of readers he is now undertaking to initiate, as one who has practiced not just one art but many.

Published only a few years before Cellini's death in 1571, the *Trattati* develop a tension already in evidence in rare moments in the *Vita,* such as when Cosimo's reluctance to pay Cellini for the Perseus clashes with the judgments of the statue's pricelessness by Florentine artists—excluding, of course, the judgment proffered by the hated and unworthy Bandinelli. The *Trattati* thus become an attempt to protect Cellini from the forces of the market he had resisted throughout his life by addressing the artists themselves as a community capable of assessing its own worth. This vision, perhaps no less than that incomplete and unsatisfying one of the autobiography, also tries to ignore the essential vulnerability of the finished work to the potentially Medusa-like gaze of others. Thus David Ricardo would write two centuries later that the value of artistic artifacts "is wholly independent of the quantity of labour originally necessary to produce them" and that the economic value of the work of art merely "varies with the varying wealth and inclinations of those who are desirous to possess them."[33] But Cellini's last writings, however tentatively—and uncharacteristically for the artist so frequently heralded as the supposedly modern "Renaissance man"—also look back to the era of guilds and corporations. The *Trattati* seek to define the artist, not as an alienated individual, but as the member of a class whose knowledge of *il fare* and ability to pass such knowledge on to others might make it, if not self-sufficient, at least the possessor of a secret "wisdom." And as such possessors of a wisdom which is only manifest in the process of making, Cellini's readers would ensure their separateness from, and at least in Cellini's eyes their superiority to, those who depended on them for the creation of beautiful things.[34]

Notes

1. The Italian text of the *Vita* is from Benvenuto Cellini, *Opere,* ed. Bruno Maier (Milan: Rizzoli, 1968). Where indicated, the English translation is from Cellini, *Autobiography,* trans. George Bull (Harmondsworth: Penguin Books, 1961); otherwise, it is my own. This passage is from Bull, 144.

2. Cited in Rudolf and Margot Wittkower, *Born under Saturn* (New York: Norton, 1963), 188.

3. See the following articles by Nancy J. Vickers: "Diana Described: Scattered Woman

and Scattered Rhyme," *Critical Inquiry* 8 (1981): 265–79; "The Mistress in the Masterpiece," *The Poetics of Gender,* ed. Nancy K. Miller (New York: Columbia University Press, 1986); "'The Blazon of Sweet Beauty's Best': Shakespeare's *Lucrece*," *Shakespeare and the Question of Theory,* ed. Geoffrey Hartman and Patricia Parker (London: Methuen, 1986), 96–116.

4. Patricia Parker, *Literary Fat Ladies* (London: Methuen, 1987). For Eve Sedgwick's work, see *Between Men: English Literature and Male Homosocial Desire* (New York: Columbia University Press, 1985); for that of Laura Mulvey, see the essays collected in *Visual and Other Pleasures* (Bloomington: Indiana University Press, 1989).

5. Jonathan Goldberg, "Speculations: *Macbeth* and Source," *Reproducing Shakespeare: The Text in History and Ideology,* ed. Jean E. Howard and Marion O'Connor (London: Methuen, 1987), 242–64; Louis Montrose, "The Elizabethan Subject and the Spenserian Text," *Literary Theory/Renaissance Texts,* ed. Patricia Parker and David Quint (Baltimore: Johns Hopkins University Press, 1986), 303–40; and "*A Midsummer Night's Dream* and the Shaping Fantasies of Elizabethan Culture: Gender, Power, Form," *Rewriting the Renaissance,* ed. Margaret W. Ferguson, Maureen Quilligan, and Nancy J. Vickers (Chicago: University of Chicago Press, 1986), 65–87; Stephen Orgel, "Prospero's Wife," *Rewriting the Renaissance,* 50–64.

6. See Judith Kegan Gardiner's review of *Representing the English Renaissance,* ed. Stephen Greenblatt (Berkeley: University of California Press, 1988), in *Modern Philology* 87 (1989): 83–89, for this characterization.

7. Gardiner calls attention to the first two examples (of Stephen Greenblatt, "Murdering Peasants," *Representing the English Renaissance,* 25; and Richard Helgerson, "The Land Speaks: Cartography, Chorography, and Subversion in Renaissance England," *Repesenting the English Renaissance,* 340) in her review, cited above; Montrose, "*A Midsummer Night's Dream* and the Shaping Fantasies of Elizabethan Culture," esp. pp. 74–77.

8. Marcel Mauss, *The Gift: Forms and Functions of Exchange in Archaic Societies,* trans. Ian Cunnison (New York: Norton, 1967).

9. Dino S. Cervigni briefly discusses the parallels between Cellini's autobiography and the picaresque genre in *The "Vita" of Benvenuto Cellini: Literary Tradition and Genre* (Ravenna: Longo, n.d.).

10. Pierre Bourdieu, "Flaubert's Point of View," *Critical Inquiry* 14 (1988): 553.

11. Cited in John Pope-Hennessy, *Cellini* (New York: Abbeville Press, 1985), 174–75. Pope-Hennessy speculates that the phrases here and elsewhere on the base of the *Perseus* were probably written with the help of Cellini's friend Varchi, and comments that "in a very real sense the base is the key to the *Perseus*."

12. See the comments of Ettore Camesasca in his edition of Cellini's *Vita* (Milan: Rizzoli, 1985), 13. On Cosimo's principate in its early years, see Giorgio Spini, *Cosimo I e l'independenza del principato mediceo* (Florence: Valecchi, 1980), esp. chap. 2.3, entitled "La construzione del poter assoluto"; and Elena Fasano Guarini, *Lo stato mediceo di Cosimo I* (Florence: Sansoni, 1973).

13. See Vickers's somewhat analogous analysis of the statue of Jupiter Cellini created for Francis's fountain at Fontainebleau: "For Cellini, Francis's 'fathering of the arts' was literal; Jupiterlike, he inseminated them with a shower of gold. Through them he took his pleasure; through them he left his mark on French culture"; in "The Mistress in the Masterpiece," 38.

14. On the dynamics of this patronage system, see the remarks of Rudolf and Margot Wittkower, *Born under Saturn,* chap. 2, "Artists and Patrons."

15. For this characterization of the *Vita,* see James V. Mirollo, *Mannerism and Renaissance Poetry* (New Haven: Yale University Press, 1984), 83.

16. For the phrase as applied to economies within which gift giving establishes the primary cycle of exchange, see Mauss's *The Gift;* and Pierre Bourdieu, *Outline of a Theory of*

Practice, trans. R. Nice (Cambridge: Cambridge University Press, 1977). Both Mauss and Bourdieu go on to insist that gift giving establishes its own forms of domination and coercion, an element to be explored more fully apropos Cellini in the discussion of the *meraviglioso* in the final section of this essay.

17. See *The Trew Law of Free Monarchies* (1597), where James argues that "as the Father of his fatherly duty is bound to care for the nourishing, education, and vertuous government of his children, even so is the king bound to care for all his subjects"; in *The Political Works of James I,* ed. Charles Howard McIlwain (New York: Russell & Russell, 1965), 55; the citation from the *Basilikon Doron* is on p.24. On James as "nourish-father" in various portraits of the period, see Jonathan Goldberg, "Fatherly Authority: The Politics of Stuart Family Images," *Rewriting the Renaissance,* 3–32.

18. See Coppélia Kahn's suggestive reading of Shakespeare's *Timon of Athens* in " 'Magic of bounty': *Timon of Athens,* Jacobean Patronage, and Maternal Power," *Shakespeare Quarterly* 38 (1987):34–57.

19. *The Masque of Queenes* (perf. 1609), in *Ben Jonson,* ed. C. H. Herford Percy and Evelyn Simpson (Oxford: Clarendon Press, 1941), 7:315. In his marginalia, Jonson notes: "The Antients expressed a brave, and masculine *vertue,* in three figures (Of *Hercules, Perseus,* and *Bellerophon*) of which I chose that of *Perseus,* armed, as I have him describ'd out of *Hesiod*" (7:302n.). In his comments on the masque in the Norton edition of *Ben Jonson's Plays and Masques* (New York: Norton, 1979), Robert M. Adams notes that "all these identifying emblems [of Jonson's Perseus, such as his sandals, wallet, shield, and sword] are to be seen on Cellini's famous statue of Perseus in Florence, which Inigo Jones had seen and Jonson surely heard about" (330n.). For Goldberg's allusion to Perseus, see *James I and the Politics of Literature* (Baltimore: Johns Hopkins University Press, 1983), 91.

20. William Kerrigan and Gordon Braden, *The Idea of the Renaissance* (Baltimore: Johns Hopkins University Press, 1989), 45; from their description regarding the expansion of the capitalist marketplace in the sixteenth century. Such expansion "touches society as a whole, and on a deep level, with a new sense of the awesomely abstract power of money: *Pecuniae obediunt omnia* (Money controls everything) (Erasmus, *Adages* I.3.87)."; idem, 43–44.

21. Such demystification of Cosimo bears comparison with that other remarkable document of the late sixteenth century which reflects on the "devaluation" of patronage, Shakespeare's sonnets. Shakespeare's 94th sonnet, his famous "They that have pow'r to hurt and will do none," can be read as an oblique commentary on the "power" of his aristocratic patron, the young man, to withhold from his poet and would-be lover nature's "gifts" and squander them elsewhere. But far from being the "lord and owner of his face," the young man who both economically and sexually finances Shakespeare's rivals becomes merely a "steward of his excellence." The pejorative use of Aristotelian and biblical terminology of the good steward betokens a degradation of one who might otherwise be a "lord." Far from controlling the "economy" and gifts with which nature has entrusted him, the patron is now conceived as being controlled *by* them, becoming in the closing line little more than a "festering lily," a flower—that "to itself" is supposedly only to live and die— suddenly met with a "base infection" that undermines both its absolutism and its aristocracy. But the sterility that closes the entire sequence, following the narrator's disastrous affair with the dark lady in the final twenty-odd poems, suggests that once the patron is forced to "audit" his value, the poet must *also* have his work quantified, weighed in strictly commercial terms, and that such commodification makes his writing *not* a powerfully "primary" vehicle but merely a copy, generating—although the reproductive term is here deceptive—*other* copies. For several insightful analyses of the sonnets and their relation to "moneyed economies," see Neil L. Goldstien, "Money and Love in Shakespeare's Sonnets," *Bucknell Review* 17, no. 1 (1969):91–106; Judith Gardiner, "The Marriage of Male Minds in Shakespeare's Sonnets," *Journal of English and Germanic Philology* 74 (1985):328–47; and

Thomas Greene, "Pitiful Thrivers: Failed Husbandry in the *Sonnets*," *Shakespeare and the Question of Theory*, 230–44.

22. "Dico . . . cerca lo scarpellare, che questo non fa l'arte più nobile, anzi più presto gli toglie dignità, perché quanto l'arti si fanno con più esercizio di braccia e di corpo, tanto più hanno del meccanico, e per conseguenza sono manco nobili"; in *Trattati d'arte del cinquecento*, ed. Paola Barocchi (Milan: Rizzoli, 1960), 1: 66. Bronzino is drawing on a tradition that placed painting above the other fine arts which goes back at least to Leon Battista Alberti, who in his 1436 treatise *On Painting* insisted that painting contains a "divine force." Relevant also to the discussion is Alberti's observation, almost a hundred years before Castiglione's book of manners, that "polite manners and easy bearing will do more to earn goodwill and hard cash than mere skill and industry"; cited in Wittkower, *Born under Saturn*, 15–16.

23. "Vi ricordo e dico, come di sopra, che la scultura è madre di tutte l'arte dove s'interviene disegno; e quello che sarà valente scultore e di buona maniera, gli sarà facilissimo l'esser buon prospettivo e architetto e maggior pittor che qualli che bene non posseggono la scultura. La pittura non è altro che o arbero o uomo o altra cosa, che si specchi in un fonte. La differenza che è dalla scultura alla pittura è tanta, quanto è dalla ombra e la cosa che fa l'ombra"; in *Opere*, 1004–5. Benedetto Varchi collected the numerous letters and treatises that formed part of the debate in his *Due lezioni* (Florence, 1547). Not surprisingly, Michelangelo (whom Cellini notes as one of his greatest influences) also argues for sculpture's supremacy as a representational rather than a mimetic art. But Michelangelo emphasizes the extent to which sculpture is capable of recognizing a hidden or Platonic essence, whereas Cellini's preference for sculpture is founded in his argument for the artist's godlike ability to be a *homo faber*. On Michelangelo's aesthetics, see Robert J. Clements, *Michelangelo's Theory of Art* (New York: New York University Press, 1961).

24. "Benvenuto, questa figura non ti può venire cosí di bronzo, perché l'arte non te lo promette" (2.73).

25. For an intriguing reading of the sexual politics of the Medusa myth, see Neil Hertz, "Medusa's Head: Male Hysteria under Political Pressure," *Representations* 1 (1983):40–50.

26. Mircea Eliade, *The Forge and the Crucible*, trans. Stephen Corrin (Chicago: University of Chicago Press, 1978), 56–57.

27. *The Passions of the Soul* (1648), in *Descartes: Selections*, ed. Ralph M. Eaton (New York: Scribners, 1955), 380.

28. "Il ricco e potente si compiace di 'essere sforzato' dall'artista"; in M. L. Altieri Biagi, "La Vita del Cellini," in *Benvenuto Cellini artista e scrittore*, special issue of *Quaderni dell'Accademia Nazionale dei Lincei* 177 (1972):94.

29. See particularly Baudrillard's preface, in which he invokes Lacan's description of the mirror stage to create an analogy with the mirror of production: "At the level of all political economy there is something of what Lacan describes in the mirror stage: through this scheme of production, this *mirror* of production, the human species comes to consciousness *in the imaginary*. Production, labor, value, everything through which an objective world emerges and through which man recognizes himself objectively—this is imaginary"; in *The Mirror of Production*, trans. Mark Poster (St. Louis: Telos Press, 1975), 19. See too Baudrillard's astute chapter on "Marxist Anthropology" in which he argues that "everything that speaks in terms of totality (and/or 'alienation') under the sign of a Nature or a recovered essence speaks in terms of repression and separation" (55–56).

30. Guido D. Bonino, *Lo scrittore, il potere, la maschera* (Padua: Liviana, 1979), 50. Bonino links Cellini's production of "narcisismo" to his social predicament of alienation; such alienation ultimately triumphs over the compensatory narcissism of the text, as the unfinished nature of the text bears witness.

31. See Camesasca's suggestion in his edition of the *Vita* that "in effetti l'autobiografia

celliniana è un dialogo fra Benvenuto e il duca Cosimo I, l'interlocutore da convincere" (19).

32. "Io promessi inel principio del mio libro di dire parte della causa che movea a scrivere questo volume, la qual causa io dissi che moverebbe gli uomini a grande sdegno del caso e compassione di me"; in *Opere*, 713.

33. Cited in Kurt Heinzelman, *The Economics of the Imagination* (Amherst: University of Massachusetts Press, 1980), 154.

34. On the interest of patrons in learning the process of *il fare* in the sixteenth century, see Richard A. Goldthwaite, "The Economic and Social World of Italian Renaissance Maiolica," *Renaissance Quarterly* 42 (1989): 1–33.

Elizabethan Music as a Cultural Mode

T. G. Bishop

Case Western Reserve University

MUCH recent work in the interpretation of Elizabethan culture has been insistently interdisciplinary in nature. Rejecting as ideologically motivated constraints many of the formal, generic, and disciplinary categories that have hitherto organized academic inquiry, practitioners have sought to construe events, customs, policies, or texts from widely disparate fields as local instances of shared general narratives, symbolic fields, and structures. The hope of this work has been to illuminate the particular historical character of instances while at the same time eliciting general habits of action or perception which can be applied more widely. At the same time, this work has sought to avoid reducing any instance to a secondary status whose meaning is simply read off in a priori terms, or whose clarity is expounded only to be trumped by a complicating alternative.

One very real difficulty, if this enterprise is to advance beyond the serendipitous, involves the extent to which diverse fields of synchronic cultural activity are in fact commensurable with one another without reductive simplification. Is mere copresence within a culture sufficient for a presumption of common features? If so, whose framework will allow those common features to be discerned? Anthropology? History? Economics? Or some new theoretical discourse whose discipline will somehow escape the charges laid against those it displaces? If, on the other hand, copresence is not of itself sufficient, with what intellectual tools are we to decide which elements can be fruitfully subjected to interdisciplinary analysis and which cannot? As yet it has proved extraordinarily difficult to produce a general methodological account of the reading of heterogenous instances of this kind, without in practice either covertly rehierarchizing them or inventing suspiciously ad hoc concepts which appear radically synthetic, but on closer examination often turn out to disguise a disappointing, sometimes even banal, flattening of nuance. Such difficulties have made much work of the last ten years by turns forceful and disappointing, according as a particular analogy has proved lucky and intuitively convincing or otherwise. Brilliance, a quality now much prized, is to this extent limiting insofar as it relies on unpredictable and intuitive connection for much of its dramatic impact.[1]

A principal source of this "hit-or-miss" difficulty, it seems to me, is that the mediations performed by such criticism must necessarily be not just between objects of attention (diaries, legal records, riots) but also between the very modes of attention, the kinds of reading, that those objects solicit, and this is an issue that many such accounts neglect. Without an appreciation of the specific contours of an example, there can be a tendency for the particularity of historical events to be steamrollered by a necessity, dictated by theoretical expectations, of finding congruence. For the possibility should be explored that signification itself operates according to different conventions, different paradigms, even different rhythms on the various levels and in various corners of a culture, and that therefore our understanding of cultural activity will need to take into account more complex features of language use from site to site than simply the sharing of "similar" verbal or ideational structures. One cannot assume that writing, reading, or signification in general are isomorphic across a culture. Rather the complex relations of similarity and difference between what I will call "cultural modes" need also to be charted. The State Papers in the Public Record Office and *The Tempest*, for example, are in important ways insulated from one another by complex institutional traditions which shape the way that they are generated and claim the close attention of their intended, and unintended, interpreters.

To become sensitive to questions such as these is to extend to the synchronic cultural moment, in its layeredness and multiplicity, both the "rhetorical nominalism" that Thomas Greene has looked for in a diachronic criticism, and the sensitivity to multiple dialectics within cultures that Dominic LaCapra has recently championed.[2] Nor should dialectic "collision" exhaust the imaginable relations between cultural strains, but also slippage, mistake, absorption, and just plain disengagement should be anticipated.[3] What emerges as crucially important is an awareness of the ways in which the different disciplines, practices, and locales of a culture *figure* "the same" events and preoccupations into different meanings. Even to use the locution "the same" is in some sense to prejudge the issue, since these figurations, though they may work by small increments, can lead to radically "different" consequences for the power, influence, and mode of operation of particular works. The well-known children's game of "Telephone" could be taken as an apt image here, or the story of the general who received the urgent request from his front-line commander: "Send three-and-fourpence, I wish to dance."[4]

This should not be taken as a rejection of interdisciplinary study, but rather a caveat that any proposals for a general "cultural poetics" need to be supplemented by something like a "cultural tropology" which would attempt to chart the particular eddies that mold and meld the flow of signification. In much the same way that a lymphatic system and a vascular one cannot be analyzed in precisely the same terms, yet figure one another complexly, the contours of systemic interimplication should never be taken for granted in interdisciplinary studies. The interpreter's movement between disciplines must be vigilantly attentive to the full range of changed conditions and enlarged (or even contracted) contexts, and the objects of interpretation brought together must be scanned with as wide a purview as possible to determine their points of contact, to define and situate their mutual illumination.

In an attempt to demonstrate what such an exploration might discover, I wish to examine some instances of Elizabethan music, attempting to chart some of music's relations to the rest of the culture and to see what, if any, models for cultural work in its period it uses and provides. How and where and along what axes does music appear, and in what ways is it like or unlike other cultural modes of the same moment? Clearly, the compass of an essay is too small to address such a question in full, since, perhaps more than for any other mode, regular and direct experience of some type of music is likely to have been general throughout Elizabethan culture. But, as a practice whose formal boundaries, at any rate, are more than usually clear, music offers the advantage of a test case for the relations between cultural modes. In the process of this exploration, I hope also to take some steps to answer a call made recently by Leo Treitler for:

> a hermeneutic sense in which music is viewed as a meaningful item within a wider context of practices, conventions, assumptions, transmissions, social relations—in short, a musical culture, which serves to endow its constituent aspects with meaning while attaining meaning from the combination of its constituents.[5]

It is not so much a question of an account of music per se therefore, as of some illuminating points of intersection between music and its milieu, to see what gets done in music that isn't or can't be done in another mode. The investigation therefore goes in two directions at once, from music to its occasion and back again, looking for their points of mutual appropriation, for what they "do with" one another.

I

The notion of a cultural "mode" advanced here to model the relations between what have otherwise been called "discourses" is itself a metaphor drawn from early music theory.[6] In this theory, giving the "mode" of a piece locates a particular class of compositions to which it belongs according to the hierarchical structure of relations between its notes.[7] "Mode" occupies the theoretical middle ground between, on the one hand, prescriptive scale and, on the other, specific tune. In regular use today two "modes" survive, designated as the familiar "major" and "minor" tonalities. In the sixteenth century, use of a mode was believed to alter psychological disposition in a particular way (though how in any particular case was much disputed).

The extension of this theoretical notion to interdisciplinary studies here imagines an entire culture as a series of discrete but related figural patternings, each defined by the variable criteria with which it orders an array of common elements (which can assume effective significance only within a mode) to produce local meanings. What is taken to be fundamental, transient, or pivotal will therefore change from mode to mode, and the particular force of an "event, custom, policy, or text" will be intimately involved with the "modality" of its occasion. Since no mode is precisely reducible to a function of another, and transition from mode to mode occurs according to a complex set of relational figures, there is always room to maneuver, to change, even to resist.

Obviously such an image for a historical culture falsifies insofar as it suggests that all possible operations are known (i.e., that the system is closed), but if we recall that the modal harmonic system only functioned in practice as a reified theoretical totality, descriptive rather than prescriptive, such a pitfall may be avoided.[8] According to this model, one cannot therefore speak properly of the "same" material presenting itself in different modes. Movement between modes, or "modulation," itself an important impetus of development in musical style through the sixteenth century, results in figurative transformation which cannot be understood simply as repetition, nor simply as difference, any more than a Dorian piece would be "the same" in Phrygian (or an F major one in D minor). The change of mode itself indicates that meanings are constellated anew, that new openings or closings become available.

To describe music as a "cultural mode" among others then is to suggest that to act in the culture musically might have different determinants and different consequences from, say, doing so poetically, or diplomatically, even if one were treating "the same" material. Different understandings, opportunities, consequences flow from acts in different modes, even in the same historical moment, and each mode has its own particular parameters for action and interpretation.

II

The notion of cultural modulation can be extended further, however, for it is not only a practice within music which can supply a convenient metaphor for the relation of cultural discourses. It also describes the effect of music itself on its participants, especially as the late sixteenth century understood and explained it. Hearers of music, that is, are confronted by and included in a translated or "modulated" ambience. Most obviously, time is segmented and arrayed differently within a musical structure; patterns of repetition and divergence are organized in ways that invite a new kind of cognitive attention. Though both the participants and the space they occupy may retain all premusical details, they can also, and very easily do, take on entirely new significances. "Modulation" is a particularly useful alternative term for figurative maneuvres therefore, because it draws especial attention to the element of boundary crossing in entering the transformed system. Thus it can describe the relation of musical to nonmusical discourse, and, as here, the relations between discursive traditions generally within a culture. "Modulation" does not merely confirm or contest, but also reviews, reflects, refracts, cites, deforms, and fragments.

The transmuting effect of music on its audience is a commonplace of humanistic writing on the subject all through the sixteenth century, and recovery of an "original" psycho-active power of music was the fondest dream of two generations of theorists and practitioners. Theories of a consonancy between the structure of the psyche and of music, taking the observed phenomenon of sympathetic vibration for their chiefest proof, provided the metaphysical basis for an understanding of music's action as a literal transformative "movement" of the proportions of the mind. The author of *The Praise of Musicke* of 1586 writes only what all who knew music theory believed when he states:

> [Music] hath a certaine diuine influence into the soules of men, whereby our cogitations and thoughts (say Epicurus what he will) are brought into a celestiall acknowledging of their natures. For as the Platonicks and Pythagorians think, al soules of men are at the recordation of that celestial Musicke, whereof they were partakers in heauen, before they entred into their bodies, so wonderfuly delighted, that no man can be found so harde harted which is not exceedingly alured with the sweetnes thereof.[9]

This mental movement, involved with theories that the soul was itself "but a Musical motion," was understood as keyed to the harmonic modes used by the ancient Greeks, and (through a link modern English still recognizes in the semantic overlap of the terms "mode" and "mood")[10] gave great power to those who could manipulate it. Hence music—at least as described by its defenders—was an important element in theories of psychology, education, and politics, as well as, inevitably, religion.

To describe Elizabethan music in terms of its own theory would yield only half-truths—theory and practice in this case being more than usually out of step—but it should be remembered that these half-truths were credited alike by audiences and practitioners, and actively shaped musical experience. It is therefore as music displays itself *for interpretation* in relation to its occasions that its particular significance as a cultural mode should be sought, rather than in either its complex metaphysics or its formal structure alone.

The claims of *The Praise* at times grow extreme: "musicke hath brought madde men into their perfect wits and senses, . . . hath cured diseases, driven away evil spirits, yea and also abandoned the pestilence from men and cities" (sig. D4–D5r). But it is important evidence that Elizabethans understood music as raising in (supposedly) precise terms the issue of modal "transposition." There is much more such evidence. Treatises, proverbs, lore, and stories of the period all stress music's recoding power. Thomas Draxe's proverb dictionary of 1616, the *Bibliotheca scholastica instructissima* (STC 7174), includes a pair of proverbs on music of this sort: "Musicians are magicians" and "Music is the eye of the ear." The first suggests the miraculous power of music to control secret orders of nature through an occult language, a direct pathway to hermetic understanding that manipulates latent hermetic structures as audible patterns. Hence music's emotive effect is through our translation into a heightened and apperceptive mode of attention. The second proverb, with its striking synesthesia, evokes this power of transformation in pointing to the new *focus* thus achieved, translating the diffuse "ear" into the more precise and localizing "eye."

Richard Hooker uses the same understanding of music as a cognitive translation in his well-known defense of its role in divine worship, arguing for its power to open alternative routes of divine apprehension for the worshiper. In part his argument, following Saint Basil, is the familiar "sugaring the pill" chestnut: music as an attention-getting but dispensable ornament for doctrine. But he takes an altogether different turn when he claims an independent cognition of divinity fostered by music alone:

> the verie harmonie of soundes being framed in due sorte and carried from the eare to the spirituall faculties of our soules is by a native puissance and efficacie greatlie available to bringe to a perfect temper whatsoever is there troubled, . . . forcible to drawe forth teares of devotion.[11]

Music has a peculiar operant grace, parallel rather than subordinate to other elements of worship, even to the Word itself. Music never merely repeats: it revises and interprets.

III

So much for theory. But what of theory's effects on practice? What consequences does a belief in the translating or "modulating" power of music, product at once of its abstraction and its inner connection to fundamental process, have on its workings in the culture at large? Does its use conform to these expectations when music comes into contact with the social, political, or religious?

A brief example of the transformation of contemporary experience by its passage into organized musical form is afforded by Orlando Gibbons's "The Cries of London," a five-part piece for voices and viol consort. Probably written around the turn of the century, when "Cries" were briefly in fashion, it charts a day's activity through London street cries. Opening with the tenor as the Watch proclaiming "God give you good morrow my masters, past 3 o'clock and a fair morning," the piece develops along a roughly chronological line, including in its musical texture as it goes early-morning pitches for fresh fish and produce, various offers of wares and services, public announcements by the town crier, and pleas for charity on behalf of mad beggars (one cries "Tom's a-cold") and poor, imprisoned women. The day concludes with the Watch's evening call of "Lanthorn and candlelight" and, in one MS, a collective "Good night." The piece is fascinating as a kind of "soundscape" of Elizabethan London, and there is reason to believe that the cries are transcribed more or less directly from common street use.[12]

The added interest of the piece for the present purpose is, however, less here than in the superposition of this motley chorus upon the well-known "In Nomine" theme (played by the alto viol). The "reportage" of the city streets is thus brought into contact with a standard art-music instrumental form of the Elizabethan and Jacobean period, usually written for viol consort or keyboard. Although a few other "In Nomine" works that include sung texts survive, the Gibbons piece is the only one of the "Cries" extant to take this further step, and it has been somewhat daring in doing so.[13] The "In Nomine" form was undergoing something of a revival in these early Jacobean years, having been very prominent in the period 1550–70 only to suffer temporary eclipse thereafter.[14] The very earliest settings of the theme are lifted directly from a section of the Benedictus of a Mass by John Taverner (hence the name "In Nomine"). In fact the plainsong theme was originally an antiphon to First Vespers for Trinity Sunday (in the old Sarum Rite), whose opening words were "Gloria tibi Trinitas," by which name Taverner's Mass is known. In some extant keyboard settings, though no consort versions, the designation "Gloria tibi Trinitas" is used instead of the Taverner derivation.[15]

In the Gibbons piece, as in all "In Nomine" settings,[16] the plainsong is prominent, even-flowing, and gently measured. Its concatenation with the amorphous snatches of street-wise bustle creates a curious and unique effect. No doubt the piece is in part a *jeu d'esprit* or a virtuoso experiment in contrastive extremes by Gibbons. But the *contaminatio* of such a "high-art" tradition with the popular and mundane also has deeper resonances.[17] The plainsong counterpointing that flows through and among the cries give them both a narrative and an aesthetic unity they could not otherwise encompass, while they move closer to appearing as vivid sparks struck off its graceful and steady serenity. Though the achivement is brittle and perhaps a little forced, and the insight confined to a coterie of the musically skilled, Gibbons's experiment offers an interpretive suggestion of the unity of London life which contemporary celebrators like John Stow or Thomas Dekker would recognize and appreciate.

Such a view of the meaning of London is not without political and social implications, whether one chooses to interpret the figuration as assertion, question, travesty, or utopian vision. And since the music does not (perhaps cannot) make clear the precise predication involved, its status is significantly different as representation of London from a picture, a sermon, a Privy Council minute. It shifts the apprehension of London life to a new level of integrity by simple juxtaposition, with economy and facility.

IV

This sense of music as a distinctly significant route of apprehension has some important consequences for its political uses. Hearing a speech on a subject is not at all the same as hearing a song, even on the same subject. Each requires a different "set" or stance toward the occasion, so that what is no longer possible for one may be negotiable for the other. For this reason, music could be and was employed as a means for renegotiating political deadlock.

An exemplary incident of this kind occurred at court in September 1602, six months before Elizabeth's death. An account of it survives in a letter written by secretary William Brown to his master, the earl of Shrewsbury, concerning the recent employment of Robert Hales, the queen's favorite court musician:

> I send your Lordship hereinclosed some verses compounded by M[aste]r Secretary [Cecil], who got Hales to frame a ditty unto it. The occasion was, as I hear, that the young Lady of Derby [Cecil's niece] wearing about her neck, in her bosom, a picture which was in a dainty tablet, the Queen, espying it, asked what fine jewel that was. The Lady Derby was curious to excuse the shewing of it, but the Queen would have it, and opening it and finding it to be Mr. Secretary's, snatched it away, and tied it upon her shoe, and walked along with it there; then she took it thence and pinned in on her elbow, and wore it some time there also; which Mr. Secretary being told of, made these verses, and had Hales to sing them in his chamber. It was told her Majesty that Mr. Secretary had rare music and songs; she would needs hear them, and so this ditty was sung which you see first written. More verses there be likewise, whereof some, or all, were likewise sung. I do boldly send these things to your Lordship, which I would not do to anyone

else, for I hear they are very secret. Some of the verses argue that he repines not though her Majesty please to grace others, contents himself with the favour he hath.[18]

The route taken by Cecil in his attempt to regain the good graces of the queen reveals not only his knowledge of her personal tastes, but his shrewd sense that refiguring his relations to her through the musical mode at this tense moment, when spoken appeals might be futile or even provocative, allows both parties leeway to reposition themselves. Music saves appearances and offers new roles through a translated formal mediation. Cecil does not have to entreat, or even directly express an intention to entreat, nor does the queen have to undertake to listen to anything but a concert: what is "told" her is not that "Cecil wishes to apologize," but that he has "rare music and songs." The disgraced lord does not speak for himself, but "is sung" by another, and Elizabeth, if she wishes to hear the music, must agree to remain silent while he is represented. It is unfortunate that the enclosed "verses" have not survived, for they might clarify the role of musical form here, and even allow us to locate the song. Nevertheless, we can see that music offers a metamorphic (and metaphoric) diversion of the quarrel for its renegotiation.[19]

This brief crisis shows a striking example of a recurrent tactic of court ceremony and exposes on a small scale the political opportunities made available by using shifts in cultural mode to articulate a complex calculus of loyalties. A more public, if less explosive, instance is the elaborate ceremony surrounding the retirement of Sir Henry Lee at the Accession Day Tournament of 1590. Sir Henry had volunteered himself into the office of "Queen's Champion" in the first year of Elizabeth's reign, and had held it ever since. Now sixty years old, he resigns the post and commends the earl of Cumberland to the queen as successor.[20] This might have been a simple process, but because the Accession Day celebration is by now a crucial element in the apparatus of Elizabethan ceremonial power, the retirement becomes encrusted with symbolic artifacts and performances, all hedging the critical moment when the march of Time on Elizabeth herself must be, however discreetly, alluded to. The result is a combination of focusing and heightening of the event with the dispersal and transmutation of its deadly import into divers media. Using a kind of sleight of hand to cover the threatening substitution, Lee's retirement is dramatized as the sudden irruption of a "unique" moment, outside "normal" time. Sir William Segar, much taken with the gloriousness of it all, narrates:

Her Majesty beholding these armed knights comming toward her [as she sat in "her Gallery Window"], did suddenly heare a musicke so sweete and secret, as euery one thereat greatly marueiled. And hearkening to that excellent melodie, the earth as it were opening, there appeared a Pauilion, made of white Taffata, containing eight score elles, being in proportion like vnto the sacred Temple of the Virgins Vestall. This Temple seemed to consist vpon pillars of Pourferry, arched like vnto a Church, within it were many Lampes burning. Also, on the one side there stood an Altar couered with cloth of gold, and thereupon two waxe candles burning in rich candlesticks, vpon the Altar also were layd certain Princely presents, which after by three Virgins were presented vnto her Maiestie. Before the doore of this Temple stood a crowned Pillar, embraced by an Eglantine tree, whereon there hanged a Tablet; and therein written (with letters of gold) this prayer following: [There follows an inscription in Latin laid out in columnar form.]

The musicke aforesayd, was accompanied with these verses, pronounced and sung by M. Hales her Maiesties seruant, a Gentleman in that Arte excellent, and for his voice both commendable and admirable.

>His golden locks time hath to silver turnde,
>(O time too swift, O swiftnes neuer ceasing).
>His youth 'gainst time and age hath ever spurnd,
>But spurnd in vaine, youth waneth by encreasing:
>Beauty, strength, youth, are flow'rs but fading seene,
>Duty, Faith, Loue, are roots and euer greene.
>
>His helmet now shall make a hiue for bees,
>And louers sonets turne to holy psalmes:
>A man at armes must now serve on his knees,
>And feed on prayers which are ages almes,
>But though from court to cotage he departe,
>His saint is sure of his vnspotted hart.
>
>And when he saddest sits in homely Cell,
>He'le teach his Swaines this Caroll for a songe,
>Blest be the harts that wish my soueraigne well,
>Curst be the soules that thinke her any wrong:
>Goddes, allow this aged man his right,
>To be your beadsman now, that was your knight.[21]

. . . These presents and prayer being with great reuerence deliuered into her Maiesties owne hands, and he himselfe disarmed, offered vp his armour at the foot of her Maiesties crowned pillar; and kneeling vpon his knees, presented the Earle of Cumberland, humbly beseeching she would be pleased to accept him for her Knight, to continue the yeerely exercises aforesaid. Her Maiesty graciously accepting of that offer, this aged Knight armed the Earle, and mounted him vpon his horse. Then being done, he put vpon his owne person a side coat of black Velvet pointed under the arme, and couered his head (in liew of an helmet) with a buttoned cap of the countrey fashion.[22]

Music plays the crucial transforming role in this scenario. It is "secret" music which first conjures and announces a transformed space in which the Temple can magically appear. And it is the song which bears the task of describing the "turning" action of time which is the key to the ceremony. Into its terms the transformation of Sir Henry from Champion to country squire is drawn. Musical form here bears an analogical political function: successive stanzas have the same setting, and change is transfigured into repetition, shaped to an underlying stability of structure which resists temporal depredations by troping them as recurrences. The musical organization of the recurring stanza reinforces this by consisting of simple variants of a single sectioned melody, playing off stasis and movement against one another and dipping to a darker "minor tonality" briefly (at "fading") before combining melodic sections to circle back to the opening. It is a simple, even common, form but here it takes on politically significant reverberations. What it presents is a "virtual image of time" (as W. H. Auden called it) as a stable and controlled recurrence which sublimes the pathos of aging and smooths any anxiety out of the transfer of office by restructuring unruly change as a varied repetition.[23] The conjunction of this particular song with the appearance of the Temple of eternal virginity is carefully motivated, especially in the light of the queen's motto, "Semper Eadem." The burden of the retirement ceremony is that Lee as "beadsman" will be merely a physically and modally translated version of Lee as "knight." In this context, music, encoded theoretically as the mode par excellence of systemic transposition, supplies a crucial allegorizing medium that does inimitable cultural work.

V

If music could open interpretive opportunities and do political work differently from other cultural modes in the period, it also took its place in relation to political and religious authority with a different, even a semi-independent stance. The crossing into music seems often to have stripped sensitive issues and texts of their actively polemic and even subversive force, or rather, to have enabled such force to appear disguised in plain sight. Nowhere is the suggestion that the meaning of an "event, custom, policy, or text" emerges according to the modality of its form confirmed so strongly as in the career of William Byrd.[24]

A devout Roman Catholic several times cited for recusancy, and once heavily fined (though whether this was paid is not known), Byrd's music nevertheless remained highly prized by monarchs, courtiers, and gentry. His first published collection of part-songs, *Psalmes, Sonets and Songs of Sadness and Piety,* sold out in its 1588 issue and was twice reprinted. It contains fourteen English psalms similar to "Sternhold and Hopkins," settings of poems by prominent courtiers (Dyer, Sidney, Oxford), and penitential and devotional songs—including a famous "Holy Innocents" Lullaby—closing with two funeral hymns for Philip Sidney, one setting English quantitative verse. In short, it is a miscellany designed to appeal broadly to courtly and devotional taste.

Song number 33 however, immediately before the Sidney hymns, is something of a daring move. The first of three printed stanzas read:

> Why do I use my paper, pen and ink,
>   And call my wits to counsel what to say?
> Such memories were made for mortal men;
>   I speak of Saints whose names cannot decay.
> An Angel's trump were fitter for to sound
> Their glorious death if such on earth were found.

This seems innocuous stuff, until the text is traced to the opening of a lengthy narrative poem on the execution of the Jesuit Edmund Campion in 1581, an event which galvanized the English Catholic community, and Byrd among them. The poem is and was thought to have been written by Henry Walpole, by his own account converted at Campion's death, later captured and executed himself as a Jesuit in 1595, seven years after Byrd published his setting. Walpole's poem appeared anonymously immediately after Campion's execution, first in MS and then in print, and the Privy Council took strong but ineffective measures to suppress it, interrogating the publisher and ordering his ears cut off. In 1588, Walpole was serving as a chaplain in the duke of Parma's army, presumably awaiting the imminent invasion of England. Byrd's setting was therefore hardly an innocent choice, and it is not unlikely that more than the three printed stanzas were sung in private.[25]

Even with the text altered in print, this publication is sailing pretty close to the wind, especially in the political climate of 1588, and the very success of Byrd's work makes it unlikely that the gesture passed unnoticed. No doubt Byrd's court sponsors shielded him, as they certainly did in his recusancy citations, but this does not quite explain why a song was countenanced where a poem, even in manuscript, was not. Perhaps, then, the song did not present itself to the same kind of attention as did the original poem: not that no one noticed or cared, but that they did not notice or care in the same way. What cannot be spoken can sometimes be sung, and sung publicly too. We might recall the songs of Lear's Fool, so obvious to us, but noted by Kent ("This is not altogether fool, my Lord") as though their bite might otherwise be overlooked.

Byrd's decision to publish this poem is precisely in line with the rest of his career. Throughout the 1580s he circulated and then published material of an obviously Catholic application with minimal restraint. His two volumes of Latin motets, the *Cantiones sacrae* of 1589 and 1591, set carefully composed biblical and liturgical texts of corporate lamentation. Over and over the faithful appear as a righteous minority surrounded by God's enemies: "O Lord, we look for thy coming, and may thou come quickly, and loose the yoke of our captivity. Come, O Lord, do not delay. Forgive the transgressions of thy followers and deliver thy people."[26] Striking references to savage martyrdom at the hands of the gentiles recall again the deaths of Campion and others. Rejoicing is kept for the day, sure but distant, when the Lord *will* ransom his faithful. As Joseph Kerman has shown, these texts and their settings are carefully assembled to provide a focus for Catholic feelings of anguish and hope.[27] The publication of the first collection after the long-expected outbreak of war with Spain can hardly be a coincidence.

In the 1590s, after moving to a farm in Essex near the Petre household, an important Catholic center, Byrd wrote and then published three settings of the Ordinary of the Mass. Under James, and in the service of the same local community, he also composed and published two enormous volumes of Propers, the *Gradualia,* for use in the annual liturgical cycle of Catholic worship. Given that manuscript circulation was a ready, tested, and comparatively safe route to recusant households, Byrd's continuing determination to publish these works and his careful supervision of their printing make, as Philip Brett has remarked, "a special statement about their importance and the authority of their texts."[28] Only once does there appear to have been trouble. The first volume of *Gradualia* appeared in early 1605; in November occurred the "Gunpowder Treason." One man taken with

Byrd's work was imprisoned, and only a single copy of the volume survives (it was reissued with its 1607 companion in 1610).[29] In the 1607 volume, Byrd appears inclined to limit himself to liturgy derived from Scripture, though even this included such risky matter as "Tu es Petrus, et super hanc petram aedificabo ecclesiam meam" (Matt. 16:18). This policy may have been intended as a kind of insurance: Byrd could claim, if challenged, that he had set only the indisputable Word, and nothing sectarian.[30] We can see here the process of weighing the vital importance of promulgating the Word against the dangers of overboldness. Byrd was not one for uncalculated risks, and in this calculation, music itself plays a part.

Nevertheless, what is most remarkable about this career, under both its monarchs, remains the intention behind it, implicit in Kerman's remarks on the originality of the 1580s motets: they are "music of a rhetorical vividness that was all but unprecedented on the English scene, and so ... music of *unprecedented power.*"[31] Recalling Hooker's remarks on the devotional force of music, on its ability to translate inner truth into the compellingly manifest, we can see Byrd's work as a bid for "power" in a very active sense: as a moving, calculated entry into a European war of faiths. From this point of view, this is the musical equivalent of the most eloquent and passionate Catholic preaching—just the kind of eloquence, in fact, for which Campion was famous. Campion's last sermon before his capture was on the subject of "Jerusalem"; Byrd's motets constantly refer to that allegorical city. And Byrd's insistence on publication corresponds strangely to Campion's famous "Brag," which so alarmed the Privy Council. Publication is then both a calculated defiance and Byrd's employment of his best talents to do what his Jesuit friend, Henry Garnet, was also doing—until his execution: to win and keep souls by setting forth the superior spiritual resources of his faith. Even where his compositional style changes, this intention remains the same. The Masses, though they lack titles, bear his name on every page, and like the *Gradualia* seek to impress on the hearer (and performer) the depths of meaning in their texts, the world's most important, in music as limpid and concise as the sentences themselves. In creating the impression of immense resonance in the simplest of liturgical moments, such as the single word "Alleluia," Byrd was also publishing the truth of his view of these texts.[32]

How much effect Byrd's efforts had we cannot know, but this is not quite the point. The musical mode apparently enabled his sectarian project to go on more or less unimpeded, if not unobserved. His music remains a public intervention in the culture of the period, a kind of exemplary Credo at once open and withdrawn. Kerman suggests that in his later works "Byrd's eye was not on history . . . but on eternity."[33] Byrd does speak, in the dedication of the *Gradualia,* of a God "qui in abscondito videt." He also asserts that "public indeed and clearly worthy are those things, which are communicated by these Songs of mine, such as they are, but also by the voices and pens of all men, as much to our descendants as to foreign nations." Perhaps history and eternity for an English Catholic in 1605 were not so antithetical.

Byrd's career suggests that the boundaries of authority and license were drawn and understood rather differently for music than for other activities, and that accounts of relations between political authority and cultural activity need to take into account the particular institutional contours of different cultural modes and the variable overlap between them.[34] As with the incident of Cecil and the queen, charged political situations have different "complexions" in different modes. Their modulation gives them new cultural meanings and new resources for action, conciliation, or dissent.

VI

The Elizabethan understanding of musical representation as standing in a translated relation to the "proper" or the "ordinary" has some interesting consequences for contemporary ideas about its effects. For example, music was held to be at once symptom and cure for insanity. Mad people took to singing ("Poor mad Tom"), but music could also cure them. Or again (predominantly male) musicians were popularly held to be effeminized by music, but at the same time had a reputation for being especially lascivious and erotically successful (hence perhaps the charges against Anne Boleyn and Mark Smeaton).[35] In both these cases, the coincidence of apparently contrary pairs registers primarily displacement—direction is comparatively less important.

This music that modulates the ordinary, registering insights in anamorphic and displaced ways, offering oblique routes of expression to the otherwise inexpressible, can become in its turn the site of trope. So imagined, music becomes a prominent and active resource in the texture of Shakespearean drama, and provides us with both the occasion and the medium for reflection on the modal complexity of Shakespeare's dramatic poetry.[36]

A good example of this appropriation of contemporary music for complex poetic purposes lies in Ophelia's sudden irruption, mad, into the court of Elsinore. Her distress is of a peculiarly lucid cast, as several courtiers remark, presenting an associatively coherent vision of Elsinore from the point of view of the triply displaced: mad, female, and singing. These three attributes are deliberately fused as common indices of her sidelong interpretive relation to the court. The stage direction in the "bad" First Quarto, which nevertheless probably records stage practice, draws attention to the conjunction: "Enter Ofelia playing on a lute, and her haire downe singing." Herself practically an emblem of displacement, this figure contains within it a further emblem: that of the paraverbal interpretive gloss, signaled by the placement of singing voice against and alongside lute accompaniment. The image is of more than one register at work at once. Ophelia's appearance pictures the entrance onto the scene of a mode of dramatic language at once oblique and precise, piercing and remote.[37] Ranged opposite Ophelia in the scene appears her exact contrary: the sane, male, and very unmusical Claudius, who attempts to contain her troublingly ambiguous songs by glossing them narrowly as "conceit upon her father," so missing or refusing any more complex intimations.

Ophelia's singing appropriates for dramatic and poetic purposes just that power of abstraction and inner connection to fundamental process which I have suggested is central to the Elizabethan understanding of music. Her songs discern general patterns in the action of the play that refuse to be localized, and touch on basic recurrences of action and consciousness, applicable at once to many instances. Her opening remark "to" Gertrude ("Where is the beauteous majesty of Denmark?") is not altogether fool, as critics have noted, and hangs in the air, at once nonspecific and sharp. Her madness realizes general habits of feeling and behavior in Elsinore in dense images of mourning and betrayal. To this achievement the fact of song rather than speech is crucial, for it is in her song fragments that this work is most vividly done.

As if to draw attention to the workings of complex displacement and signal Shakespeare's awareness of how his dramatic language here exposes its own "undersong" operations, Ophelia's first song is a fragmented variant of the popular ballad, "Walsingham." In its circulating version, this was the lament of an aging male speaker for the young lover who had left him because "Love liketh not the falling fruit / From the withered tree." Ophelia's version converts this into the lament of a woman for the death of an older man.[38] Fragmentation and metamorphosis of the popular version in Ophelia's impromptu performance create a revisionary relation ("new song": "old song") immediately observable by those who know the ballad.[39] The tension created between the lurking original and its revision indexes the complex work of transposition and condensation being done by Ophelia's "madness" on the events of the play as a whole. The older version may itself gloss the scene in secret ways, as for example in identifying one source of Ophelia's derangement:

> Yea but Love is a durable fire,
> In the mind ever burning,
> Never sick, never old, never dead
> From himself never turning.

If the old ballad sums up what Hamlet seemed to accuse her of back in the nunnery scene, the new version turns this around into a grief-stricken response, followed at once by the "Valentine's Day" riposte, an accusatory version of the same reaction formation to Hamlet's calumnies. The coordinates established by this layering of possibilities then serve to translate, by condensation and displacement, all the surrounding action of the play: Gertrude's remarriage, Laertes's hypocrisy, Polonius's exploitation, Hamlet's betrayal. Madness and music correspond as modes of cognition that organize into observable pattern what is otherwise inchoate but pervasive. Musician joins lunatic, lover, and poet.

This use of music reappears in the similarly allusive and revising song of Ophelia's gravedigger. The latter's ditty is also based on a famous miscellany poem, Lord Vaux's "The Aged Lover's Farewell to Love." The grim irony of this for Ophelia's grave again suggests an interpretive relation between the song and the scene of its singing, and again this is signaled by the clown's getting Vaux's poem "wrong." The clown's "speech by the card" and Ophelia's madness are thereby coordinated as both standing aside from the "ordinary" public language of Elsinore, just as their songs "stand aside from" the well-known originals. In both songs youth transmutes into age, and love is revealed as just death cosmetically disguised. (Hamlet's encounter with his own love for Yorick reconfirms the conjunction.) It is almost as though the gravedigger is a demystified and antisentimental version of Ophelia, and indeed, he claims the grave is his.

This complex playing of song against scene and song against song provides a model of both a psychological and a political unconscious for Elsinore. The role of song in the scenes is to show the interpretive work of transposition and condensation being done by "madness" or "clowning" through significant variation of the popular ballad tradition. And here the question of the shifting modalities of Shakespearean dramatic language arises. Ophelia's musical madness, as represented by Shakespeare, undermines the notion that there can be only one mode of relation between characters and the language they speak, a relation that must be designated "intention." This becomes clear if we ask simply: "What does Ophelia mean by her songs and speeches?" Clearly she means nothing "by" them, since we are impressed in the scene above all by her innocence of meaning in this sense, as though meaning were an upwelling current in her language, upon which, oblivious, she rides (an image later played out at her death). And yet her songs and fragments mean "through" her, in ways that can be specified. Nor is it entirely satisfactory to speak of her actions and words as "unconscious," for she displays forms of behavior that might be taken for calculation—such as her distribution of flowers—if they did not also seem so abstract. What we perceive is just that her consciousness is modal in a different way from those around her. And this implies that Shakespearean representation is capable of registering its subjects in several modes even in a single scene, that it does not always configure character and language in the same way, and that therefore identical protocols of reading cannot be applied at all points.

This is an important lesson for criticism in that it must call into question any claim that Shakespearean characters always have control over or intend the full range of nuance that their language can support. A recent version of this claim, for instance, seems to be put forward by Harry Berger, Jr. in his theory of "imaginary audition," a practice of reading based on the premise that "every interlocutory act is partly a soliloquy in which the speaker constitutes himself as the theater audience he shares confidences with or tries to persuade, affect, deceive.... This perspective converts [his] speech to continuous self-interpretation or interrogation."[40] Ophelia's fundamentally "intentionless" language and the complex relation to music that reveals it cast into doubt the apparently global nature of this claim, and suggest instead that a multiple array of shifting modalities governs the relation between character, language, and situation. The contours of this array must be felt for carefully in the language that a particular play or character has access to. It is as often the conflict of modes as of actions that energizes the Shakespearean scene, for these plays, like their culture, configure modes together in a bewildering and constantly creative medley of juxtapositions.

VII

In the currently supportive climate for interdisciplinary ventures, anthropology and psychoanalysis have been heavy contenders for attention, but music has not. In this, music continues to display the relative distance and abstraction that made Byrd's sectarian activities possible four centuries ago. The complexity of Ophelia's example suggests there is still much work to be done on Elizabethan music as a cultural practice, one with a "poetics" distinct enough to be in turn used and troped within drama or politics. We have as yet no satisfactory way to describe the relations between music and the culture it springs from and informs. Nor is this by any means an easy task to imagine, since it may require the abandonment of some distinctions often considered basic, such as that between narrative and rhetoric. It also seems likely that rhetorical terms will bear only poorly on musical modes of figuration so that even the so-called "master tropes" of various cultural theories will have to be thought out anew. Is the relation of the "In Nomine" plainsong to the street cries in Gibbons's piece, for example, metaphor or metonymy, synecdoche or irony? How would one choose between these? Or should such an inquiry begin again, and ask in the most basic terms how meaning is apprehended in both fields? Perhaps the common metaphor of a "language of music" is at once too easy and too hard a metaphor, and perhaps this very conceptual difficulty calls into question the adequacy of a solely linguistic model for the production of meaning. For example, it appears that musical structures, qua musical, cannot perform some logical operations basic to language, operations such as predication, denotation, and even negation. And yet this is not a handicap to music's ability to be semantic, to reap its own harvest.

Elizabethan music was an energetic and vital part of its culture. It produced major works of artistic intelligence and pervasive forms of sensibility that need to be accounted for if a full understanding of the period's complexity is ever to emerge. The usefulness of the concept of "mode" in avoiding certain kinds of interpretive reduction already suggests how an accurate map of the figurations peculiar to music would teach us a great deal about the way cultural meanings are generated.

Notes

This paper grows out of an NEH Summer Institute at the Folger Library in 1989. I wish to thank the institute's director, Leeds Barroll, and its members for their encouragement and criticism, and the staff of the Folger for their assistance. The comments of Ross Duffin, Elise Bickford Jorgens, and Larry Rosenwald at a symposium on Elizabethan song in Cleveland, and of audiences at the New England Conference on British Studies, and the Comparative Literature conference at the University of Tulsa were also helpful. Philip Brett in particular has been unfailingly generous in his patience with this nonmusicologist. Errors of fact or interpretation that remain despite such good counsel are mine.

1. In this I share some of the reservations voiced by Christopher Hill about Stephen Greenblatt's recent book, *Shakespearean Negotiations;* see Hill's review in *History and Theory* 29, no. 1 (1990): 100–104.

2. Thomas M. Greene, *The Light in Troy* (New Haven: Yale University Press, 1982), 19–27; Dominic LaCapra, *History and Criticism* (Ithaca: Cornell University Press, 1985), chap. 2, esp. 63–69.

3. Raymond Williams's analysis of "dominant," "emergent," and "residual" cultures in this respect appears to me to determine its organizing categories too early on a teleological basis, and therefore to beg the question of how one is to fix boundaries to the categories in the double dialectic. This may seem a scholastic quibble, yet it can be important. For example, one of the favored candidates for the "emergent" banner in seventeenth-century England, the "philosophical rationalism" of Bacon, Descartes et al., appears to have developed at least in part from a neglected revival in English universities around 1600 of a pan-European Aristotelianism, which would surely come under the category of "residual" (see Charles B. Schmitt, below, n.6). While there is nothing to prevent the emergent and the residual, in Williams's scheme, from being part of a continuum (indeed, that is part of the point), such close connection must call into some question a posited opposition. See Raymond Williams, *Marxism and Literature* (Oxford: Oxford University Press, 1977) and John D. Cox, *Shakespeare and the Dramaturgy of Power* (Princeton: Princeton University Press, 1989), ix–xv.

4. "Send reinforcements, I wish to advance." The story also draws attention to the peculiar transformations a hierarchy can practice on meaning.

5. Leo Trietler, "History and Music," *New Literary History* 21 (1990): 301.

6. I put Foucault's well-known coinage in quotation because its usefulness in the present context is unclear to me. For one thing, I am not sure whether music is a discourse in the sense normally understood by such analysis, though music theory probably is. More generally, the phrase deliberately intends to reduce its objects to a continuum of certain types of content formulations, and it is precisely this continuum that I wish to argue can be significantly disrupted by "modal" translation, and potentially by formal figuration in general.

7. On this very complicated topic, see the entry by Harold S. Powers on "Mode" in the *New Grove Dictionary of Music and Musicians,* 12:376–450.

8. Powers makes a similar point, distinguishing emphases rather than absolutes: "Modal systems used for classification are closed and often symmetrical in some ways as well; they are constructions used for ordering purposes. . . . Musically functional modal systems, on the other hand, have to be open-ended and capable of making room for new musical modes, which may come into the system through borrowing, variation, proliferation, inspiration and in many other ways" (*New Grove*, 12:377).

9. *The Praise of Musicke*, 1586, reprinted in *Anglistica & Americana*, vol. 99 (London: Olms, 1980), sig. C4^v–C5^r. *The Praise* (STC 4757) is an anonymous work. In 1589 it was evidently understood as by John Case, the Oxford philosopher, for in that year William Byrd published a broadside setting of a poem by Thomas Watson, entitled "A Gratification

unto Master John Case, for his learned book, lately made in praise of Music" (STC 4246). Howard Barnett, in "John Case—An Elizabethan Music Sholar," *Music and Letters* 50, no. 2 (1969):252–66, has shown that Watson's poem refers to the English work, and that therefore he and Byrd believed it to be Case's. Case certainly wrote the Latin text on the same subject, *Apologia musices* (STC 4755), that appeared in 1588 from the same press— Joseph Barnes at Oxford—and he was otherwise involved with music and the theater at the university. There remain, however, reasons for doubting Case's authorship. For a recent review of the issue, see Charles B. Schmitt, *John Case and Aristotelianism in Renaissance England* (Montreal: Kingston-McGill University Press, 1983), 256–57. Byrd's six-part song (of which only three parts survive) is reconstructed in *The Byrd Edition*, vol. 16, ed. Philip Brett (London: Stainer & Bell, 1976), 16–32, 188.

10. Philologically, these terms are quite distinct, "mode" deriving from Latin *modus* = way, method, and "mood" from Old English *mod* = disposition, mental state. Their almost inextricable confusion in modern English (e.g., in the grammar of verb "Moods") is an interesting essay on the relation of rhetoric and psychology.

11. Richard Hooker, *Laws of Ecclesiastical Polity, Book 5*, ed. W. Speed Hill (Cambridge: Harvard University Press, 1977), 152. The language of "temper" here indicates the affinity with "Case."

12. Gibbons's "Cries" appears in *Consort Songs*, ed. Philip Brett, *Musica Brittania*, vol. 22 (London: Stainer & Bell, 1967), 114–26. Future references to this series will be cited as *MB*. The piece has also a second part, repeating the "In Nomine" motif, where much the same ground is covered, though the full chronological sequence is not so clear. The volume contains several other examples of "Cries." See also David Wulstan, *Tudor Music* (Iowa City: University of Iowa Press, 1986), 44–47.

13. The three other "vocal in Nomines" are on texts taken from the 1561 Anglican Psalter. They appear as Nos. 38–40 in *MB*, vol. 22.

14. See Oliver Neighbour, *The Consort and Keyboard Music of William Byrd* (Berkeley: University of California Press, 1978), chap. 2; also the entry *s.v.* by Warwick Edwards in *New Grove* with its bibliography. The form lasts on until Purcell, who writes one example.

15. Keyboard pieces designated "Gloria tibi Trinitas" that use the plainsong occur in a narrow tradition. There are six by Blitheman in the Mulliner Book (ca. 1565, *MB*, vol. 1, ed. Denis Stevens [1954]), and one by Bull, his pupil, in the Fitzwilliam Book (No. 44), which also includes one of the Blitheman pieces (No. 50), retitled "In Nomine." In the late 1640s, the antiphon name designates seven of the "In Nomines" in the hand of Thomas Tomkins in Paris Conservatoire Réserve MS 1122 (*MB*, vol. 5, ed. Stephen Tuttle [1955], passim). Tomkins's MS also has four "Gloria tibi Trinitas" pieces (including the Fitzwilliam Book piece), and several marked "In Nomine" of Bull. Tomkins seems to have regarded the names as completely interchangeable. No consort "In Nomine" by Gibbons uses the antiphon name (four survive), though it is not unlikely that he knew of it as an alternative: Tomkins was his colleague in the Chapel Royal, and his junior organist after 1621, and Bull was organist there also before his 1613 debacle. Tomkins dedicated a song to Gibbons in 1622 and succeeded to the senior organist post upon his sudden death in 1625. Nevertheless, all awareness of the original antiphonal context of the plainsong seems to have disappeared fairly early, though Paul Doe (*MB*, vol. 45 [1988], xxiii and 149) has conjectured that the form retained, at least in the sixteenth century, a crypto-Catholic association in some quarters. If so, this may have persisted as late as the Fitzwilliam piece of Bull, copied by Francis Tregian, Jr., a prominent Catholic imprisoned in the Fleet from 1608 until 1619. Tomkins was not a Catholic.

16. The exception is an elaborate "In Nomine Fantasia" for six viols by Alfonso Ferrabosco, Jr., where a highly active version of the motif appears in all voices once from top to bottom. The piece, which survives in several MSS, is printed in *MB*, vol. 9 (1955), 122–26, 226.

17. As an aesthetic strategy it also has intriguing links with Shakespeare's work, for whom this was a presiding habit of imagination.

18. Talbot Papers, vol. M fol. 36. The letter is reprinted in Edmund Lodge's *Illustrations of British History*, 2d ed. (London: Chidley, 1839), 2:575. The only surviving song attributed to Hales is in Robert Dowland's 1610 collection, *A Musicall Banquet* (STC 7099). It is not impossible as a candidate. No author is given for the "ditty," which is perhaps not surprising given that Cecil was still alive. Most other songs in the volume have named, deceased authors.

19. This appears not to have been the only occasion on which Hales performed such a service. Sir Henry Wotton later recalled a similar use of him by Essex. See Diana Poulton, "The Favourite Singer of Queen Elizabeth I," *The Consort* 14 (July 1957):24–27.

20. See E. K. Chambers, *Sir Henry Lee: An Elizabethan Portrait* (Oxford: Oxford University Press, 1936), 135–40.

21. John Dowland's music for this poem can be found in *The English Lute-Song*, vols. 1–2, ed. E. H. Fellowes, rev. Thurston Dart (London: Stainer & Bell, 1965), 36. I give here the version of the text found in Dowland's 1597 *First Book of Ayres* (STC 7091), which is probably the original. A closely similar version appears in Peele's commemorative volume "Polyhymnia" of 1590 (STC 19546). Though this has led to its ascription to Peele, the likely author of the poem is Lee himself. The version Segar prints varies significantly from these, and does not fit Dowland's music as well. While there is no precise evidence that Dowland was the composer of the song sung by Hales, it seems most likely, the more so as a Dowland setting of a later Lee poem that alludes back to this appears in *A Musicall Banquet* (above, n.10). On the "Polyhymnia" text, see D. H. Horne, ed., *The Life and Works of George Peele* (New Haven: Yale University Press, 1952), 1:169–73.

22. Sir William Segar, *Honor, Military and Civil*, 1602 (STC 22164), sig. R3^r–R4^r. A speech most likely delivered by Lee on this occasion appears in John Nicholls, *The Progresses and Public Processions of Queen Elizabeth*, 2d ed. (London: Nicholls for the Society of Antiquaries, 1823), 3:197.

23. W. H. Auden, *The Dyer's Hand* (New York: Random House, 1948), 504.

24. A general account of Byrd's life can be found in E. H. Fellowes, *William Byrd*, 2d ed. (Oxford: Oxford University Press, 1948), 1–46, but a new biography is now overdue. An important short account of Byrd's religious music in the Catholic cause is Joseph Kerman's "William Byrd and the Catholics," *New York Review of Books*, 17 May 1979, 32–36.

25. See also Kerman, "William Byrd," 32, who includes the traditional, though unconfirmed, account of Walpole having Campion's blood splash on his clothing as his limbs went into the cauldron. The second and third of the printed stanzas in the 1588 issue were altered to remove any direct reference to Campion. No doubt this helped make them acceptable for publication. The song appears in E. H. Fellowes, ed., *The English Madrigal School* (London: Stainer & Bell, 1920), 14:183–89. Byrd's original setting for solo voice and instrumental consort is known in seven MSS independent of the printed version (see Brett, ed., *The Byrd Edition*, 16:144–47, 195). For Walpole, see Augustus Jessopp, *One Generation of a Norfolk House*, 3d ed. (New York: Putnam, 1914), esp. chap. 4 and nn. The poem survives in four MS versions as well as in print, one in the hand of Sir John Harington, Sr. in the Arundel Harington MS. See *The Arundel Harington Manuscript of Tudor Poetry*, ed. Ruth Hughey (Columbus: Ohio State University Press, 1960), 1:106–11; 2:57–66. The printed verson of 1582 (in STC 4537) occasioned an immediate parody by Munday (in his STC 18262). In March 1594, John Bolt, a musician and former servant of Sir John Petre, Byrd's principal patron, was examined by Coke for having books "on Campion's matter," one of which was Walpole's poem: *P.R.O.–S.P. Elizabeth*, vol. 248, no. 38, *Calendar of State Papers–Domestic*, 3:467.

26. "Domine, praestolamur adventum tuum, ut cito venias, et dissolvas jugum captivitatis nostrae. Veni, Domine, noli tardere. Relaxa facinora plebi tuae et libera populum

tuum." See *Cantiones sacrae,* ed. Alan Brown, *The Byrd Edition,* vol. 2 (London: Stainer & Bell, 1988).

27. Kerman, "William Byrd," 32–34 and in detail in his *The Masses and Motets of William Byrd* (London: Faber, 1981), chap. 3.

28. Philip Brett, "Text, Context and the Early Music Editor," *Authenticity and Early Music,* ed. Nicholas Kenyon (Oxford: Oxford University Press, 1988), 109. On the *Gradualia,* see *The Byrd Edition,* vol. 5, ed. Philip Brett (London: Stainer & Bell, 1989), vii–xx; Kerman, *Masses and Motets,* 216–340.

29. *Byrd Edition,* 5:xiv.

30. I owe this suggestion to discussion with Philip Brett, and see ibid., xiii.

31. Kerman, "William Byrd," 34; my emphasis.

32. See Kerman, *Masses and Motets,* 350–51.

33. Ibid.; *Byrd Edition,* 5:xxxi, xxxvi.

34. Also relevant to the "noticeability" of musicians in the period is their not infrequent use as spies. Morley and Ferrabosco Sr. were both involved in spying, and Dowland seems to have thought himself involved in it at one point (see *New Grove,* s.v. Morley, Ferrabosco, Dowland). Perhaps the dismissal of heresy proceedings against John Taverner on the grounds that he was "but a musician" is also connected.

35. Or indeed against John Bull, who was accused when he fled England being "as famous for the marring of virginity as he is for fingering of organs and virginals." Letter of December 1613 from George Abbot, archbishop of Canterbury, to the English envoy in Brussels, quoted in *New Grove,* 3:441.

36. Of all his playwright contemporaries, Shakespeare seems to have been most engaged with the poetics of music. Though songs are included in many plays of the period, none shows the complex figurative relation to the dramatic action of Shakespeare's characteristic use. Compare, for example, *Measure for Measure*'s "Take, O take these lips away," which seems incidental but is not, with *Volpone*'s "Come, my Celia," which does not seem so, but is. This does not mean that all songs in Shakespeare bear such a complex function, but many do. See Auden, *The Dyer's Hand.*

37. The figurative resonances of voice against lute in both poet and musician in the Renaissance have still not been fully explored, though excellent work has been done by both John Hollander, *The Untuning of the Sky* (Princeton: Princeton University Press, 1961) and John Stevens, *Music and Poetry in the Early Tudor Court* (London: Methuen, 1961). Important also are James Winn, *Unsuspected Eloquence* (New Haven: Yale University Press, 1981) and Elise Bickford Jorgens, *The Well-Tun'd Word: Musical Interpretations of English Poetry, 1597–1851* (Minneapolis: University of Minnesota Press, 1982).

38. The issues surrounding the ballad are complex. The best-known example of what may be a much older ballad-type, since other poems with a similar structure survive, the poem is usually cited from an MS version attributed to Sir Walter Ralegh. The text of this "Ralegh" version appears in *The Poems of Sir Walter Ralegh,* ed. Agnes M. C. Latham (London: Constable, 1929), 184–86, and also Josephine Waters Bennet, "Early Texts of Two of Ralegh's Poems from a Huntington Library Manuscript," *Huntington Library Quarterly* 4 (1941):469–75. However, only one of the three MS texts of this version known ascribes it to "Sir W. R.," so it may not be his. On the other hand, the poem was presumably available in the 1590s without ascription through its publication in Deloney's very popular anthology *The Garland of Goodwill* entered to J. Wolfe, 5 March 1593. ("Presumably" because no copy survives before 1628—STC 6553.5—where, as also in all later copies, the poem is anonymous.) If Ralegh's authorship of "Walsingham" was known, Shakespeare's choice parallels the borrowing of Lord Vaux's "Aged Lover" for the gravedigger from Totell's *Miscellany,* where too no ascription is given. Deloney's is in fact likely to be the version Shakespeare knew since he seems to have used his *Garland* also in *2 Henry 4* (2.4.36) for Falstaff's "King Arthur" fragment. It is also worth noting that the third ballad in

Deloney has the refrain lines "adown, adown, down, down, down" and "call him down a" Ophelia refers to in her scene. See also the Arden *Hamlet,* ed. Harold Jenkins (London: Methuen, 1982), 529–32; Peter Seng, *The Vocal Songs in the Plays of Shakespeare: A Critical History* (Cambridge: Harvard University Press, 1967), 131–42.

39. Such an allusive revision is not uncommon in the practice of the ballad repertory (Byrd's "Why do I use . . . ?" is in some ways an instance, where revision skirts a known danger). See D. Fowler, *A Literary History of the Popular Ballad* (Raleigh-Durham: Duke University Press, 1968); Diana Poulton, "The black-letter broadside ballad and its music," *Early Music* 9, no. 2 (October 1981): 427–37.

40. Harry Berger, Jr., *Imaginary Audition* (Berkeley: University of California Press, 1989), 46.

The Commodity of Names: "Falstaff" and "Oldcastle" in *1 Henry IV*

Jonathan Goldberg
The Johns Hopkins University

ALTERNATIVE Shakespeares: Political Shakespeare, Puzzling Shakespeare, Reinventing Shakespeare, Bad Shakespeare: Shakespeare Reproduced, Shakespeare Revealed: these are not only names of recent books, but new names for the author central to the canon of English literature. Renominations aimed at unsettling that centrality—or showing its complicity with the institutions of modernity—they raise the worry that the name is only resecured for further institutional appropriation. This situation can be glimpsed too in the editorial work associated with the Oxford Shakespeare (produced under the aegis of Stanley Wells and Gary Taylor), whose inclusion of two plays called *King Lear* in the 1986 one-volume *Complete Works* begins the work of destabilizing the texts that have gone under the magisterial name—but, as I have argued elsewhere, only begins it.[1] For the point is not (as Wells and Taylor seem to think) that the Oxford Shakespeare has given readers another play to add to the canon, but that it provides further evidence for the canon's contingency. Factitious Shakespeare.

The pages that follow continue that argument by pursuing another editorial decision made in that volume—the printing of *1 Henry IV* without "Falstaff." My argument attends necessarily to bibliographic details—to the evidence that the play once had "Oldcastle" in it, and to the argument that it ought to again—but its implications are broader. Denying "Falstaff" to its readers, the Oxford Shakespeare could seem to be taking away a textual support for the canonical edifice. Paradoxically, I will be arguing in behalf of "Falstaff," but in order to remark the improprieties of the proper name and the instability of its textual properties. Thus, although the argument that follows is directed against an Oxford editor, it aims to further his project, and to offer criticism another tool—a (de) foundational one—for dismantling Shakespeare.

Preparing the way for the decision enacted in the one-volume Oxford Shakespeare, in 1985 Gary Taylor published an essay, "The Fortunes of Oldcastle," in which he argued that editors must restore the name "Oldcastle" in their editions of *1 Henry IV*. "Oldcastle is what Shakespeare wrote; . . . Oldcastle is what Shakespeare meant; . . . Oldcastle is what his contemporaries understood," Taylor summed up his case, continuing: "If editors nevertheless refuse to restore Shakespeare's name for the character, then they might as well confess that they care more about an artificial *post hoc* consistency than they do about the integrity of the individual work of art."[2] Parts of Taylor's argument are indisputable: there was once—in its original performances—a play by Shakespeare in which a character named "Oldcastle" appeared; we know that because of the documented evidence that Shakespeare was compelled to change the name because it had given offense, presumably to Oldcastle's descendants, Sir William Brooke, Lord Cobham, the Lord Chamberlain at the time of the play's initial performance, and to his son, Sir Henry Brooke;[3] moreover, as many before Taylor have pointed out, the part involves Puritan posturing, claims to vocation, biblical allusions, all apt for Oldcastle, a proto-Protestant martyr celebrated in such texts as Foxe's *Acts and Monuments*. Given such evidence, Taylor's case would seem compelling, and the editorial whimper that no one had ever thought of restoring the name—that no text of the play from its first printing on has ever had the name in it—is nothing but what Taylor calls it, pusillanimity in the face of tradition, a slavish worship of transmission of the sort that one finds in edition after edition until the advent of the New Bibliography sent editors back to the beginning and to the possibilities of restoring "what Shakespeare wrote." Here, Taylor claims, the choice is clear: we know the author's original intention, we know the original reading; how can we ignore what we know? "What says Monsieur Remorse?" (1.2.109).[4]

The case presented thus far is, in Taylor's terms, external: it depends upon secondary knowledge about a performed version of the play that may—or, as I will be arguing, that may not—be identical to the first printed versions, facts about a historical Oldcastle that may—or may not—be the referent for the play's pious lines. Taylor's further external arguments are equally open to suspicion. Noting persistent references to the name "Oldcastle," and arguing from them for the possibility of the retention of that name in subsequent performances of *1 Henry IV,* Taylor refuses to take seriously the possibility that the play called *Sir John Oldcastle* and not *1 Henry IV* is meant in the instances he cites. Taylor's belief that no one could have confused Shakespeare's play with Henslowe's property is belied by the evidence of the 1664 Folio, and its subsequent reprintings through Rowe, which include *Sir John Oldcastle* as Shakespeare's. Moreover, even if subsequent to the 1598 printing of *1 Henry IV*, a version of the play with Oldcastle in it was staged, there is no way of knowing whether its text was the same as the one that was printed; the argument that follows insists that the Oldcastle version of the play cannot have been identical to the one with Falstaff in it.

Taylor, however, has, or claims to have, internal evidence as well to support his argument that the earliest texts of the play are identical to that original performance save for the change of names in which "the integrity of the individual work of art" was violated by the forced removal (the censorship) of the original names by yet another external agent. Two places in *1 Henry IV*, he argues, give evidence that nothing but the name has been changed. "The only verse line in which the character's surname appears," Taylor writes, "would be metrical if a three-syllable name had originally stood in place of the two-syllable 'Falstaff'" (85). The line in question occurs at the end of 2.2. when the prince turns to Poins after they have easily robbed the robbers:

> *Prince.* Got with much ease. Now merrily to horse:
> The thieves are all scatter'd and possess'd with fear
> So strongly that they dare not meet each other;
> Each takes his fellow for an officer!
> Away, good Ned—Falstaff sweats to death,
> And lards the lean earth as he walks along.
> Were't not for laughing I should pity him.
> *Poins.* How the fat rogue roared.
>
> (2.2.99–106)

"Away, good Ned, Oldcastle sweats to death": thus Taylor would have the line read. That way it would have ten syllables, the ten syllables we are to suppose it originally had. But would it be a more metrical line by the addition of that extra beat? Certainly not a more regular one: Oldcastle's name interrupts the iambs, while the line with "Falstaff" in it, although short by one syllable, is regular; the caesura before the name functions as a weak beat, and the accent on Falstaff's name occurs where one would expect it to be in a line of iambic pentameter. To claim that Shakespeare's line only is metrical with Oldcastle's name in it is to argue that it is the number of syllables in a line that makes it metrical, that Shakespearean versification is simply a matter of arithmetic.

That assumption is palpably incorrect; the line is metrical either way. There is, in short, no internal proof here that originally the line had Oldcastle's name in it. Moreover—and this is something that Taylor only glances at in a footnote, something that editors only put in small type at the bottom of the page—these lines are printed as prose in the earliest editions. "The Quarto sets the whole speech as prose, but it is clearly verse," Taylor notes (85n.4). *"As Pope; prose QqF"* the Arden lemma reads. Ever since Pope rearranged these lines as verse, editors have succumbed to his relineation as if it discovered the essential poet buried in the prose. "Shakespeare may have intended verse but failed to make the lines clear," Humphreys comments about the end of 2.2 in his Arden edition (p. xx); "the comic narrative stimulates him to metre while the wit-play stays in prose." That "comic narrative," in Humphreys's account, is nothing less than the destiny of the English nation, embodied in Prince Hal, the future Henry V; as Hal escapes from his low companions and turns the tables upon them, he must "naturally" rise to verse. Versification assures us of the moral purity of the princely robber—and the lines are snatched away from the prosaic compositor who misunderstood the stimulant that moved the author's hand to stray into something that looked like prose. Humphreys divines Shakespeare's divine(ly) right intentions. Humphreys's comments follow upon Pope's agenda in his edition of Shakespeare, to give Shakepeare the poet's pretensions, rescuing him from the depredations of the actors and the printers. Printed as verse, some, but scarcely more than half of these lines have ten syllables; some of them even scan. These lines are only "clearly verse" because they have been printed that way ever since 1725. Taylor's internal evidence here lies not in the text but in that slavish respect for tradition he so abhors.[5] *"Nature* and *Homer* were, he found, the same."

Taylor's second piece of internal evidence is a pun, when the Prince names his companion "my old lad of the castle" (1.2.41). The phrase certainly depends upon the fact that Oldcastle was once the character's name. But does it secure the argument that in the original staging the character named Oldcastle was so addressed? While one could argue that the pun works better after the name had been changed—in which case it would allude to the suppressed name—it is perfectly possible that the text originally had this rather lame pun. Taylor himself, however, provides a way of adjudicating this issue, although it undermines his argument.

Looking to the plays in which Falstaff figures—*2 Henry IV, Henry V, Merry Wives of Windsor*—Taylor notices in each of them a moment in which a space is opened in which Oldcastle's censored name is recalled. This is most palpably the case in the epilogue to *2 Henry IV* with its insistence that Falstaff is not Oldcastle, but it is equally the case in moments in the other plays when the character's name is forgotten—when, for instance, Fluellen needs to be prompted to supply the name of "the fat knight with the great-belly doublet" (4.7.50),[6] or when Mrs. Page claims to Mrs. Ford that she has forgotten the name of the knight who has supplied her husband with a page. "I have forgot his name," Fluellen says (4.7.52); "I can never hit on's name," Mrs. Page insists (3.2.21).[7] Each time, as memory lapses, a pause occurs—and then the name, "Sir John Falstaff"; each time, as Taylor powerfully argues, the audience is reminded of another name that cannot be recalled, made to recall what the play cannot.

The pun on Oldcastle could be like these moments, for what makes the pun possible is the fact that "old lad of the castle" is not a proper name but, as the Arden editor puts it, "a cant term for roisterer" (1.2.41n.). Oldcastle is not named in the term—the pun depends upon the dispersal of his proper name. Of course, this possibility is there either in an original version in which Oldcastle is the character's name or in the Falstaff version. But what if *1 Henry IV* gave evidence, as the later plays do, of the forgetting of Falstaff's name—and with it the recall of a version of the play with Oldcastle in it? "What says Monsieur Remorse?"

From the start, he desires another name:

> *Fal.* Marry then sweet wag, when thou art king let us that are squires of the night's body be called thieves of the day's beauty: let us be Diana's foresters, gentlemen of the shade, minions of the moon; and let men say we be men of good government, being governed as the sea is, by our noble and chaste mistress the moon, under whose countenance we steal. (1.2.23–29)

From the start, he has many names—"Sir John Sack—and Sugar" (1.2.110); "Sir John Paunch" (2.2.63); "Ribs . . . Tallow" (2.4.109). Sir John does not seem to have a proper name. What it is has been forgotten.

When he plays the king, he attempts to summon up the name of the sole companion his son must not cast off, that one "virtuous man" he has "often noted" in the prince's company. "I know not his name" (2.4.414). The prince prompts his recollection, and soon the swelling belly delivers the name: "and now I remember me, his name is Falstaff. If that man should be lewdly given, he deceiveth me" (2.4.419–21). The joke is so good that it comes again, after the prince and his companion switch parts. Now the prince, speaking as his father, singles out a monster. "I would your Grace would take me with you: whom means your Grace?," Falstaff, playing the prince, interrupts; to be answered: "That villainous abominable misleader of youth, Falstaff, that old white-bearded Satan" (2.4.454–57). Twice, then, a pause interrupts the production of the name; first, to supply the virtue lacking in the old name; then, to dispel the possibility that the new name has quite effaced the old, "that old white-bearded Satan." From the start, Falstaff says, he wishes that he and the prince "knew where a commodity of good names were to be bought" (1.2.81). As they exchange parts in this play-within-the-play they jostle over the name the boon companion has acquired thanks, if not to Diana herself, then to her Lord Chamberlain. He too puts in a disguised appearance in the play, clothed, like "Oldcastle," in the guise of a pun, in the possibility that the proper name can be dispersed. "What ho! Chamberlain!" Gadshill calls (2.1.46)—Gadshill, the setter of the robbery, the thief whose name also is not quite proper since it also names the place of the robbery; "'At hand, quoth pick-purse'" (2.1.47), the chamberlain, arriving, replies to the thief's call, his first line a citation of a proverb. He doesn't own the line—it is not properly his. Is it the Lord Chamberlain's line, a line that belongs to the hand that struck out "Oldcastle," and that allowed the name to be recalled, but only in a proverb? "My old lad of the castle; . . . is not a buff jerkin a most sweet robe of durance?" (1.2.41–42). "What says Monsieur Remorse?"

The gaps, the multiple names, the glances at the queen and her chamberlain, these, I would argue, are as compelling as the instances that Taylor cites for the plays with "Falstaff" in them; like them, they make the argument that the *1 Henry IV* we have is not the play that originally had "Oldcastle" in it but a text revised to remark the censored name and even the agents of that censorship.[8] The outside has entered the inside, and the external agents of censorship and suppression cannot be distinguished from the hand writing. The absent name is marked by "damnable iteration," as Falstaff calls it (1.2.88); it is paralleled by a censorship represented in the play when the king forbids mention of another name:

> *Hot.* He said he would not ransom Mortimer,
> Forbade my tongue to speak of Mortimer,

> But I will find him when he lies asleep,
> And in his ear I'll holla 'Mortimer!'
> Nay, I'll have a starling shall be taught to speak
> Nothing but 'Mortimer', and give it him
> To keep his anger still in motion.
>
> (1.3.217–23)

Instead, to keep the censors at bay, another name is insisted upon:

> *Fal.* No, my good lord; banish Peto, banish Bardolph, banish Poins—but for sweet Jack Falstaff, kind Jack Falstaff, true Jack Falstaff, valiant Jack Falstaff, and therefore more valiant, being as he is old Jack Falstaff, banish not him thy Harry's company, banish not him thy Harry's company, banish plump Jack, and banish all the world.
> (2.4.468–74)

"I do, I will," the prince responds. And so does Gary Taylor.

What Taylor proposes is not restoration but censorship of the texts we have. This is most apparent when Taylor turns to what the text would mean were "Oldcastle" to appear in it. The claim is that just as the lexical substitution would restore an originary text, so the name would secure and fix historical referentiality. "Oldcastle" in the text would be the real historical Oldcastle; his lines would now refer us to that figure—he would be that figure—and it would be apparent that Shakespeare's depiction of him was a scoffing representation of the Protestant martyr.[9] "Oldcastle really was a soldier," Taylor writes; "Sir John's appearance at the King's side, in the council before the battle of Shrewsbury (5.1), would therefore not have seemed as incongruous with 'Oldcastle' as it does with 'Falstaff'" (93). What "really was" enters the text, securing congruity—despite the representation of Sir John in the scene. Its meaning would be contained within the historical referent; the play would be delimited to a singular history. History, in this way of thinking, always is one and the same, it is the locus of truth—of incontestable facts; meaning is likewise univocal. Oldcastle—in the play, in real life—"really was" a Protestant martyr, and his depiction in the play once he has his proper name would confirm Taylor's suspicion that Shakespeare was a papist (100). All of Taylor's claims meet in the final sentences of the essay; Oldcastle's name secures, in Taylor's words, "the recovery and restoration of the original authoritative *logos*" (100). What's in a name, another Shakespearean character asks. Taylor's answer, the original, singular *logos,* in fact covers many names. In the place of Oldcastle's name one could read: God, Shakespeare, History, Meaning—multiple names for the singular origin supposedly to be found lodged in Oldcastle's name. For Taylor, all these are one and the same. Such is the fantasmatic nature of the so-called proper name.[10]

These restorations, made in the name of "the integrity of the individual work of art" and, congruously, "the integrity of the individual"—call him Oldcastle, or Shakespeare—relentlessly reduce multiplicity to singularity. This text of *1 Henry IV* is the one and only text, unrevised. The character's name is likewise fixed, referring to the real. But in these claims, Shakespeare's hand is being held firmly in the censor's grip, for the exterior has violated the very integrity Taylor wishes to secure; claiming to free Shakespeare—and to allow him artistic autonomy—Taylor ties him to a singular historical referent, and a singular meaning. Through the proper name, all sorts of propriety are secured in the transcendental name of the *logos.* Scorning the priesthood—the editors—who worship idolatrously the received, transmitted text, Taylor's restoration would return editors to the one true faith, making the author central to the canon of English literature his scribe. "New Presbyter is but old Priest writ large."

The evidence reads otherwise. *1 Henry IV* is a play written not with one hand, but with two. It opens upon the scene of censorship, punctuates its referentiality at the very moment it names Falstaff and with him the suppressed name of Oldcastle. When it puns upon "Oldcastle"—or assigns Gadshill a name that is also the name of the place of the robbery—it disperses the proper name and punctures the fantasies of propriety that Taylor would secure. History enters the text, the writer is in history, but not as some stable ground of singular meaning and determination. The historical is a field of contestation and submission, and so too is the Shakespearean text. And while Taylor's restoration claims to reground the text in history, his historical restoration would remove the traces of the history that produced the earliest texts of *1 Henry IV.* It would stop history in the *logos.* It would produce a cleaned up text, one in which there could be but one meaning.

So doing, Taylor repeats something that can be seen in the text of *1 Henry IV* after it was submitted to the censors. For, as editors regularly note, the text of *1 Henry IV* is a remarkably clean one, one made proper by the demands of the censors that a cleaned up text be produced to replace the offending one.[11] In Taylor's account, only the names have been changed (John Jowett supplements the argument by seeing the suppression of an original Harvey and Russell as congruent changes in the text).[12] Yet, if only the names had had to be changed, the compositors might have been told to perform a simple act of mechanical substitution of names. The clean text of *1 Henry IV* does not suggest that behind it stood authorial foul papers, however, but a scribal transcription. The clean printed text suggests that there was more to changing the text than changing the names, that the foul papers had grown so foul in revision that they had become illegible, or that the author had rewritten so much that only a fair copy would do.[13] Yet, here and there, in the margins of *1 Henry IV*, a stray Russell and Harvey put in an appearance, signs that the copiest (a scribe who might also have been the author) or the compositor, busily attending to much else, had lapsed in the performance of the merely mechanical task of substituting new names for the old ones. And once, even, *Old.* appears in the margins, not, as it happens in *1 Henry IV,* but in its sequel. Its appearance, which Taylor takes as further support for his argument that Falstaff was once Oldcastle, that the two characters are identical, in fact embarrasses his case.[14] Not merely because it suggests that more was involved in printing the play than substituting the name, but in its very insistence on the name that was supposed to be suppressed. The Lord Chief Justice addresses Sir John: "I think," he says, "you are fallen into the disease, for you hear not what I say to you." And the fat knight replies: "Very well, my lord, very well. Rather, and't please you, it is the disease of not listening, the malady of not marking, that I am troubled withal" (1.2.117–21). Not marked out, in the margin, is the speech prefix *Old.* for this speech in defense of not marking. *Old.* remains—thanks to whose hand?—to mark what the censor—inside the play and outside it—would have marked out. This double structure of the mark remarks the proper name, denying it all the proprieties of an originary *logos;* the name is written within a dispersal that refuses self-sameness, a history of marking and remarking. It is produced and erased at once, remembered and forgotten in a relationship between the margin and the text, the outside and the inside, that never can be stabilized through some originary meaning, some fixed history, some text restored to singular propriety, an inside protected against all time from the outside. This mark, intentional or inadvertent, rebellious or accidental, original or secondary, remarks the limits of Taylor's originary designs upon the Shakespearean text, a lapse in the mechanisms of censorship made in whatever name.

Notes

The argument presented here was developed in the course of a seminar offered in the fall 1988 semester at Johns Hopkins. I am grateful to the participants for much stimulation and for a give and take that makes it difficult to claim that everything in this paper is my own (the notion is, of course, under pressure in the essay itself). In particular, I must mention Beth Pittenger and Michael Deneen, who wrote papers on this topic; although I have not had their essays before me as I have been writing, it is doubtless the case that they have influenced what I wrote (this too is implicit in the argument made in the paper).

1. See Jonathan Goldberg, "Textual Properties," *Shakespeare Quarterly* 37 (1986): 213–17, which discusses the arguments for the decision to include two *King Lear*s in *William Shakespeare: The Complete Works*, ed. Stanley Wells and Gary Taylor (Oxford: Clarendon Press, 1986).

2. Gary Taylor, "The Fortunes of Oldcastle," *Shakespeare Survey* 38 (1985): 100. Further page references will be cited in the text.

3. The history of the acceptance of the notion that Oldcastle became Falstaff is detailed in Rudolph Fiehler, "How Oldcastle Became Falstaff," *Modern Language Quarterly* 16 (1955): 16–28; Taylor fills out the Cobham connection in "William Shakespeare, Richard James and the House of Cobham," *Review of English Studies*, n.s., 38 (1987): 334–54.

4. William Shakespeare, *The First Part of King Henry IV*, ed. A. R. Humphreys, Arden edition (London: Methuen, 1960); all citations are to this edition unless otherwise noted.

5. The question of verse-prose distinctions is an enormously complicated one, and nothing in my argument really depends upon the rightness of the Q1 imprint except insofar as it testifies to a much more fluid relationship between prose and verse in Elizabethan practice than that of the eighteenth century. All sorts of evidence, including scribal and authorial manuscripts of the period, suggest that in many instances verse and prose were not always distinguished; on this, see a forthcoming essay by Stephen Orgel, "Acting Scripts, Performing Texts." Pope's decisions about versification, like those of many editors subsequently, have been motivated by the desire to raise the stature of characters by having them, whenever possible, speak verse.

6. William Shakespeare, *King Henry V*, ed. J. H. Walter, Arden edition (London: Methuen, 1954).

7. William Shakespeare, *The Merry Wives of Windsor*, ed. H. J. Oliver, Arden edition (London: Methuen, 1971).

8. These markings of Queen Elizabeth (the allusion to her as Diana is unmistakable and is noted in J. Dover Wilson's 1946 Cambridge edition of the play) and the Lord Chamberlain must give pause to anyone who thinks that Elizabethan censorship is easily comprehended. In the case of *1 Henry IV*, it is worth noting that while we think we know who caused the suppression of Oldcastle, we really do not know why—nor does the play in its present form tell us. In its present form, however, it does show that censorship could be remarked, names could be named in the glancing of metaphoric substitution, supplantation of the proper title with a generic one—and that these lapses could survive unremarked. Taylor's notion that a play presenting Oldcastle in an unfavorable light could not be endured fails to consider how the *Famous Victories,* hardly flattering in its portrait, could have made its way on stage or in print—in the very same year as *1 Henry IV* appeared, its

title page announcing it *"As it was plaide by the Queenes Majesties Players."* The pertinence of the *Famous Victories* to the composite character of Falstaff—derived not only from that play's Oldcastle, but also from several other characters (a point about origins that also disturbs the notion of the propriety and proper naming of characters)—has often been documented; see, e.g., James Monaghan, "Falstaff and His Forebears," *Studies in Philology* 18 (1921):353–61; D. B. Landt, "The Ancestry of Sir John Falstaff," *Shakespeare Quarterly* 17 (1966) : 69–76. Falstaff's punning name has also occasioned a number of notes; see, e.g.: Robert F. Willson, "Falstaff in *1 Henry IV:* What's in a Name?" *Shakespeare Quarterly* 27 (1976) : 199–200; Norman Davis, "Falstaff's Name," *Shakespeare Quarterly* 28 (1977) : 513–15; G. Walton Williams, "Some Thoughts on Falstaff's Name," *Shakespeare Quarterly* 29 (1979) : 82–84.

9. As the title of his essay suggests, Taylor depends upon J. Dover Wilson's *The Fortunes of Falstaff* (Cambridge: Cambridge University Press, 1943) for his historic reconstruction. It is, of course, the case, that what Dover Wilson offers is not the real character, but an interpretation of it, one marked by a high moral tone, one that can find little to say in behalf of Falstaff. (On the ideological ramifications of his work, see Graham Holderness, *Shakespeare's History* [Dublin: Gill & Macmillan, 1985], 90–95 passim.) This is by no means the only version of the character possible, nor is it one prevailing in criticism which, on the whole, has found itself more attracted to the old reprobate than not. Moreover, it is worth noting that the very title of Taylor's essay enacts the argument I am presenting here; it simply replaces a name, and restores the true reading; but it also therefore loses its name in the allusion, and the true reading it would substitute is not the only one. Against Dover Wilson one could martial not only previous "sentimental" defenders of Falstaff like Bradley, but also his contemporary New Critical opponent Empson, or, finally, various new historicists (notably Stephen Greenblatt) who read *1 Henry IV* as a more contestatory historical site. Above all, one would have to reckon with the sheer popularity of Falstaff, even, as Walter Cohen has argued in *Drama of a Nation* (Ithaca: Cornell University Press, 1985), 225–26, his mobilization for revolutionary politics: these would not disappear if he were given another name, much as Taylor might wish that to be the case.

10. That fantasmatic is, of course, explored in much theoretical work, especially that of Derrida and Lacan, and it is upon that work that this critique relies. But even within a philosophical approach that is in many respects closer to Taylor's suppositions, these fantasies about the self-identity and absolute guarantee of the proper name come into question. Saul Kripke, in *Naming and Necessity* (Cambridge: Harvard University Press, 1980) imagines an originary moment in the baptismal scene of naming; but what the name means thereafter is confirmed by chains of transmission which can never be returned to that originary moment. Kripke stops the chain only by assuming that the discourses of science offer an objective real against and through which the identity of the proper can be secured, but this is an intensely problematic gesture once the historicity of scientific truth is introduced—as problematic as the theological guarantees that Taylor assumes. It is nonetheless notable that Kripke does not for a moment assume that a proper name, as transmitted, as used, cited, etc., ever can correspond to its originary ground. "What is true is that it's in virtue of our connection with other speakers in the community, going back to the referent himself, that we refer to a certain man" (94). That going back, I would argue, is an infinite regress; and even when we look at a particular person at a particular time—call him Shakespeare—it is impossible to say that his "integrity" assures some unbreached interiority. The conditions of writing are never absolutely free, nor is it possible to separate external censorship from internally imposed censorship, nor is it necessary to see the historic and its transmissions as solely a field of error that could somehow be restored to a truth (claimed to be historical) without error. That phantasm haunts all rationales of copy-text and their intense dehistoricization. For a recent exploration—and explosion—of the

construct of foul papers (the author's hand) as the guarantee of texts, see Paul Werstine, "Narratives about Printed Shakespearean Texts: 'Foul Papers' and 'Bad Quartos,'" *Shakespeare Quarterly* 41 (1990) : 65–86.

11. See, e.g., Humphreys, lxviff. Like many editors, Humphreys wishes he could claim that authorial foul papers stand behind the earliest printings of *1 Henry IV*, but he marshals the evidence for "signs of fair copy" (lxvii), including reasonably standardized speech prefixes and an attention to "minute details" (lxviii) of pointing and elision that suggest scribal intervention. Similarly, David Bevington in his volume edited for the Oxford Shakespeare (1987), finds "Shakespeare's corrected papers" or "a scribal copy" behind the remarkably "clean" Qo and Q1 (90). (Not the least remarkable feature of the editing of this play is the way in which the derivative quality of the so-called Q1 has been ignored.) Bevington also takes up the question of Oldcastle and defends the retention of Falstaff. It should be clear that he and I are not making the same argument; he would have the name secure a final intentionality represented by Shakespeare continuing to write with the name of Falstaff, and while I agree that that retroactivity bears upon the original remarking in *1 Henry IV*, I part company with the assumptions made about what the name secures. Bevington avers that with the name "Falstaff" the author makes a "fictional . . . contract" (108) with the audience. That, however, is Bevington's fiction, and it, as much as Taylor's, is tied to the phantasmatic properties believed inherent in the proper name. If Falstaff's name, especially as explicit substitute, secures anything, it is the impossibility of such stabilization through the proper name.

12. In "The Thieves in *1 Henry IV*," *Review of English Studies*, n.s., 38 (1987) : 325–33. Jowett's essay is capable of being read otherwise, against its grain (as I have been reading Taylor). By itself, it reads almost as a parody of Taylor's method, rifling the pages of history to try to discover some proper names—of real historical figures—who would have found themselves offended by the play's Harvey and Russell. When it turns to the marks of those names in the text of *1 Henry IV*, the essay tries, desperately, not to see revision taking place after the original performance, wishes, that is, to make the revision merely nominal. Nonetheless, Jowett also finds evidence that a new character emerges in revision, as the original Russell splits to become sometimes Bardolph, sometimes Gadshill. Although it would take more than a footnote to work this out, in my reading of the evidence presented by Jowett, a compelling case can be made for this revision as postdating the original performance. And in terms of the argument made above—about the pertinence of the name of Gadshill, the "setter" of the robbery (and perhaps of the robbery of the original names as well)—it is worth emphasizing the impropriety of Gadshill's name, a proper name and a place name as well, for it intimates what is true of all proper names, in whatever version of the play we have or might have had—that the proper name is always subject to dispersal.

13. If so, then another of Taylor's scenarios is called into question, the desire he projects upon Hemmings and Condell, staying the printing of *1 Henry IV* so that they might reprint the original text. If all that would have taken was the substitution of names, why would they have needed another text? By Taylor's own account, they had the text in hand already.

14. A further sign of this embarrassment can be seen in Jowett's commentary in Stanley Wells et al., *William Shakespeare: A Textual Companion* (Oxford: Clarendon Press, 1987): "The prefix 'Old.' for Falstaff at 1.2.122/374 probably stands for Oldcastle (a conceivable alternative is 'Old man')," 351. What leads Jowett to conceive this alternative? Presumably, Taylor's thesis that Shakespeare was done with Oldcastle when he moved on to subsequent plays (the prefix shouldn't be there if Taylor's chronology is correct, or if *1 Henry IV* is to be preserved in its "integrity" as an "individual work of art"; a fine instance of how historic fixing is allied to suppressive singularity). And why the substitute, by what logic is it generated? A logic of the generic by which Shakespearean foul papers preserve such

names, which always come to be individualized, but also, and powerfully opposing this ideology of the proper, because the name "Oldcastle" (that cant term) triggers the generic and its destabilization of the proper name. The text of *2 Henry IV* keeps putting into Falstaff's mouth the lines, "I am old, I am old," insisting on a relationship to Oldcastle through the generic suggestion that exceeds his name. "I am old" does not name Oldcastle properly, but neither does his proper name.

Spenser's Saluage Petrarchanism:
Pensées Sauvages in *The Faerie Queene*

Jonathan Crewe
Dartmouth College

WHEN we speak of "Petrarchanism" we are generally thinking in the first instance of *lyric* poetry written in the wake of, and in emulous imitation of, Petrarch's lyrics. This lyric poetry, embodying some remarkably durable codes of cultural inscription and visionary description, is what largely constitutes for us a Petrarchan literary "tradition." No doubt a great deal is now included under the broad rubric of Petrarchanism that only questionably belongs there, yet it is to what we think of as stable and recognizable—otherwise "conventional"—discursive codes that the term "Petrarchanism" generally refers. In particular, the term identifies codes of overtly heterosexual, idealistic, masculine devotion on one hand, and of visionary representation of the woman on the other; these codes seem stable and recognizable enough to go under Petrarch's name by whatever subsequent lyric poet they are produced, and in however parodic, extended, subversive or revisionary a guise they appear. Even so-called anti-Petrarchanism tends now to be regarded as a de-idealizing mode of Petrarchanism.[1]

However, it is not lyric Petrarchanism that I primarily want to consider here, nor am I concerned with the proper limits of the term, if such there are. My interest is in the cultural embedding and dissemination of Petrarchan codes in forms other than lyric ones, a process at once pursued and reflexively thematized by Spenser among others. This process of embedding and dissemination is so well advanced by the time Spenser begins to write that it can hardly be regarded as a new departure from lyric Petrarchanism; rather, it seems like the ongoing realization of popularizing and self-dispersing ambitions inherent in lyric Petrarchanism from the start.[2]

I want to concentrate on Spenser's embedding and dissemination of Petrarchan codes in pastoral, particularly in *The Faerie*

Queene. Instead of propounding a thesis or invoking a single interpretive model from the start, I want to rethematize this Spenserian process briefly in some of the critical terms now available to us before moving on to a conclusion. The point of doing it this way is partly to rehearse a set of issues in the hope of making some critical progress in dealing with them, and partly to enact rather than dictate a critical repositioning of Petrarchanism. To the extent that this procedure unavoidably entails a repetition of Spenser's process, I hope to make it repetition with a historical and critical difference in the end.

The word "saluage" in my title will be recognized as a familiar Spenserian locution. "Saluage" can denote "savage," "wild," "fugitive" and "pertaining to the woodland" as in French *sauvage*, and it is applied by Spenser to various situations in which those implications of pastoral are being invoked rather than the more civil Theocritan or Vergilian ones. Yet Spenser's complicated punning on that term may also include "salvage" or "salvaging."[3] If so, the process of Petrarchan dissemination in saluage pastoral will never be fully separable in Spenser's view from a salvaging operation. Certainly the question of what is being saved from what and for whom is repeatedly raised by Spenser's Petrarchan embeddings, and it is from that perspective that I want to begin.

Consider the well-known and much-discussed episode of Una among the saluages in book 1, canto 6 of *The Faerie Queene*.[4] There, having been abandoned by her protector-manqué Redcrosse, and having been pursued by his rapist alter ego Sansloy, she is saved by a saluage people who subsequently attempt to deify her. When she resists, they deify her ass, obscene pun conceivably intended or unavoidable. This forest refuge from the chivalric world of male identification through struggle soon turns out, however, to be a place of dangerous entrapment. It becomes such a place as soon as the terrified Una's self-possession begins to reassert itself. She shifts from being a damsel in conspicuous distress, and hence an object of pastoral sympathy, to being a "beauty sovereigne" and hence an object of pastoral wonder. Her manifestation of beauty gets its conventional due when the saluages "all prostrate on the lowly plaine, / Do kiss her feet" (1.6.12).

This saluage attempt to deify Una can of course be read as Protestant, iconoclastic parody of Petrarchanism as an idolatrous cult. The point will then be that the truth Una signifies rather than the beauty she manifests isn't recognized by saluages; they are thereby doomed to remain merely savages living in a pagan backwater, unable to join the long march of world-historical Protestantism.[5] Additionally, the episode can be read as an anxiously witty critique of the regiocentric, Petrarchan politics of the English cult of Elizabeth, to which Spenser had so notably contributed in *The Shepheardes Calender*. The point I want to make, however, is that the Petrarchan deification of Una, which seems to secure her a place in the pastoral community and protect her from any further violation, not only threatens to objectify her as a powerful idol, but thereby exposes her to threatening communal demands that seem only barely held in check. As an object of sympathy, Una has caused the saluages to lay aside what Spenser calls their "rusticke horror" and threateningly satyrlike aspect, displaying instead a "semblance glad." Yet as the episode unfolds, Spenser implies that if there had been no ass on to which the community's objectifying will and demand could be displaced, Una's effort to resist their deifying attempt in the name of truth might well have turned the happy faces back into one of rustic horror. Even when they are displaying a "semblance glad," the "grenning" faces of these saluages seem very close to being snarling and incipiently devouring ones. Una's Petrarchan triumph among the saluages thus seems constraining, while the distinction between the idol and the object of sacrifice seems precarious. What happens in the narrative tends to confirm the threat posed by the saluages; Una has been saved by them only to need saving again by a properly converted satyr type called Satyrane. Thus the possibility that her "sovereigne beautie" might be her long-term salvation in a world in which any single woman—any Una—is constantly exposed to sexual assault is first invoked and then questioned in this saluage setting. At best, the Petrarchan guise—in which, from the official standpoint of book 1, Una is misrecognized anyway—buys a little time for her, and allows a temporary displacement of communal desires onto a sacrificial surrogate.[6]

It is to some of the unrealized implications and potentialities of this scene that Spenser evidently returns in book 6 of *The Faerie Queene,* in the episode in which Serena, wandering alone in a "desert" landscape thanks to the negligence of her "courteous" protectors, falls into the hands of another band of saluages, this time explicitly hungry cannibal ones. One could terminate the process of thematization right here in the name of a justified feminism by saying, as a number of critics have done, that in this episode Petrarchan admiration and extended blazoning of the woman are further disseminated, but are then also clarified and literalized as cannibalistic.[7] Here Petrarchan representation of the woman's "sovereigne beautie" seems to shift from figurative equivalence toward literal identity with cannibalistic butchery. What members of this implicitly masculine community are greedily eyeing as they gaze at Serena are the choicest cuts:[8]

> So round about her they them selues did place
> Vpon the grasse, and diuersely dispose,
> As each thought best to spend the lingering space.
> Some with their eyes the daintiest morsels chose;
> Some praise her paps, some praise her lips and nose;
> Some whet their knives, and strip their elboes bare:
> The priest him selfe a garland doth compose
> Of finest flowres, and with full busie care
> His bloudy vessels wash, and holy fire prepare.
>
> (6.8.39)

This drastically "misplaced" Petrarchanism, in which an epideictic rhetoric of visionary admiration and a poetics of "floral" composition are at once implicated and de-idealized, issues in an extended and still highly conventional blazon, in which cannibalism is now fully inscribed:

> Her yvorie necke, her alablaster brest,
> Her paps, which like sweet sleeping pillows were,
> For loue in soft delight thereon to rest;
> Her tender sides, her belly white and clere,
> Which like an Altar did itself uprere;
> To offer sacrifice diuine thereon;
> Her goodly thighes, whose glory did appeare
> Like a triumphall Arch, and thereupon
> The spoiles of Princes hang'd, which were in battel won.
>
> (6.8.42)

Pausing over all the subtleties of these passages would detain us too long, but I will note in passing, first, that the passage's simultaneous exposure and retraction of the woman's genitals makes them indeterminably the object over which men battle and fame is produced, or the site at which even warlike princes are "despoiled," what they have lost becoming, in effect, the grisly ornaments of female triumph. Second, this threatening body of the woman is already—or always and already—in the process of conversion into a sacrificial object through which masculine authority can be reclaimed. This possibility is realized as the saluage community erects an "altar," anticipated in the reference to Serena's "belly," on which she will be sacrificed; her altar can, so to speak, be altered. Finally, and still pertinently I hope, the Spenserian punning on "battle/battil" (eating) makes cannibalism into the war of the sexes pursued by culinary means. All this might strongly support a feminist critique, perhaps above all a militant feminist critique, of Petrarchanism as a cultural code.[9]

That, however, is not the critique I wish to elaborate, or at least not yet. Admittedly, an assimilation of Petrarchanism to cannibalism is occurring in the episode, in the process of which its codes of female inscription are being recharacterized as ones of uncivil butchery. Yet it is the deferral of the cannibal moment that allows the Petrarchan discourse to be produced. This deferral, on which the community first agrees in order to fatten Serena up for the kill, and which the savage priest then piously prolongs, also allows cannibalism to be economized. The stripping of Serena before the final devouring means that she can be visually carved up and devoured over and over again in anticipation. Such, perhaps, is the meaning, exposed by Spenser, of Petrarchan *de*scription of the woman. Deferral additionally constitutes the visual and discursive field of the community, some members of which fix on the daintiest morsels with their eyes only, while others additionally praise her choicest parts. The cannibal feast isn't therefore, as one might initially have expected, an immediate act of voracious dismemberment and lawless struggle over the body. Rather, anticipation and deferral of this savage moment, which would predictably be one of communal anarchy and privation rather than repletion, enables the single body of the victim to "feed" the gaze of the entire community in the interim. This economical spacing of cannibalism allows every member of the community to sample the best cuts, though not without invidious anxiety. It even converts the waste space-time of deferral into a form of communal capital that individuals can "spend." The result may still be that sense of insufficiency (of starving while gazing) that has so often been remarked in critiques of scopophilia, yet it can also be said that there is something rather than nothing in this spectatorship for every member of the saluage community. In short, a rational economy of voyeuristic consumption seems to be getting staged in this episode around the exposed and all too conventionally represented body of the Petrarchan woman. Moreover, this economizing of cannibalism permits a symbolic order to be constituted or maintained in the potentially lawless, self-consuming cannibal community. The priest indeterminably asserts or reconstitutes his authority by preserving Serena as an object of sacrifice. Her body will feed the community and her blood, ritually shed, will be offered on the altar to the tribal deity.[10] Profane and sacred appetites thus appear equally well catered for, while the separation between these appetites seems capable of being effected with almost surgical exactness. (Or so it may seem, no Portia being present to quibble over drams and scruples.)

The appearance in this episode of a rational if still precarious voyeur economy rather than just an instance of scopic violation may force us to reexamine Spenser's staging of the opposition between cannibal and civil society. Insofar as this staging is Spenser's precondition for whatever critique of Petrarchanism follows in the passage, and is equally the precondition for whatever self-critique he may be performing as he recognizably implicates his own Petrarchanism, it is a precondition to which we may feel bound to do justice. I believe it is also a precondition to which we can usefully attend as a way of expanding the range of the discussion rather than shifting its grounds. Recognizing this precondition doesn't, in other words, lead us beyond or away from a feminist critique, but eventually back to it in what I hope is an informatively extended historical and cultural perspective.[11] The narrator in book 6 gives an account of the saluage nation before Serena comes on the scene. We are told that these saluages are a thriftless, unproductive band of outlaws who live on what they can steal:

> ne did giue
> Them selues to any trade, as for to driue
> The painefull plough, or cattell for to breed,
> Or by aduentrous marchandize to thriue.
>
> (6.8.35)

They steal even or especially from the vulnerable poor; we might thus add that they appear self-excluded from outlaw romance as we like it, of the Robin Hood type. As outlaws stigmatized from the beginning as cannibals, these saluages respect no borders, and indeed their raids entail repeated boundary crossings. If this is already beginning to sound familiar, it isn't surprising; one of the intertexts of this episode is Spenser's *View of the Present State of Ireland,* in which cross-border depredations as well as reduction of the "thriftless" Irish to literal cannibalism are graphically described.[12] Even in the narrative of book 6 we have quite recently heard an exchange between Artegall and Calidore in which the former expresses relief at having escaped from the "saluage island" of book 5 into the more congenial realm of Renaissance civility in book 6. But the familiarity goes a good deal further than that. The drawing of a transgressed borderline between a realm of law and one of outlawry, between a productive economy and one of improvident poverty, and between civil selfhood and that which is radically Other, is a commonplace of Renaissance cultural inscription, particularly characteristic of its colonial self-inscription in the New World and elsewhere. Just as commonplace is the self-justifying stigmatization of the Other as taboo-violating in some particularly horrible manner; the accusation of cannibalism is not the only one, but it is an important one apparently dictated by some of the economic presuppositions of Western (especially Protestant) culture.[13]

The disproportion between the shocked Renaissance discourse of cannibalism and properly attested instances of it even in the New World make it seem as if cannibalism is the only logically possible answer to the question about how communities can survive without recognizable Western forms of production and thrift, and when even their outlawry hasn't enough to prey on. Such communities must logically devour themselves. But if it is a logically possible answer it is also a logically impossible one since the cannibal community must then be considered a wholly self-consuming and hence rapidly disappearing one.[14] In the absence of an endlessly expansionist technology, not even having neighboring tribes to eat can long arrest this logic of self-consumption. The cannibals' continued marginal form of survival must then be accounted for, and this, I believe, is what leads Spenser to envisage their barely sustainable scarcity economy as a parasitic one in which cannibalizing others plays an indispensable if periodic part. This is the scarcity economy to which a law-abiding productive economy is opposed in book 6. How does this opposition read out, or, more precisely, how are we to read it out?

We know from Montaigne's essay on the cannibals as well as the extensive commentary it has provoked that positing a radical, normative difference between Western civil society and the cannibal Other uncontrollably results in a radical inversion. Insofar as the opposition aspires to produce difference in an extreme form, it succumbs to specularity in which the aggravated or depraved cannibalism of the normative Western society is disclosed—thus the western civil Self turns out to be the twin of the cannibal Other, only more so and with less justification. (No noble savagery goes with "our" cannibalism.) A more complex result is that a problematic of translation immediately arises, not just as a matter of contingency, but necessarily and constitutively. In Montaigne's essay, we are never sure that the cannibals' language is being correctly translated, and in that sense we can actually not claim to know anything for sure about them, not even that they are cannibals. Such is the ethnographic predicament at its extreme. A putative translation is however being made, and insofar as that is occurring, there is a sense in which cannibalism is being reintroduced to—or reinscribed in—a Western culture in which it is unknown, at least legally and officially speaking. Implicitly, reverse translation, which may still be no translation at all, will be occurring in the New World (or in Ireland) as the colonizing powers translate themselves or are translated into native terms.[15] In these endless processes of translation, valorized differences threaten to crumble and boundaries to blur; eventually, the alien can no longer necessarily be recognized in nor expelled from anyone's construction of the proper.

The terms of this problematic as well as its complexity are fully apparent in Spenser's passage in book 6. Contradictions immediately surface in the narrative as it seeks to produce cannibal culture as Other. It is not clear from the narrative standpoint whether the saluages are a disorderly rabble preying on their thrifty neighbors or whether they are community ordered according to different principles—or rather, with respect to different founding taboos—from those that constitute the narrative standpoint: they are successively described as orderly and monstrous. Implicit in this contradiction is the question about whether they are really improvident or provident in their own way, and if so, what construction of providence they inhabit. As it proceeds, and despite scandalized interjections from the narrator, the narrative seems bound to resolve initial contradictions into a steady recognition that the cannibal community is orderly, is not unnatural in the sense of being monstrous, and is self-disciplined through the agency of its priest despite its nomadic existence.[16] It seems paradoxically less hard on the strange woman it proposes to devour than is the chivalric culture out of which she has dropped. The uncontaminated purity of her blood is affirmed by the pagan priest, and can accordingly be offered in sacrifice to the tribal deity while her body parts are eaten by the tribe. In the culture from which Serena has become an outcast, she bears the taint of having been led astray by her guilty desires, implicitly those of her wanton blood.

Such, then, is the saluage community into which Serena has wandered. Let us recall before concluding that her "sovereigne beautie" hasn't saved her in the chivalric world, partly because she has nothing to do and no protector in it once her admirer has been seduced into bonding with the enchanting Sir Calidore.[17] Serena's mediating function seems to have been fully performed once that has happened, and she becomes redundant. This state of redundancy can be construed as her "desert" or deserted existence. The radically displaced Petrarchan woman—ironically displaced *from* the world of courtesy and civility—is reconstructed in the saluage episode as the sacrificial victim sustaining a cannibal economy in both the broad and narrow senses of that term. In this process of recharacterization, however, a final eerie effect needs to be recognized. The discourse of cannibalism in the passage is infiltrated by a language of providence and grace, and the sacrificial preparations recall Christian communion, albeit with apparently differential intent:

> Then when she waked they all gaue one consent,
> That since by grace of God she there was sent,
> Unto their God they would her sacrifize,
> Whose share, her guiltless bloud they would present.
>
> (6.8.38)

> But them the priest rebuking, did aduize
> To dare not to pollute so sacred threasure,
> Vow'd to the gods; religion held euen theeues in measure.
>
> (6.8.43)

Insofar as Christian communion is differentially recalled, the apparently desired antithesis between cannibal and civil society expands into a putative global antithesis between pagan and Christian culture. In terms of this antithesis, the savage sacrifice must logically be regarded as an anthropological survival which is also the regressive, literal antitype or demonic parody of Christian communion. Implicitly, perhaps, for the Protestant Spenser, Catholic communion belongs to the side of regressive parody, not yet having undergone the symbolic translation of English Protestantism. Insofar as Ireland remains Catholic, it will remain a "saluage island" rather than a civil community in this sense as well. Worse, it will be resisting translation, and its idolatrous cult of the virgin must then be regarded as a literal, cannibalistic fixation on the wrong object which displaces the Christian eucharist, erases the figure of Christ, and rebarbarizes sacrifice.

It goes almost without saying that this expanded cultural anithesis will be subject to exactly the same problems of inversion, specularity, and problematic translation as those that arise from the more limited antithesis between civil and cannibal society. This will especially be the case insofar as the English cult of Elizabeth simultaneously displaces and translates the Catholic cult of the virgin.[18] While the savage sacrifice can be read from the Protestant standpoint as an instance of failed symbolic translation, it can no less be read as a disconcertingly successful reverse translation revealing the symbolic order of English Protestantism to be a fictional one in which the sacrificial objectification of the woman is constantly being denied and dissimulated. Moreover, this reverse translation will be occurring between two *symbolic* orders, not between a symbolic and a literal one as Spenser in his Protestant capacity might wish.

Since, however, all this is happening in Spenser's book of courtesy, not of holiness, the point may be slightly different and even more general. Through unavoidable "mistranslation," it may begin to seem as if the definitively Renaissance system of courtesy, in which women are ostensibly included, valued and protected, sacrificially devours them; likewise Renaissance Christian culture, organized around the figure of Christ as symbolic victim, dissimulates its own cannibalistic sacrifice—its constitutive dismemberment and symbolic consumption—of the woman's body.

Now, it is possible to imagine these observations being made with a certain intent to shock or in a shocked state. It is in a shocked state that I take Stanley Cavell, for example, to be writing in an influential essay, strongly informed by Montaigne's essay on the cannibals, on Shakespeare's *Coriolanus*.[19] In that essay, one of the few that does seriously confront the issue, Cavell discerns in the Rome of *Coriolanus* a self-consuming economy of pure cannibalism. Through the well-known Shakespearean pun on Rome as "room," the Mother City paradoxically becomes an enormous void in which all are starving. In Rome, no object of sacrificial consumption can be found or can suffice if it is found, and no psychic or maternal economy of nurturing bounty can be recovered. From Cavell's point of view, Coriolanus's anguish arises from the fact that he cannot successfully occupy the position of the nourishing father who feeds all Rome;[20] from the point of view of my own discussion, he seems also to withdraw from any position in which he can symbolically be consumed by the Roman people. He will not expose his body to view.

For Cavell, practically all politics are forever threatened by collapse into this cannibal politics. The collapse can be averted only by regenerating a sharp antithesis between cannibal politics as bad ones and eucharistic politics as good ones. This large difference will subtend a further distinction between the aggressively savage discourse of *Coriolanius* on one hand and a wished-for, perhaps ritualistic, civil discourse on the other. Regenerating this saving difference as an absolute one may, however, be regarded as an effect of shock, and as a form of reentry into circular or specular problematic. In my own conclusion, I want to try for something else, even if that only means situating the saving difference in a different place and articulating it in a more fully problematized way.

At the narrative level, it may be impossible or pointless to try and conclude whether Serena is better off in chivalric society, in the desert into which she is expelled from it, or in the cannibal community in which she regains a sacrificial, community-sustaining function—and perhaps a shred of paradoxical dignity on that account. Each of the choices seems unattractive, and the last-minute rescue of Serena by Calepine doesn't necessarily put an end to the problems of the displaced Petrarchan woman. In order to be rescued she has to be seen naked by Calepine, and the effect of this unwanted exposure to the "courteous" or "civil" male gaze seems to be a mortification so profound as to cast doubt on the desirability of the rescue. Serena is "savingly" subjected to a gender-differentiated mode of discourtesy from the effects of which recovery may not be easy in a Renaissance courtesy world in which life and death are civil rather than natural states.[21] Yet it is not with this narrative outcome that I want to conclude. The point I want to make is that the particular dissemination of Petrarchan codes in this episode *is* one that primarily saves them in and for a scarcity economy of consumption. What the difficult translation between saluage and civil society in the episode ineluctably seems to disclose is not a reliable economic abundance on the side of the civil that would justify providential constructions and obviate any need for cannibalism.[22] Rather, what is disclosed in the process of translation, but also in book 6 as a whole, is a precarious *general* economy, signified by repeated invocations of Fortune, to which all are subject.[23] It is an economy of erratic ups and downs, or windfalls like Serena's arrival among the saluages, but of a continuing scarcity that requires windfalls to be economized. The Serena episode implies that it is the supposedly productive civil economy as much as, or rather than, the saluage one from which the cannibal principle can't structurallly be excluded. (If this cannibalism is regarded only as a supplement, it will be a dangerous one in Derrida's sense). Indeed, it is into that civil economy of providence and thrift that the cannibal principle may have to be reimported from the New World (or from Ireland) in the guise of translation.

If we are to explain under what necessity this importation occurs, perhaps it is that of an emergent early modern imperative of consumption that is excessive with respect to any previous constructions of thrift or abundant production. The emergence of this particular imperative has widely been discussed in recent work on the Renaissance, as has its profoundly disruptive effect on many existing codes of social and economic inscription, particularly those regarding cornucopian abundance and hospitality.[24] In the light of this broader discussion, the episode of Serena can be regarded as the rehearsal of a consumer economy in which the woman will be both the object of unsatisfied consumption and the prototype of everything to be consumed. The codes of Petrarchanism are *intelligibly* being saved in this economy, which they may always and already anticipate, and in the emergence of which they may acquire their peculiar dominance. This saving process is subjected by Spenser to what can still be regarded as a singularly damaging exposure—it is the codes rather than the body of the woman that get exposed in the Serena episode—but Spenser's critique remains seemingly inseparable from, and may importantly facilitate, the economic functioning or refunctioning of those codes. Undoing this relationship between critique and dissemination, as Spenser may historically be unable to do, remains a challenge to which our forms of critical theory might enable us to respond.

Notes

1. For the English Renaissance sonnet tradition, these points are well made by Joel Fineman, *Shakespeare's Perjur'd Eye: The Invention of Poetic Subjectivity in the Sonnets* (Berkeley: University of California Press, 1986). In that book, Fineman also suggests that Shakespeare's male homosexual revision of Petrarchanism in sonnets 1–126 at once "unmasks" heterosexual Petrarchanism and identifies the male homoerotic version as the only one rigorously consistent with visionary admiration and a poetics of "likeness."

2. I am not suggesting that Petrarch occupies an authentic position of origin. What Petrarch derives (or successfully appropriates and "fixes") from a broader romance tradition of female admiration, or from Dante's *rime petrose* and other sources, has extensively been discussed inter alia by Robert Durling in his introduction to *Petrarch's Lyric Poems* (Cambridge: Harvard University Press, 1976): 1–33. The "Petrarachan" tropes in question may in every case be ones subject to a long history of narrative embedding and lyric disembedding. Petrarch's fixing of these tropes as well as his self-production (self-fixation) in the act of doing so has been well discussed, for example, by John Freccero, "The Fig-tree and the Laurel: Petrarch's Poetics," *Diacritics* 5 (1975): 34–39.

3. The notion of "salvage" primarily applies, according to *OED,* to situations of marine recovery at the time Spenser is writing, and an interest in this issue as well as in the laws governing it is evident in book 5.4.4–20 of *The Faerie Queene.* My discussion may, however, depend to some degree on an "unauthorized" extension of the term, yet it is an extension that is arguably occurring in Spenser's representation of "saluage" events, especially in book 6, in which losses and recoveries are so consistently thematized.

4. Edmund Spenser, *The Faerie Queene,* ed. J. C. Smith and E. de Sélincourt (Oxford: Clarendon Press, 1960), 30–31. While my discussion of this episode doesn't aspire to go beyond the commonplace and uncontentious, it is informed by well-established critical traditions of the kind summarized in Hugh Maclean, ed., *Edmund Spenser's Poetry* (New York: Norton, 1982), 64–68, and A. C. Hamilton, ed., *The Faerie Queene* (London: Longman, 1977), 86–89. I do, however, wish to acknowledge here Donald Cheney's pioneering *Spenser's Image of Nature: Wild Man and Shepherd in "The Faerie Queene"* (New Haven: Yale University Press, 1966), and, in general terms, Theresa M. Krier, *Gazing on Secret Sights: Spenser, Classical Imitation, and the Decorums of Vision* (Ithaca: Cornell University Press, 1990).

5. The Una episode can accordingly be read as one of fairly catastrophic pedagogic failure, in which the suspended state of "wonder" leads on to no higher recognition (the reverse, if anything). One of the main Petrarchan justifications thus appears to fall away early in the poem.

6. This term may seem to invoke a model of the sacrificial community as expounded in René Girard, *Violence and the Sacred* (Baltimore: Johns Hopkins University Press, 1972), 1–68. It does so only marginally, however, insofar as Una's arrival might be *inferred* to avert a crisis of violence inside the savage community. This doesn't seem to be a particularly strong or necessary inference, and the sacrificial "economy" in question is one that I read otherwise in due course. In connection with Bataille's sacrificial discourse, Derrida raises the question, pertinent to my later discussion, of the move from a restricted to a general economy. See Jacques Derrida, "From Restricted to General Economy: A Hegelianism without Reserve," in *Writing and Difference,* trans. Alan Bass (Chicago: University of Chicago Press, 1976), 251–77.

7. For a good critical summary as well as important intertextual discussion of this issue, see Krier, *Gazing on Secret Sights,* 113–18.

8. It is possible that Petrarchanism can be regarded, on account of its broad cultural dispersal, stabilization and "mechanization," as a technology of the gaze in the sense given to that term by Teresa de Lauretis, *Technologies of Gender: Essays on Theory, Film and Fiction* (Bloomington: Indiana University Press, 1987).

9. What is being displaced and/or contained here is no doubt a considerable anxiety regarding the woman as an all-devouring figure, from whose "belly" everything may come, but into which it also threatens to disappear again.

10. It isn't quite clear whether an act of communal *re*constitution is occurring in this episode as a result of Serena's arrival. This possibility is certainly consistent with my own later argument.

11. In some important respects the following discussion (regarding, for example, the dialectic of same and other, and the eucharist as sacrifice) is paralleled or anticipated by Peter Hulme, "Caribs and Arawaks," *Colonial Encounters: Europe and the Native Caribbean, 1492–1797* (London: Methuen, 1986), 78–87. I should emphasize that in my own discussion nothing is implied about the real nature of New World native economies, nor, in my view, does a profound interest in other economies as such inform Spenser's work. Rather, the elision, projection, and reappropriation of such economies appears to be part of a dynamic in which a general economy—call it that of early modernity, or of capital—is being constituted.

12. For some discussion of the "borderlands" of Spenser's *View* see Kenneth Gross, "Mythmaking in Hibernia: *A View of the Present State of Ireland," Spenserian Poetics: Idolatry,*

Iconoclasm, Magic (Ithaca: Cornell University Press, 1985), 78–112.

13. In recent unpublished work, Jonathan Goldberg has discussed "sodomy" as a taboo-violation attributed to a particular native aristocracy by Balboa. This violation licenses Balboa to slaughter all these natives (and "feed them to [his] dogs") on behalf of the "people," an action in which the native power structure in conveniently displaced.

14. Not entirely a predicament, however, since radical nontranslation can be reclaimed in and *as* translation, in which the native "original" is effectively erased.

15. "Translation" of Western religious skepticism into a mode of self-insinuating power in the New World is implied in Stephen Greenblatt's "Invisible Bullets: Renaissance Authority and its Subersion, *Henry IV* and *Henry V*," in *Political Shakespeare: New Essays in Cultural Materialism*, ed. Jonathan Dollimore and Alan Sinfield (Ithaca: Cornell University Press, 1985), 18–47. This essay may say more about European power production (or about a mechanism under which power can imaginarily be constituted) than about any insidiously successful projection of power into the New World. Each side translates and retranslates the other.

16. The historical unthinkability of a nomadic-pastoral economy—its offensively absurd yet undeniably successful persistence—is implied in the discussion of Irish "Bollies" in Spenser's *A View of the Present State of Ireland*, ed. W. L. Renwick (Oxford: Clarendon Press, 1970), 49–51. These Irish nomads not only survive in the unenclosed pasturelands of Ireland, thus escaping English pursuit and incorporation, but seem almost indistinguishable as communities from the self-sustaining "herds" they raise. *OED* gives only one pertinent citation for "Bollies:" the term suggestively denotes "hobgoblins" (i.e., threatening, spectral apparitions).

17. It seems to be part of the problem with courtesy in book 6 that Calidore's fatal enchantment as "ideal" courtier works primarily on men. It is far from clear that there is any place in the text of courtesy for women. At least one of the mechanisms of exclusion involved in book 6 is the homosocial one identified by Eve Kosofsky Sedgwick in *Between Men: English Literature and Male Homosocial Desire* (New York: Columbia University Press, 1985). The "economy" of such exclusion is strongly thematized by Spenser in book 6; it could no doubt be discussed under the rubric of fetishism, but that is not what I have chosen to do here.

18. See inter alia Louis Adrian Montrose, "Eliza, Queene of the shepheardes' and the Pastoral of Power," *Renaissance Historicism: Selections from "English Literary Renaissance*," ed. Arthur F. Kinney and Dan S. Collins (Amherst: University of Massachusetts Press, 1987), 34–63.

19. Stanley Cavell, "*Coriolanus* and Interpretations of Politics (Who does the wolf love?)," *Themes out of School* (San Francisco: North Point Press, 1984), 60–96.

20. The figure of the "nourish-father," strongly invoked by James I on behalf of his own kingship, is well discussed by Coppélia Kahn, "'Magic of bounty': *Timon of Athens*, Jacobean Patronage, and Maternal Power," *Shakespeare Quarterly* 38 (1987): 34–57. A broader discussion of this figure can be found in Debora Kuller Shuger, "Nursing Fathers: Patriarchy as a Cultural Ideal," *Habits of Thought in the English Renaissance: Religion, Politics and the Dominant Culture* (Berkeley: University of California Press, 1990), 218–50.

21. In Krier's discussion of the episode, this mortification is well recognized, while a wish to humanize the intersubjective gaze is also expressed. Part of the difficulty, however, is that this mortification becomes evident in the book of *courtesy*, as an effect produced within the field of humanism rather than in a field of savage otherness.

22. What might be called Weberian Protestantism, in which individual prosperity within a general productive economy is believed to signify providential approval, can be regarded as the fantasy belied in this passage.

23. It might be suggested that this is the economy figured by Greek as distinct from

chivalric romance in book 6, but also in some of the late Shakespeare plays. An attempt at "civil" mastery of this economy of random Fortune may accordingly be figured by the heroes of book 6. The scopic rupturing in book 6 of Colin Clout's "closed," Acidalian economy of grace—characterized by maternal abundance and balanced gift exchange—implies the drastic *loss* of any such economy, though in book 6 that ideal poetic economy of pastoral is already lost insofar as Colin is a figure recalled from the past. In "Consuming Texts: Spenser and the Poet's Economy," *Voice Terminal Echo* (London: Methuen, 1986), Jonathan Goldberg finds the poetic economy of *The Shepheardes Calender* to be already one of "excessive" consumption and self-consumption, in which a cannibalistic principle seems to be operating.

24. See, in addition to Goldberg, Lorna Hutson, *Thomas Nashe in Context* (Oxford: Clarendon Press, 1989); Jonathan Haynes, "Festivity and the Dramatic Economy of Johnson's *Bartholomew Fair*," *Journal of English Literary History* 51 (1984): 645–48; Karen Newman, "City Talk: Women and Commodification in Jonson's *Epicoene*," *Journal of English Literary History* 56 (Fall 1989): 503–18; Joan Thirsk, *Economic Policy and Projects: The Development of a Consumer Economy in Early Modern England* (Oxford: Clarendon Press, 1978). Insofar as women inhabit the consuming community, as we may suppose them to do in the Spenser passage—no matter how constitutively masculine the position of "saluage" spectatorship may be—they evidently can do so only as self-cannibalizing subjects and objects of consumption.

Making History Straight: Collecting and Recording in Sixteenth-Century Italy

Stephanie Jed
University of California, San Diego

THIS essay began as a reflection on the story of the first tyrant-slayers, Harmodius and Aristogiton, who, in book 6 of Thucydides' history of *The Peloponnesian War*, were lovers. Thucydides tells us that their love was so strong that even the tyrant Hipparchus, who was also in love with Harmodius, could not succeed in destroying their love. Hipparchus tried every means of flattery to win the love of Harmodius for himself. But his entreaties failed, and so he decided to insult Harmodius by forbidding his sister to take part in a procession of basket carriers. This insult, according to Thucydides, was but the last in a series of "erotic" offenses which induced the lovers, Harmodius and Aristogiton, to plot against the life of the tyrant.[1]

Aristotle, in the *Politics*, tells this story as well, featuring, however, the insult to the sister as the cause of the violence. In Aristotle's account, the love between the two men is relegated to the background.[2]

In the pseudo-Platonic dialogue *Hipparchos,* another verison is offered. Harmodius and Aristogiton are friends, not lovers. Harmodius has an unnamed lover who is successfully seduced, this time, by the flattery of the tyrant. This lover leaves Harmodius for the tyrant Hipparchus. The two friends Harmodius and Aristogiton, not bound together by a sexual tie in this narrative, take revenge against the tyrant for his offense to Harmodius.[3]

Finally, in a much later version of the third century A.D., received from tradition by Justinus, the tyrant is slain because he has raped the sister of Harmodius.[4] In this account, every trace of relationship and rivalry between the male lovers has disappeared. The story, it would seem, has now been made straight; Harmodius' sister, after various narrative vicissitudes, has come to occupy the ground on which acts of political violence are constructed. A homoerotic offense has been transformed into a heterosexual act of violence. Definitions of tyranny and justifications for tyrannicide from this moment on will depend upon some reference to the tyrant's lust and his violation of women.

In this essay, I want to discuss "making history straight" in relation to a much later event of tyrannicide. On the night of 6 January 1537, Lorenzino de' Medici, according to historiographic accounts, devised an elaborate ambush against his cousin, Alessandro de' Medici, the duke of Florence.[5] Alessandro purportedly had a weakness for insulting noblewomen and climbing convent walls. And Lorenzino, capitalizing on this weakness, lured Alessandro into his bedroom and persuaded him to remove his arms; a woman, Lorenzino said, had agreed to satisfy Alessandro's lust for her on that very night. So, Alessandro waited in Lorenzino's bed unarmed for Lorenzino to bring back the woman. Instead, Lorenzino came back with his henchman Scoroncolo and together they finished off the duke. Once again, the heterosexual motive for political assassination, inherited from the history made straight of Harmodius and Aristogiton, had been called into play.

Historiographic representations of this event include, in addition to the heterosexual motive, other novelistic details as well. For example, various histories tell us that Lorenzino, in order to muffle Alessandro's screams during the attack, put his hand in Alessandro's mouth. Alessandro then clamped his teeth down on Lorenzino's hand so hard that he practically bit off his thumb. Blood gushed from Lorenzino's hand so fast as to force him to seek medical treatment in Bologna before notifying key people in Florence of what he had done. Much is also made in the historiography of Lorenzino's melancholy, his brooding over books, and his resemblance to Brutus.

Contrary to what we might expect, such motifs are not unique to the more "literary" historiographic texts, penned and published by men of letters, but they are produced, as well, in unedited reports and correspondence, written by men of varying degrees of literacy, in the days following the assassination.[6] It is in this common ground between "literature" and "historical records" that we may investigate the relation between the heterosexual motive, or history made straight, and the documentation projects of the state. What interests me here are the recording and collecting procedures by means of which the state constructed and naturalized masculinity and heterosexuality in order to contain the disruptiveness of Alessandro's assassination.

The state in question here is not Florence but Milan, a client state of the Emperor Charles V. Milan was the site of the emperor's Italian administration, and the emperor administered the Florentine situation through Marino Caracciolo, the governor of Milan. Alessandro de' Medici was the emperor's appointment in Florence.[7] And bureaucratic control of Florentine affairs from Milan was such that the assassinated Duke Alessandro was replaced in a matter of days by another imperial appointment, Cosimo de' Medici. An army of humanist exiles resisted the appointment of Cosimo, but this resistance was crushed by imperial forces. In the period of Alessandro's reign, 1530–37, one can palpably mark the transfer of power from Florence to Milan in the disintegration of institutional records in the Florentine state archive and in a new kind of record keeping about Florence in the form of reports to Caracciolo, conserved in the state chancellery of Milan.

The records of the Milanese chancellery for the year 1537 thus constitute one important locality of writing in which the authority of Charles V's imperial state was constructed and deployed. For the chancellery of Milan, in this period, was an important site of the contest between Charles V and the French King François I for domination over Europe. Imperial domination of Italy was maintained from the Milanese writing offices. And Italy was an economic key to subjugation of the world.[8] This claim to domination was, in part, produced in the reports to Caracciolo, which constructed a dependency of local Italian needs upon imperial management.

Complaints of commanders about overdue salaries to soldiers, complaints about the financial burden and offensive behavior of the occupying troops, reports of mutinies, military budget requests, all helped to support the authority of imperial administrators by representing the administration of Italy as dependent on the resources of imperial domination. Illustrating the extent of this dependence, the imperial ambassador to Genova wrote to Caracciolo in November of 1537: "Milan's necessities are so great that [the gold and silver of] seven Peru's wouldn't be enough to take care of them."[9] In this way, the Milanese chancellery was constructed as a kind of settlement office administering Italy as an internal European colony.

In the context of this enormous burden that the Milanese administration placed on the finances of the empire, news of the assassination of Alessandro had a tremendous impact. For it meant that unexpected additional expenditures, especially military, would be required to command continued loyalty to the emperor in the wake of this disruption. It also meant that more writing would be required from imperial agents, whose assignments included reporting to Caracciolo on every development. Soon after the assassination, imperial agents from all over Italy wrote to Caracciolo to report to him whatever they knew of the Florentine crisis and to help him with the task of managing that crisis. These reports, written as they were by imperial loyalists, at times imagined even the sentiments of the emperor. "His Majesty," one correspondent wrote from Asti, "would have good reason to complain, because news was being made in Italy and there was already too much news, especially with the Turks approaching, and both the Pope and his Majesty were quite concerned to put an end to any new uprisings."[10] These reports thus constitute an important resource for understanding the construction of an official record and the power of this record in containing disruption.

Official knowledge about the Florentine crisis was constructed, in the first place, by privileging a particular kind of coverage of events and by claiming that other points of view were responsible for the crisis provoked by Alessandro's assassination. The case of the cardinal Salviati, opponent of imperial domination, shows us, for example, how the Milanese chancellery required critical voices to change their tune if they wanted to become part of the official record. On 14 January Caracciolo wrote to Salviati and other opponents of empire, inviting them to change their allegiances and offering them material rewards for imperial service:

> I wanted to remind you that now is the time to perform great service, . . . repressing every insurrection . . . and making everyone straight on the straight path to universal gain [driciando ognuno al camino dritto et più expediente al benefitio universale]. And you can be sure that his imperial majesty . . . will keep good accounts of the services performed for the personal and universal gain of the state [benefitio particulare et universale di quello stato]. Your honor and profit will acrrue from those services.[11]

Using the terms *drizzare* (to straighten) and *dritto* (straight), Caracciolo made clear that "making everyone straight" entailed not only repressing anti-imperial sentiments and activities but forging a written link with the chancellery of Milan. The cardinal Salviati's response to Caracciolo's letter showed that, in his case, at least two obstacles would have to be overcome before such a link could be operative. In his letter, we can begin to see the particular conditions of writing imposed upon imperial correspondents. And we can see how these conditions of writing contributed to the process of making history straight.

In his response to Caracciolo's invitation, the cardinal Salviati showed he was willing to write back, but that two major snags would prevent him from performing his duties as imperial correspondent. The first consisted in the fact that, unlike every other man who wrote to Caracciolo, Salviati did not see the Florentine matter as under control. He reported "great confusion and anguish"[12] in Florence and large-scale troop movements of the exile armies. He expressed his anger that the imperial troops were not observing the terms of the peace accord: the Florentines had stopped fighting, as the agreement stipulated, but the imperial troops continued to advance, destroying the city and committing atrocities against its citizens. Although many other correspondents also wrote about the troop movements of the exile army, they did so in reports on the 2500 Spanish reinforcements about to arrive or in the context of affirming Florentine loyalty to Charles V. "News keeps coming in," says one typical letter from Parma, "that there has been no change in Florence and the people of that city appear to be on our side [imperiali] and all of the fortresses are loyal to his Majesty."[13] Against the background of this rosy media coverage, Salviati's more critical picture of anguish and war crimes was unlikely to get a spot.

But there was also another important obstacle that prevented a writer like Salviati from fulfilling the duties of an imperial correspondent and that was his eccentricity in relation to the imperial postal network. Salviati begins his letter to Caracciolo, written five weeks after Caracciolo sent his, underlining the fact that the imperial postal agents do not know how to locate him. He writes: "If Ridolfi and I had received the other letters you say you sent, we would not have delayed in responding, but those letters were neither delivered to us in Rome before our departure, nor upon our arrival in Florence, where we think you probably addressed them."[14] Another imperial correspondent reinforces the exclusion of men like Salviati from the imperial loop by claiming that Salviati was to blame for the death of Alessandro and that Caracciolo was naive to write to him at all.[15]

The case of Salviati suggests at least two of the qualifications necessary for the job of imperial correspondent: coverage affirming Florentine loyalty to the imperial cause and well-established connections within the imperial postal system. Other qualifications that distinguished the careers of successful imperial reporters pertained to the methods and conditions of collecting information about the Florentine crisis. The development of an automatic writing reflex on the part of imperial agents; the ability to fill up a page with news on a routine basis; consciousness of a writing network; the development of standards for testing the reliability of news sources; these were all keys to the Milanese chancellery's success in containing the Florentine crisis. The definition, through writing, of a body of knowledge and the practices by which such knowledge was compiled give us some clue as to how reports about Alessandro's heterosexual desires functioned in the exercise of imperial power.

The construction of knowledge about the Florentine crisis was characterized by a sense of both urgency and routine. Imperial correspondents wrote to Caracciolo immediately upon being awakened in the middle of the night as a matter of routine, whether or not they had anything to say. For example, Bernardo Sanctio, an imperial ambassador, manifests in his letter to Caracciolo of 12 January the signs of having been woken up with the news of the murder of the duke. He begins his letter: "In this hour whose date is 2 o'clock in the night."[16] He then proceeds to betray the fact that he has not quite understood what he has been told about the Florentine events by confusing the names and the details of what he has heard. And Giovanni Antonio, a Bolognese postal clerk in the service of Caracciolo, also writes in great haste and excitement to Caracciolo on 9 January, telling him that Lorenzino has passed through Bologna. He was in such a great hurry to report this news to Milan that he seems not to have waited for the ink to dry. The signs of this haste are the particles of sixteenth-century dirt that stuck to the ink and that are still there today on the paper.[17] The "reality" embedded in these representations of confusion and urgency was that crises in imperial power could be effectively managed by prompt and automatic reporting to Milan.

On the side of routine, there is a letter of Alfonso Piccolomini to Caracciolo, written from Siena on the 30th of May, five months after the assassination. His letter represents the more humdrum routines of being an imperial reporter. He writes: "From here, I have no news to report that isn't old to you. Still, to fill up the page, I will say that I have understood from the last dispatches from Florence that the Count is carrying forward the peace negotiations . . . The Turkish threat seems to be reviving."[18] Whether or not there were matters of urgency to report, the job of the imperial reporter was to fill up the page with a standard repertoire of news items about Florence and the Turks, the Turks and Florence. What was important was the compilation or combination of "facts" on the page, not the complex realities these facts might have denoted. The routine juxtaposition of news about Florence and the Turks became a standard for naturalizing the image of Florence as Other with respect to the aims of empire. An efficient use of writing was the method for managing this otherness.

On 12 January Captain Speciano, the imperial envoy in Piedmont, reported to Caracciolo that the Marchese del Vasto was using the imperial writing network quite efficiently on behalf of the emperor. As soon as the death of the duke was confirmed, the marchese sent Pyrro Colonna to Florence in the mail coach with diplomatic credentials for two Florentine imperialists "in addition to a condolence letter for the Duchess, and three blank sheets with signatures so that [Colonna] could write to whomever necessary."[19] In the context of the imperial network, filling up blank pages with authorized writing was tantamount to affirming imperial power. References to this network, therefore, abound in the letters to Caracciolo. Phrases like "you have probably already heard [this] from another source" and "I am sending you this news so that, if you like, you can pass it on to so-and-so" underline the awareness among imperial writers of the role of the network in promoting imperial power through the circulation of writing.

Imperial correspondents consistently emphasized their various obligations to the network, especially the obligation to write everything of importance for the maintenance of imperial power, to write reliably and without omissions. As one correspondent put it, he was writing because he didn't want to "leave anything in his pen."[20] And his sentiment was registered in the letters of many correspondents, for whom omission was like defaulting on an imperial loan. The transmission of unreliable information constituted, on the other hand, a sort of betrayal of the imperial network, a betrayal that was in conflict with the first obligation to write without omissions. The conflict consisted in the fact that it was not always possible to verify the reliability of every piece of news *and* send it quickly on to Milan. For this reason, the issue of reliability was constantly represented in reportage on the Florentine crisis. And the care reporters took to qualify the reliability of the news they were transmitting was constructed in relation to Lorenzino's "horrrendous" betrayal of the duke. One message of these collected records seems to be that a report on Lorenzino's betrayal of empire was proof of the reporter's own loyalty.

Now, as we know, Lorenzino, according to these reports, betrayed the duke by murdering him instead of bringing, as he had promised, the woman Alessandro was desiring. What is interesting to note is that this heterosexual motif emerged in these reports in relation to the issue of reliable information. For example, on 11 January Alessandro Landriano, the imperial envoy to Parma, wrote to Caracciolo about the episode, taking care to assure the governor that the truth of the story had been confirmed by various sources:

> I think you have received some other letters in which I communicated the horrendous death of his most illustrious Duke Alessandro de' Medici and although I wrote that it was of dubious truth, now it is coming to be confirmed that last Saturday at 8 o'clock in the evening, while His Excellency was *coming from pleasure,* he was disemboweled by Lorenzo de' Medici.[21]

And Bernardo Sanctio, providing the fullest account of the incident, also took great pains to qualify his report by referring to conflicting opinions. He wrote on 13 January:

> Having arrived in Bologna, I have found *true information* about the Florentine event and so [I write] to your lordship. *They say* that because the Duke was the cousin and very close friend of Lorenzo, a very melancholy young man, and because he had total trust in Lorenzo, Alessandro used Lorenzo as a pimp to obtain a certain noblewoman. *Others say* it was a nun. *Others say* it was a widowed sister of Lorenzo. *All concur* that one Saturday night Alessandro arranged to go to Lorenzo's house to have there a woman.[22]

Sanctio never abandons this balanced style in his report, taking pains, at a later point, to interpret even the motive for the assassinastion from several perspectives:

> *Lorenzo says* the only motive of his action was to liberate his city. *Others say* it was the honor of his sister. *Many say* that it was the melancholy humor of this young man whom they say was very oppressed by his constant pensiveness and resemblance to Brutus. Whatever was the cause, the poor Duke carelessly let himself get caught in the trap and because of his lack of caution, he lost his life and moved the affairs of Florence once again on the chessboard.[23]

Whatever was the truth of the incident, it is clear from these reports that all of the correspondents strived to provide reliable information to the Milanese chancellery about Alessandro's lust for this woman; they seem to have sensed that information about the duke's sexuality was somehow important to the containment and maintenance of imperial authority. Bernardo Sanctio, for example, underlined the importance of the episode by reporting it in the context of the Florentines' continued loyalty to the empire. Following his account of the duke's sexual desires, Sanctio reported, once again in his inimitable balanced style, on the loyal sentiments of the "people":

> Some say that the People wanted to make Cosimo de' Medici the new Duke. Some others say that the people sent word to Salviati and Ridolphi asking them to give a new form of government in this city. All affirm that the city, for now, remains loyal to his Majesty.[24]

On 10 January 1537, Lopez de Soria, the imperial ambassador to Venice made a direct link between the duke's heterosexual exploits, the murder, and the importance of informing the emperor. He wrote in a postscript:

> I have since heard that Lorenzo murdered the Duke in his own house, where the Duke was accustomed to going often with a woman; this matter is of great importance for the affairs of Alessandro's lineage; and no one knows this better than your most Reverend Sanctity. For this reason, it is of great importance that his Majesty be quickly informed.[25]

The urgency of this news for the emperor is underlined by the fact that in midsentence Soria interrupts the work of his scribe and takes over the writing himself with another pen.

The presence of these reports in the Milanese state chancellery produces a kind of eerie effect, encouraging us to reflect on the procedures through which reports to the Milanese chancellery constructed masculinity and heterosexuality as appropriate knowledge for governing. Masculinity was represented in the reports to Caracciolo as the passion, expressed by many correspondents, for creating writing networks among the loyal supporters of empire. In the context of Alessandro's assassination, this loyalty and faithfulness to the imperial cause were further constructed in relation to Lorenzino's betrayal.

Lorenzino was repeatedly represented in reports as the archtraitor, who not only surpassed Marcus Brutus in the number of knife wounds he inflicted on the duke, but who also betrayed the "poor" "trusting" duke's hopes for an evening of sexual domination. The collection of reports affirming this betrayal had the double effect of, first, reinforcing the loyalty among male supporters of empire, and, second, naturalizing male heterosexual lust as a part of that bond among men. In this way, the heterosexual motive or history made straight became linked to technologies of governing. If the assassination of the duke had a real potential, as many thought, of disrupting the imperial rule, this disruption was effectively contained by the documentation project of the Milanese state.

About fifty years after Alessandro's death, the event was reconstructed, printed and reprinted, in illustrations and in verse. Lorenzino was represented, in these later reconstructions, as a traitor so dangerous that the devil refused to welcome him to hell for fear that he would betray Pluto and try to usurp his domain. Alessandro was figured at his own state funeral, denouncing Lorenzino's act of betrayal and addressing Charles V and each and every Florentine who remained loyal after his assassination. The many editions of these works, presumably for a large reading and listening public, served to naturalize the figures of Lorenzino and Alessandro in the literary mythology of Charles V's empire. What interests me here is how the naturalization of Lorenzino as Other from the loyal imperial subject served to further, on a larger scale, the reproduction of empire as a masculine domain.

The "Lament" of Lorenzino is constructed as a dialogue in terzarima between Lorenzino and the devil. The devil, after denying Lorenzino permission to join the worse traitors in hell, wants to know what could have possibly motivated Lorenzino to commit such an act of betrayal:

> What were you lacking? O Lorenzino,
>   clothes, horses, servants,
>   you had day and night under your rule.
> What? Were you perhaps lacking cash?
>   Didn't you have your pocketbook full?[26]

"Every person in the world,"[27] continues the devil, hates Lorenzino for turning his back on the benefits of working for Charles V and choosing instead to oppose him. That is, every person in the Christian imperial world, extending, by this time, from Europe to the Americas to Asia, hates Lorenzino. Lorenzino's alienation from the Christian world is emphasized by the fact that neither God nor the devil is willing to accept him. And his otherness with respect to empire is explicitly constructed in terms of his allegiance to Islamic peoples and places. "Since I don't think God will ever forgive my sin," Lorenzino says, "I think I will go to Turkey to refute the faith . . . I don't believe that in pagan parts of of the world, there is one Tartar, Moor, Turk or Catalan who has been crueler than I."²⁸

Lorenzino, in these verses, was elevated from the historical man who betrayed the duke to an "emblematic type" of the traitor. As an emblematic type, he joined the world of heroes and villains of chivalry whose stories were mass produced and collected in the same verse format. There is some evidence to show that books of chivalry constituted the preferred reading of the conquistadores charged with the task of spreading imperial values in the New World.²⁹ These verses representing Lorenzino, collected along with other chivalric verses about loyalty and treachery, Christianity and Islam, can thus be seen as instruments of imperial power.

The world was a very different place in the 1580s than it was fifty years earlier. One mark of this difference was the proliferation of collecting as a means of constructing otherness and containing disruption. In the fifty or so years that ensued from the collection of reports in the Milanese chancellery about Lorenzino's betrayal to the wide distribution of printed verses about the event, collecting had become one important European mode of knowing and controlling the world. Collections of travel accounts, maps, new world objects, botanical specimens, antiquities, and verses like the ones about Lorenzino dominated the world of the cultural elite. As Defert has discussed in his important essay "Collecting the World," the publication of collections of travel narratives constituted an important moment in state formation. Monumental publishing projects of this period like Ramusio's *Naviggationi e viaggi,* whose publication began in 1550, and Hakluyt's *Principall Navigations,* whose publication began in 1582, constructed Venetian and English statehood by collecting the Other in the context of "the heroes and hopes" of the nation.³⁰ And as Paula Findlen has so beautifully analyzed in her work on the museum, sixteenth-century collectors constructed a space of male bonding in their sharing of "facts."³¹

The development, in the middle and latter parts of the sixteenth century, of an imperial network of male collectors was required to ensure a certain control over the explosion of knowledge brought about by imperial expansion. Imperial authority, in the second half of the century, could no longer be supported by the reports of imperial correspondents alone. Supplementary, semigovernmental networks of male loyalists, who would collect, classify, and define every bit of imperial reality, were needed to contain the information crisis. Libraries like the Escorial were charged in this period with the task of collecting and ordering knowledge for the promotion of Christendom.[32] And the founding of private libraries and museums constructed a bridge between local, national, and imperial interests.

In 1544, Paolo Giovio, a museum founder and imperial historiographer from Como, represented this link between collecting and empire in his letter to a Venetian minister residing in Milan. After commenting, in some detail, on the political "health" of Italy, Giovio asked the Venetian minister to donate the windows for his "Sacred Museum" in Como.[33] This letter with its juxtaposition of national ideals and the financial needs of a private museum, has several implications for our understanding of collecting. First, it shows that the collecting enterprise required the collector to create a series of financial and cultural contacts in order to sustain the viability of his project. Second, we can see how the institution of the museum participated in the construction of a cultural identity, that of the nation, an identity which greatly exceeded the boundaries of the museum's locality. And, finally, we get a glimpse of how this link between a locality and a larger cultural concept served the political/cultural aims of both collector and empire. Empire was served by the construction of common interests that transcended localities, ultimately crossing national boundaries. While the collector was served by the construction of a network through which to attract male visitors to his home.

If the purpose of the museum was to bring an imperial image of "the world into the home," this world was inevitably followed by an "endless flow of goods, information, and visitors."[34] Scholars, for example, came to the Museum of Giovan Vincenzo della Porta "from the furthest corners of Europe drawn by its fame."[35] And Aldrovandi boasted that "everything in my museum is seen by many different gentlemen who, passing through this city, visit my *Pandecchio di natura* like an eighth wonder of the world."[36] Many of these visitors arrived with letters of introduction that revealed the importance of personal contacts in constructing the intellectual communities of sixteenth-century Europe. One professor wrote to Aldrovandi, for example, asking him to receive his friend in his museum and to treat him with courtesy "for love of me."[37] This informal male network of collectors and scholars continued undisturbed through the eighteenth century. Bonding in particular over their desire for news about the Indies, these men were instrumental in the production of a unified European culture supporting the aims of empire.[38]

Although sixteenth-century collections in Europe and England—whether they were called libraries, museums, or studios—were essentially open to any scholar or collector of appropriate rank, one purpose of collecting was to close off or defend the collector and the imperial point of view from disturbing bits of knowledge. In his preface to the Mercator-Hondius *Atlas* (1636), Henry Hexham reinforced this somewhat defensive image of collecting by representing Mercator's collection of maps as a substitute for contact with the world. He wrote that, with the aid of a map collection,

> the greate Monarches, Kings and Princes of this Universe, may representively *in their Cabinets* take a view of the extention and limits of their owne Kingdomes, and Dominions . . . And if they be in hostility with their neighbour Princes may peepe upon those places, townes and Forts, which lye most advantagious & commodious to satisfie their ambition . . . Here the Noble-man and Gentle-man by speculations *in his closset*, may travell through every Province of the whole world. Here the Marchant sitting in his counting-house, may know what marchandises every Countrie affordeth, what commodities it wanteth, and whither he may transport, and vent those which are most vendible, to return gaine and profite into his purse.[39]

Once again, in these words, we can see the strong connection between collecting and imperial profit. If the practice of collecting created a European cultural network to support the aims of empire, it also protected the collector from the effects that network had on the cultures it collected. By circumscribing knowledge within the confines of two book covers or four walls, the collector was able to retain some semblance of dominion over knowledge. At least part of the attraction of sixteenth-century collecting must have been this possibility of dominating the world in the comfort of one's own study.

This composite image of the collector, at once a solitary figure and part of a male cultural network supporting imperial domination, brings us once again to the question of gender. For embedded in the solitary space men constructed for collecting was the desire to represent men's domination over women, to contain their disturbance by means of correspondence among men. If, in 1537, reports to the Milanese chancellery constructed heterosexual domination as appropriate knowledge for governing, this construct persisted through the eighteenth century in the activity of collecting and in correspondence among collectors. In early eighteenth-century England, when the Bodleian opened its doors to all people, one German traveler wrote:

Every moment brings fresh spectators and, surprisingly enough, amongst them peasants and women-folk, who gaze at the library as a cow might gaze at a new gate with such noise and trampling of feet that others are much disturbed.⁴⁰

Once again, as in the case of reports on the Florentine crisis, women appear in the records of collecting only to confirm their own domination, only to uphold imperial definitions of masculinity, only to perform the task of making history straight.

John Comenius, the Dutch educator, defined the museum in 1657 as

a place where a Scholar, apart from other Men, sits alone, addicted to his Studies, while he reads Books, which being within his reach, he lays open upon a Desk, and excerpts all the best things out of them into his own Manual, or marks them with a Dash or an asterisk in the Margin.⁴¹

A somewhat chilling description of our own activities as scholars, this definition also stands for a long-standing tradition of collecting understood as an instrument of power. The power in question is the power of male address, men talking and writing to men, masculinity emerging from particular social practices that empower males as agents of history, women either arriving at certain moments to satisfy male lust or trampling in the library, making history straight. To leave it like this would be to say nothing new. It is important above all to analyze this construction and then to establish different centers of power. In this project, we might follow the example of Paolo Giovio, our sixteenth-century collector from Como. He used his collection of the past, based on the principles of male address and male agency, to write a history of his own time. I would like to suggest that we, too, might write a history of our own time and a history of our gender, a history of female address and agency. In such a history, the study of relations among women today and our different structures of producing knowledge might serve as a useful lens through which to study the past.⁴²

Notes

The conception of this essay depends, in part, on the terminologies and methods employed by Bernard S. Cohn and Richard Saumarez Smith in their work on British imperial rule in India. It would be cumbersome to annotate my borrowing of such terminologies as "technologies of governing," "documentation projects," "appropriate knowledge," etc., and somewhat inaccurate in the sense that my debt to their work is more general and extensive. See, in particular, Bernard S. Cohn, "The Anthropology of a Colonial State and Its Forms of Knowledge," a paper prepared for an International Symposium held at Mijas, Spain, 5–13 November 1988, whose theme was "Tensions of Empire: Colonial Control and Visions of Rule"; and Richard Saumarez Smith, "Rule-by-records and rule-by-reports: complementary aspects of the British Imperial rule of law," *Contributions to Indian Sociology,* n. s., 19, no. 1 (1985): 153–76. I am especiallly indebted to two colleagues in anthropology, Jennifer Robertson and Maria Teresa Koreck, for their generous discussion of the ideas in this paper. In particular, I am grateful to Maria Teresa Koreck, who works on the issue of "making histories" in relation to twentieth-century Mexican archives (and who made the unpublished paper by Cohn available to me). Our discussions have led me to think about the construction of state archives and libraries in Italy and the power such institutions have had over historical developments and our research methodologies.

    1. Thucydides, *The Peloponnesian War,* trans. Charles Forster Smith (Cambridge: Harvard University Press, 1952), 6.54.

    2. Aristotle, *The Politics,* trans. Benjamin Jowett (Oxford: Clarendon Press, 1885), 5.10.

    3. Sture Brunnsåker, *The Tyrant-Slayers of Kritios and Nesiotes,* 2d ed. (Stockholm: Svenska Institutet i Athen, 1971), 21.

    4. Marcus Junianus Justinus, *Nelle historie di Trogo Pompeio* (Venice: Zopino & Vincentio, 1524), 15v–16.

    5. Many sixteenth-century historiographers narrated the event of the murder of Alessandro de' Medici, including various details. My own condensation here is a digest of the following writers: Paolo Giovio, *Gli elogi vite brevemente scritte d'huomini illustri di guerra, antichi e moderni,* trans. (into Tuscan) by Lodovico Domenichi (Florence, 1554), book 6; idem, *La istoria del suo tempo,* trans. Lodovico Dominichi (Florence: Torrentini, 1550–52), book 38; Jacopo Nardi, *Istorie della città di Firenze* (Florence: Le Monnier, 1858), vol. 2, book 10; Filippo de' Nerli, *Commentarj dei fatti civili occorsi dentro la città di Firenze* (Trieste: Colombo Coen, 1859), book 12; Bernardo Segni, *Storie fiorentine* (Milan: Società Tipografica de' Classici Italiani, 1805), vol. 2, book 7; Benedetto Varchi, *Storia fiorentina* (Milan: Società Tipografica de' Classici Italiani, 1804), vol. 5, book 15.

    6. The unedited reports and letters I refer to may be found in the Archivio di Stato di Milano in the collection of documents entitled "Cancelleria dello Stato di Milano" (hereafter cited as CSM).

    7. Federico Chabod, *Lo stato e la vita religiosa a Milano nell'epoca di Carlo V* (Torino: Einaudi, 1971), 39.

    8. Ibid., 11, 19.

    9. Ibid., 52–53 and n.

    10. Speciano to Caracciolo, 21 January 1537, CSM 14, fol. 37: "Sua Maestà haveria havuto giusta causa de dolersi, perchè si dava causa a notivà in Italia che pur ce n'erano troppo massimamente espettandossi il Turco, et era non manco interesse di Sua Santità che di Sua Maestà che cessasseno questi nuovi timulti."

    11. Caracciolo to Ridolfi, Salviati, Strozzi (in rough draft), 14 January 1537, CSM 13, fol. 417: "ho voluto recordarli che hora il tempo è che la gli può fare servitio grande . . . reprimendo ogni seditione . . . et driciando ognuno al camino dritto . . . al benefitio universale et Vostra Signoria Reverendissima può essere sicura che la Cesarea Maestà . . . tenerà bono conto delli offitii si farano in benefitio particulare et universale di quello stato et ne seguirà honore et utile a Vostra Signoria Reverendissima."

    12. Salviati to Caracciolo, 17 February 1537, CSM 13, fol. 426 (autograph): "in Firenze, trovamo le cose in gran confusione et travaglio."

    13. Landriano to Caracciolo, 14 January 1537, CSM 13bis, fol. 64: "Qui si ha nuova

anchora come in Fiorenza non è successo per hora nuovità alcuna e che li populari di quella città si monstrano Imperiali e che le forteze tutte stano a devotione di Sua Maesta."

14. See n. 12: "Se il Reverendissimo de Ridolfi o io havessimo recevute le altre lettere che Vostra Signoria Reverendissima ci dice . . . haverci scritte . . . non haremo tardato a risponderli . . . ma né in Roma avanti el partire nostro ci furon date, né ancora arrivati in Firenze, dove pensiamo più presto le indirizasse."

15. Speciano to Caracciolo, 16 January 1537, CSM 14, fol. 27.

16. Sanctio to Caracciolo, 12 January 1537, CSM 12bis, fol. 28: "In questa hora che somo adi ij di nocte."

17. Antonio to Caracciolo, 9 January 1537, CSM 20, fol. 268.

18. Piccolomini to Caracciolo, 30 May 1537, CSM 20, fol. 146: "Di qua non ho cosa da render in cambio a quello di nuovo, ch'io non pensi essergli vecchia, pur per empir il foglio, dirò che per li ultimi avvisi ho di Firenze intendo che 'l signor Conte continovi tuttavia la practica di comporre quelle cose a commune quiete . . . Le cose del Turco pare che vadino rinfrescando."

19. Speciano to Caracciolo, 12 January 1537, CSM 14, fol. 9: "con lettere credentiali . . . oltra quella alla Signora Duchessa ove si condole, et tre bianchi sottoscritti per potere scrivere a cui serà bisogno."

20. Landriano to Caracciolo, 17 January 1537, CSM 13bis, fol. 71: "non mi pare tenire in la pena alcuna cossa."

21. Idem, 11 January 1537, CSM 13bis, fol. 62: "penso . . . ne habbi recevutto de le altre ne le quali li ho significato la morte horenda dello illustrissimo Signor Duca Alexander de Medici e anchora ch'io lhabi scritta dubiosa pure si va accertando come Sabato passato alle octo hore de nocte, venendo Sua Excellenza da Piacere fu sventrato da Laurentio de Medici"; emphasis mine.

22. Sanctio to Caracciolo, 13 January 1537, CSM 12bis, fol. 32: "Essendo arrivato in Bologna ho trovato vera Informatione del caso de Fiorenza et così ad Vostra Signoria. Dicono che essendo el Signor Duca cugino e molto amici stretto de Lorenzo . . . giovene molto malinconico et fidandose extremamente in dicto Lorenzo, lo usò per mezano per otenere una certa gentildonna. Altri dicono una Monicha. Altri una sorella vidua de dicto Lorenzo. Tutti concorreno che uno sabbato ad sera conpose de ire a sua casa per havere li una donna"; emphasis mine.

23. Ibid., fol.33: "la cause che habia mosso dicto Lorenzo de Medici ad tale effecto da lui è narrato essere stato solo per liberare la patria. Altri dicono per honore della sorella, molti che è stato uno humore malencolico de questo giovene del qual dicono essere molto oppresso per stare sempre cogitanbondo et de effigie simile al Bruto, quaecumque fuerit causa, il povero Duca se è lassato pigliare alla trappola et per sua advertentia ce ha posta la vita et ha anchor mosse le cose de fiorenza in su el tavoleri . . ."; emphasis mine.

24. Ibid.: "Dicono alchuni chel Populo havea voluto fare creare de novo Duca . . . il Cosmo de Medici. . . . Alcuni altri dicono che il populo ha inviato ad dimandare li Reverendissimi Salviati et Ridolphi per dare nova forma al governo de quella città. Questo se afferma per tutti che la Città sino ad questa hora sta alla medesma devotione di sua Maestà."

25. Soria to Caracciolo, 10 January 1537, CSM 12, fol. 144: "Ho doppo inteso che il detto Lorenzo . . . amazzò il Duca in casa sua dove soleva andare spesso con una donna il detto duca; questa cosa è di molta importanza per le cose di sua casata; so che vostra Reverendissima Sanctità el sa meglio che altro; per ciò importa asai che sua Maestà sia presto avisata."

26. Lorenzo Ghibellini da Prato, "Il Lamento che fa in fra se Lorenzino de Medici che amazzò l'Illustrissimo Signor Alessandro de Medici Duca primo di Fiorenza" (Florence: Giovanni Baleni, 1584): "Che ti mancava à te ò Lorenzino / veste, cavalli, servitori, e fanti, /

haveivi giorno e notte à tuo domino / Che ti mancava à te forse contanti, / che non tenevi la tua borsa piena."

27. Ibid.: "Tu se in odio al mondo à tutta gente."

28. Ibid.: "Tanto che mai non penso che da Dio / questo pecato mi sia perdonato . . . Mi penso . . . ire inTurchia à rinegar la fede/ . . . Non credo nelle parte de pagani / un piu di me sia stato si crudele / Tarari, Mori, Turchi, ò Catelani."

29. Irving A. Leonard, "Conquerors and Amazons in Mexico," *The Hispanic American Historical Review* 24 (November 1944): 568, 570. Lucien Febvre and Henri-Jean Martin, *The Coming of the Book*, trans. David Gerard (London: Verso Editions, 1984), 207–8. Cohn, in "The Anthropology" (10), refers to "the creation of emblematic heroes and villains, as individuals and types" in "popular" texts as one means by which British rule in India was legitimated.

30. Daniel Defert, "Collecting the World: Accounts of Voyages from the Sixteenth to the Eighteenth Centuries, " *Dialectical Anthropology* 7, no. 1 (September 1982): 16.

31. Paula Findlen, "The Museum: Its Classical Etymology and Renaissance Genealogy," *Journal of the History of Collections* 1, no. 1 (1989): 65. I am grateful to my colleague John Marino for bringing this comprehensive and illuminating essay to my attention.

32. Ibid., 68.

33. Cited by Chabod, *Lo stato*, 215n.

34. Findlen, "The Museum," 69.

35. Ibid.

36. Ibid., 72.

37. Ibid.

38. Gigliola Fragnito, "Il museo di Antonio Giganti da Fossombrone," *Scienze, credenze occulte, livelli di cultura* (Florence: Olschki, 1982), 510–11; Defert, "Collecting the World," 16.

39. Henry Hexham, Preface, in Gerhard Mercator, *Atlas: or, A geographicke description of the world*, trans. Henry Hexham, Introduction by R. A. Skeleton (Amsterdam: Theatrum Orbis Terrarum, 1968), Iv; emphasis mine. Cited and discussed by José Rabasa, "Fantasy, Errancy and Symbolism in New World Motifs: An Essay on Sixteenth-Century Spanish Historiography" (Ph.D. diss., University of California, Santa Cruz, 1985), 234.

40. Cited by Findlen, "The Museum," 72.

41. John Amos Comenius, *The Orbis Pictus*, trans. Charles Hoole (1728) (Syracuse, N.Y.: C. W. Bardeen, 1887), 120–21. Cited, in part, by Findlen, "The Museum," 70.

Translating Montaigne's Crypts: Melancholic Relations and the Sites of Altarbiography

Timothy Murray
Cornell University

> The text, then, is not only based upon the approach of a Word that is always lacking; it also postulates a pre-existing reader who is missing in the text, but authorizes it. The text is produced in relation to this missed present, this speaking, hearing other. Writing arises from the separation that makes this presence the inaccessible other of the text, and the author himself (the "I") a multiple, iconoclastic passer-by in his own fragmented work. (Michel de Certeau, "Montaigne's 'Of Cannibals'")[1]

I would like to open this essay on the "ends" of Renaissance and Baroque autobiography by citing a few words chosen by John Florio to translate a line written by Michel de Montaigne: "The deadest deaths are the best."[2] Suggested by this line is a dual drive, *pulsion*, of the end which motivates the comparative study of texts and images. While the phrase "deadest deaths" exemplifies the drive of the end to effect difference through repetition, its adjunct, "the best," identifies the finite, the fixed, or the complete as something not merely attainable but also valuable. Attainable and valuable, that is, to a critical tradition fixated on the worth of its ends, its aims, and sustained by self-reassurances that what it is about counts for something, for something almost always political in the best of senses, for something more worthy, that is, than the sum of its own doubled figuration, "a dead end."

For many comparative scholars of Renaissance and Baroque studies, the best deadest deaths would be tantamount to the ending of the worst worse. That is, for many of us "the end" of Renaissance and Baroque studies would be the ultimate demystification of the oppressive patriarchal and colonial systems of mastery, subjection, and subjectivity so kindly passed on to us by the period which we study—and perversely lament. The perversion stems, of course, from our melancholic bond to the departed objects of our study. Not able to ascertain exactly *what* it is that we think we have lost, we shift the onus of incapacity onto our own weakened condition as critics, dissatisfied not so much with the "lost" objects of study themselves as with the moral destitution of our critical relation to them.[3] It might thus be said that the endless public manifestations of discomfort with the methods of comparative Renaissance and Baroque studies double as narcissistic forums of self-torment and self-punishment, in which contemporary readers devour themselves as the "objects" of study, indirectly enacting revenge on the ambivalent love object, the Renaissance and Baroque text. So it is that metacriticism realizes the potential, always and already there, to mimic the complex of melancholia which behaves, in Freud's words, "like an open wound, drawing to itself cathectic energies . . . from all directions, and emptying the ego until it is totally impoverished."[4] Or as Florio has anglicized the romantic aphorism of Montaigne, "The deadest deaths are the best."

My end here is not, however, to lament the bankrupt state of Renaissance and Baroque studies but rather to settle anew into the dark cabinets of reading in order to situate what I'll be calling *the melancholic relation* as a position of strength for the contemporary reading of autobiography. In discussing the complex relation of the French musings of Montaigne to Florio's English translation of the *Essais,* which appeared in three early editions, in the years 1603, 1613, and 1632, I intend to discuss the melancholic relation as something different from the disease of melancholia as well as from the melancholic aspect of genius. And rather than being a fixed figure, like Dürer's *Melencolia* or Timothy Bright's "Melancholicke friend: M," the melancholic relation will be said to provide contemporary readers with a representational trajectory that disturbs and unsettles the delusions of mastery over the enigmatic figurations, folds, and spaces of intertextual and intercultural otherness. And while evoking many contemporry theorizations of the Baroque as the textual trace of optical perspective, this trajectory will foreground Medusa-like figures of enigmatic representation which always have seemed capable of wounding and disrupting the narcissistic continuum of the phallologocentric tradition and its perspectival architectonics.[5]

Phallic Exposure

The lines from Montaigne which open this essay appear in the 1595 edition of his essay "To Philosophize Is to Learn How to

Die," book 1, chapter 20 (or chapter 19 in Florio's translation on which I will rely throughout). It is in this early chapter of the *Essais* that Montaigne aligns his autobiographical project with the celebration of a philosophical method whose end is to simulate death: "It is uncertaine where death looks for us; let us expect her everie where: the premeditation of death, is a fore-thinking of libertie. He who hath learned to die, hath unlearned to serve. . . . To know how to die, doth free us from all subjection and constraint" (34). At issue in Montaigne's writing is the trajectory of our relation to death, not so much our phenomenal knowledge of it, "to know death," as our knowledge of its phenomenological practice, "to know *how* to die," that is, its forethought, its premeditation. Thinking, here, effects death's imaginative construction, exercise, and practice. In this context, freedom from constraint and subjection entails the enactment of the autobiographical condition, or rather, what Louis Marin calls the condition of "autobiothanatography," that is the discourse of self as the necessary supplement of "writing one's own death as death."[6]

Montaigne describes his method in "Of Exercise or Practice," an essay recounting the author's almost literal return from the dead: "I wholy set forth and expose my selfe: It is a Sceletos: where at first sight appeare all the vaines, muskles, gristles, sinnewes, and tendons, each severall part in his due place. . . . I write not my gests, but my self and my essence" (210).[7] Such a virtual relation to death, in which reflection enacts essence, is also one of the elements posited by Walter Benjamin, in *The Origin of German Tragic Drama,* as constituting the Baroque. Benjamin writes that "[Baroque] mourning is the state of mind in which feeling revives the empty world in the form of a mask, and derives its enigmatic satisfaction in contemplating it. For feeling is bound to an *a priori* object, and the representation of this object is its phenomenology."[8] For Montaigne, moreover, feeling is as much a product of the mouth as of the eyes, of language as of sight. As Montaigne so aptly describes his condition: "I learned this custome or lesson, to have alwaies death, not only in my imagination, but continually in my mouth" (35). With these words, Montaigne situates not only the Baroque fixation on death but also its mental incorporation as the most valuable exercise of individual liberty.[9] For to have death always in one's mouth, that is, as Freud would say, to incorporate the object of loss into itself "by devouring it," is to exert narcissistic control over one's alienated relation to the organic representation of death.[10] This could be said to be the ultimate end of the *Essais;* "to the end," as Montaigne writes in "The Author to the Reader," "that losing me (which they are likely to doe ere long) they may therein find some lineaments of my conditions and humours" (A5v).

Resonating throughout Montaigne's essays, then, is the celebration of autobiothanatography, a textual method of bringing the subject (author as well as reader) eye to eye/mouth to mouth with virtual loss. But unlike melancholia itself, this method spurns the total withdrawal from the world typical of both the illness and the genius in favor of a continual remembrance of death—that a priori condition—within the intersubjective realm of feeling and desire. In one of the more revealing moments when Montaigne comes "mouth to mouth" with death, he goes so far as to situate the incorporation of death at the furthest limits of desire:

> I am not so much given to melancholy, but rather to dreaming and sluggishness. . . . There is nothing wherewith I have ever more entertained my selfe, than with the imaginations of death, yea in the most licentious times of my age. . . . Being amongst faire Ladies, and in earnest play, some have thought me busied, or musing with my selfe, how to digest some jealousie, or meditating on the uncertaintie of some conceived hope, when God he knowes, I was entertaining my selfe with the remembrance of some one or other, that but few daies before was taken with a burning fever, and of his sodaine end. (34)

Thinking on the frontiers of feeling (not to mention the supplementation of thinking feelingly by the writing of autobiography) is paramount to the mental conditioning prescribed by Montaigne, who frequently reflects on man's alienation from his own body whether in the state of "carnall copulation" or in the state of death itself.

In "Of Exercise or Practice," Montaigne brings together these two states of death, the sexual and the physical, to stress the difficulty, indeed, the virtuality, of containing one's body and/or death in one's mouth:

> There are many creatures, yea and some men, in whom after they are dead, we may see their muskles to close and stirre. All men know by experience, there be some parts of our bodies, which often without any consent of ours doe stirre, stand and lye downe againe. Now these passions, which but exteriourly touch us, cannot properly be termed ours. (208)

While Montaigne boasts in the prior passage of his ability to contemplate death in the midst of passion, he here acknowledges that certain "passions" figure the corporeal independence of death from its total incorporation. Elsewhere, Montaigne argues that these same stirring muscles be taken seriously as something much more substantial than a merely figural threat to thought. In "Of the Force of Imagination," he recounts how philosophers have been troubled historically by the challenge of their exterior members to the independence of their will to learn how to die, by "these muscles and veines, that rise and fall without the consent, not only of our will, but also of our thought" (43). One frightening remedy of such corporeal liberty surfaces in "Of Exercise or Practice" when Montaigne recounts how some philosophers "have frankly deprived themselves of the dearest and best parts of their body, as of their eyes, and members of generation, lest their over-pleasing, and too-too wanton service, might in any sort mollifie and distract the constant resolution of their minde" (205). Even though Montaigne continually distances himself from any recommendations of such radical practice, his writings can be said similarly to want to contain the distracting independence of certain bodily members, not to mention the attendant fear of their loss. It is as if to curb the worst consequences of such a mind/body split that Montaigne takes pen in hand to reshape the passions of philosophy.[11] Montaigne's philosophizing thus might be read not only as the premeditation of death but also as the forethought of recent theorizing of autobiography as the performance of phallologocentric loss.[12]

If considered further in a psychoanalytical context, Montaigne's philosophical forethought could be said to double as a phantasm of autobiographical foreskin, that is, as a fore-thinking inscribed in a nexus of castration anxiety alternating between attraction and repulsion in the profoundest sense. The memory of phallic exposure remains to be, after all, one of the catalysts prompting the chapter on philosophy and death. In exhorting his readers to be attentive to the many means and ways death might surprise us, Montaigne asks whether we remember, among other less prurient examples, how "*Cornelius Gallus* the Praetor, *Tigillinus* Captaine of the Romane watch, *Lodowike* sonne of *Guido Gonzaga,* Marquis of *Mantua,* end their daies beweene womens thighs?" (32). While Montaigne's point here is that death can arrive at the most inauspicious moments, his texts sketch out a very fragile distinction between the acts of dying and of thinking death when executed between female thighs. In fact, a similar threat of phallic vulnerability hovers over Montaigne's account of the historical terrain of philosophizing. Again, from "Of Exercise or Practice":

> for a man to acquaint himselfe with death, I finde no better way than to approach unto it . . . We have notice but of two or three former

ancients, that have trodden this path; yet we can not say, whether altogether like unto this of mine, for we know but their names. No man since hath followed their steps; it is a thorny and crabbed enterprise, and more than it makes shew of, to follow so strange and vagabond a path, as that of our spirit: to penetrate the shady, and enter the thicke-covered depths of these internall winding crankes. (209)

Although Montaigne never prohibits "the thicke-covered depths," he cautions more than once that their penetration—learning how to die—entails the threat of accident and overexposure. The forethought of death lies here, as throughout the *Essais*, on the epistemological rim of a conceptual "vagina dentata." Even when Montaigne prudently endorses "a very great conflict and power of imagination" (40), in "On Imagination," he casts its feminine dangers in the guise of the castrating Medusa: "Now they wrong us, to receive and admit us with their wanton, squeamish, quarrellous countenances, which setting us a fire, extinguish us" (42).

That the practice of philosophy is somehow gender bound, inscribed in the containment of squeamish countenances, is borne out further by John Florio, in one of his dedicatory epistles to the first edition of the English translation. This is when Florio praises his friend, Maister Doctor Guinne, for scholarly assistance in untying the philosophical knots of Montaigne's prose. "So was hee to mee in this bundle of riddles an understanding *Oedipus*, in this perilous-crook't passage a monster-quelling *Theseus* or *Hercules*."[13] Similarly praised throughout the *Essais* is a methodological manipulation of the threatening phantasms of memory and imagination, a procedure which bears an uncanny resemblance to the strategy of defense also made famous by the monster-quelling Perseus. It was Perseus, of course, who transformed his shield into a screen of representation to deflect the deadly threat of the desired Gorgon, Medusa.[14] And so it goes, in turn, that the preceding series of passages recalls the charge of feminist theoreticians that the end of philosophical prose, learning how to die, consistently situates itself in a defensive relation to the generic death threat of woman, especially when woman is made desirable by her cunning and enigmatic presence, as are the mythological figures alluded to above, the Sphinx, Medea, and Medusa.[15]

Virility Incorporated

In the melancholic trajectory sketched above, the figure of the enigmatic woman is relegated to the position of "the abject" insofar as she is figured as nothing more than a wound in the well-oiled hinge of philosophical, or, as Luce Irigaray would say, homosocial, desire.[16] What makes this deadly transfiguration of the feminine so significant in Montaigne is the fact that he construes it as a mere offspring of accident, really less active than passive, less rational than irrational—that is, not as truly melancholic in the classical sense of passion's submission to reason. Nor is it truly melancholic in the strict Freudian sense of the process of sadomasochistic torment which leaves the ego totally impoverished. Figured instead as a phantasm of a willful exchange gone wrong, that of the philosophical wanderer buried alive in the "internall winding crankes" of exploration, Montaigne's abjection of the feminine suggests that the melancholic trajectory in the *Essais* may be a literary mechanism effecting incorporation, as it is theorized by Nicolas Abraham and Maria Torok.[17] By incorporation, Abraham and Torok mean something other than the process of introjection normally associated with the Freudian processes of mourning and melancholy. They understand introjection to correspond roughly to a procedure of narrative supplementation: words replace loss through which the presence of an object—initially the mother's breast—gives way through metaphorization to an auto-apprehension of its absence. An essential feature of Abraham and Torok's system of introjection, distinguishing it from Lacanian language acquisition as the inscription of the Law of the Father, is the symbolic role of the mother whose constancy (which they compare to the God of Descartes) is the necessary guarantor of linguistic signification. Through introjection, words are able to replace the maternal presence and give way to newer introjections.

In contrast to introjection, Abraham and Torok describe incorporation as the denial of the denial of loss (of the mother). Otherwise put, incorporation constitutes the refusal of mourning itself to the extent of censoring the inconsolability of loss, of dispensing with the painful procedures of psychic reorganization. "In lieu of this relief outlet, there will remain only to counter the fact of the loss with a radical denial—by feigning to never have had anything to lose."[18] Within the wider spectrum of what I'm calling the melancholic relation, incorporation is the lament that cannot be spoken. And, in the specific context of Montaigne, incorporation would entail the foreclosure of philosophical lament, of "learning how to die." The result would be a "phantom" installed by the ego in a "secret crypt" where a phantasmatic world sustains a separate and occult life. "All the words which will not be able to be spoken, all the scenes which will not be able to be recalled, all the tears which will not be able to be shed will be swallowed at the same time as the trauma which caused the loss. Swallowed and preserved. The unspeakable lament installs a secret tomb in the interior of the subject. Alive in this crypt, reconstituted from memories of words, of images, and of effects, lies the objective correlative of the loss as a complete person with its own topical structure, in the same way as the traumatic moments—real or imagined—that had rendered the introjection impracticable."[19] What Abraham and Torok term *cryptophoria* is the condition of not being able to do otherwise than bury a lost clandestine crime or pleasure by establishing it as a hallucination, a phantom, an "intrapsychic secret."

Cryptation is especially difficult to analyze for two specific reasons. First, the undetected phantom, so Abraham and Torok believe, can skip generations, thus creating a "familial" disturbance in the transgenerational sense of the term. A bit further on I will develop the literary significance of this possibility that a subject or a text could be thought capable of carrying an ancestor's phantom. Second, the phantom constitutes itself in resistance to figural translation. It is marked by both *objectification* (what is undergone is not a wound to the subject but the literal loss [incorporation] of an object) and *demetaphorization* (taking literally what is understood figuratively). In so doing, cryptation feeds on "antimetaphor" and thus thwarts interpretation: "Incorporation entails the phantasmatic destruction of the act itself by which metaphor is possible: the act of putting into words the original oral void, the act of introjecting."[20]

A concrete example of the hallucinatory logic of cryptation can be provided by applying it to the periphrasis described by Montaigne: "For so much as this syllable [death] sounded so unpleasantly in their eares, and this voice seemed so ill-boding and unluckie, the Romans had learned to allay and dilate the same by a Periphrasis. In lieu of saying, he is dead, or he hath ended his daies, they would say, he hath lived" (32). Termed by Puttenham, "the Figure of ambage," of "darkness or obscurity" *(OED)*, periphrasis is one trope of many which would be taken literally by the device of antimetaphor flourishing in the dark chambers of the melancholic trajectory. In so doing, cryptation would turn Montaigne's periphrasis inside out. Harboring the verb "live," without its referent "dead," the incorporated periphrasis would turn "he hath lived" into "he lives buried."

What remains important here is the counterrevolutionary vigor of the hallucination which can easily remain undetected by the most radical forms of psychoanalysis and reading, while yet haunting the guardian of the crypt with strange and incomprehensible signs, unexpected sensations, and unusual acts. Turning back to Montaigne, I would like to dwell on the possible eruption of such a counterlogical phantom in the essay "Of the Force of Imagination." I am interested in Montaigne's presentation of the case history of the woman-child, Marie, who became known as Germaine when once "upon a time leaping, and straining himselfe to overleape another, he wot not how, but where before he was a woman, he suddenly felt the instrument of a man to come out of him" (41). Montaigne then complicates the potential interpretation of this confounding folkloric fantasy by associating the event with a condition which he cryptically aligns with some kind of incorporation: "It is not great wonder that such accidents doe often happen, for if imagination have power in such things, it is so continually annexed, and so forcibly fastened to this subject, that lest she should so often fall into the relaps of the same thought, and sharpnesse of desire, it is better one time for all to incorporate this virile part unto wenches" (41). One approach to this passage about Germaine might suggest that Montaigne foreshadows the theory of penis envy endorsed by Freud (another sort of "Germa[i]ne") and that the solution to such envy is to give to women the "virile part" they always imagine to be wanting. But another approach might dwell just as productively, although more indirectly, on the counterlogic of the nexus incorporation/virile part/wenches. Prompted by the case of Marie, we might reconsider the broader case history of the text(s) of Montaigne. What if the figure privileged in Montaigne's essays on death, those exposed "veines," were taken as exemplary of "antimetaphor," as a literalized figure of what "hath lived" unremarked in the historical text? What if these "veines" exemplify less the organ of writing, the phallic *énoncé*, than the clandestine *matter* written, those skeletal traces lying between marbled sheets, those inside/outside folds of the text, or the marbled tomb, the crypt of bookish enunciation? What if "veines" were an enigmatic phantom of *jouissance (mater)* rather than a phantasm of lack *(pater)*?[21]

Translation Gendered

One place from which to evoke such a phantom lying marble bound might be the melancholic site of translation itself. It might well be Florio's project that embodies the sort of mysterious "memorial of something I would have done after my death" (34) which Montaigne's curious friend found lying on his writing table. In the pages that remain, I would like to consider the significance of the prefatory monuments to Florio's three editions as dark (female) cabinets incorporating the "virile parts" of Montaigne's text.

One anonymous prefatory poem first printed in the second edition of 1613 clearly states "How poore remembrances, are statues Toomes / And other monuments that men erect / To Princes, which remaine in closed roomes / Where but a few behold them; in respect / Of bookes, that to the universall eye / Shew how they liv'd, the other where they lye."[22] The end of translation, as Florio's many prefatory texts continually profess, is to show how to live, not how to die. Yet the figure of life remains universal throughout Florio only insofar as it is inaccessible, born not so much of mourning or loss as harbored by antimetaphor. Commenting on Montaigne's text in the first edition's dedicatory epistle to book 2, Florio wonders "but is hee then so capriccious, so opiniative, so paradoxicall? I graunt, sometimes extravagant, often od-crocheted, and ever selfe-conceited to write of himselfe out of himselfe" (R2^v). Curiously, Florio's description of the translator's source text as something "od-crocheted," as something made inaccessible by the foundation of its mutated textual self (of itself from outside itself), is echoed in a text by Jacques Derrida on the subject of Nicolas Abraham and the *anasemia* of translation. *Anasemia* is Abraham and Torok's term for the process, through narrative, of revealing the traumas surmounted by a subject and encrypted in prior significations whose phantoms are both regressive and reflective. In "Me—Psychoanalysis," Derrida analyzes the project of translation in terms of its constitutive relation to the anasemic, autobiographical writing of the self:

> The very "messages" that the text conveys must be reinterpreted with new (anasemic and symbolic) "concepts" of sending, emitting, mission, or missive.... The very value of authenticity ("authentic concepts") will not, it seems to me, emerge from this transmutation with its ordinary meaning intact.
> To translate otherwise the concept of translation, to translate it into itself outside itself. Absolute heterogeneity, signaled by the "outside itself" which extends beyond or on this side of sense, must still be translated, anasemically, into the "in itself."[23]

If anasemic writing always already effects the translation of self from outside itself to in itself, then its refiguration by a translator as sensitive as Florio could be expected to multiply the transmutations effected by translation. And this is precisely how Florio describes his undertaking in a note, "To the curteous Reader," appearing only in the first edition of 1603:

> some errors are mine, and mine by more than translation. Are they in Grammer, or Ortographie? as easie for you to right, as me to be wrong; or in construction, as mis-attributing him, her, or it, to things alive, or dead, or newter, you may soone know my meaning, and eftsoones use your mending: or are they in some uncouth termes; as entraine, conscientious, endeare, tarnish, comporte, efface, facilitate, ammusing, debauching, regret, effort, emotion, and such like; if you like them not, take others most commonly set by them to expound them, since there they were set to make such likely French words familiar with our English, which well may beare them. (A5^v)

Regarding the link between translation and *anasemia,* this passage suggests that Florio establishes linguistic correspondences paradoxically grounded in the transmutations of sense and rhetorical propriety. He writes, like Montaigne, from outside himself to in his self. If the readers feel compelled to right these wrongs ("if you like them not"), they should follow the guidelines set by Florio in choosing synonyms which seem less uncouth. But even when these substitutions result in "others most commonly set by them to expound them," they ultimately subscribe more to the interior standards of English taste than to the exterior verity of French signification. It is fitting to note, in light of this subversion of sense by the senses, that Florio's translation has been praised by Tom Conley for the rampant allegorical violence which makes his English work, in Conley's words, "the *only* translation of Montaigne."[24]

Florio's apology for translation in the opening lines of "To the curteous Reader" frames his practice as one running counter to the ends of Occidental philosophy. He defends translation's sustenance of a field of desire and a genealogy of representation far removed from the end of learning how to enact one's own phallologocentric death:

> Shall I apologize translation? Why but some holde (as for their free-hold) that such conversion is the subversion of Universities. God holde with them, and withholde them from impeach or empaire. It were an ill turne, the turning of Bookes should be the overturning of Libraries. Yea but my old fellow Nolano tolde me, and taught publikely, that from translation all Science hadst's of-spring. Likely, since even Philosophie, Grammar, Rhetorike, Logike, Arithmetike, Geometrie, Astronomy, Musike, and all the Mathematikes yea hold their name of the

Greekes's and the Greekes drew their baptizing water from the conduit-pipes of the Egiptians, and they from the well-springs of the Hebrews or Chaldees. And can the wel-springs be so sweete and deepe, and will the well-drawne water be so sower and smell? (A5r)

Despite Florio's sour wit, translation should indeed be recognized as a subversion of the universities. For Florio suggests that to philosophize is first to learn how to translate, how to give life to the conduit pipes linking nations, peoples, and intercultural texts in such a way that the mossy slippage of transmission, transmutation, and transference remains, much like the texts of Montaigne, more significant than any return to source or origin.[25] Nor should this difference be taken lightly as something merely formulaic or blandly philosophical. For, as it is situated and situates itself within the phallogocentric tradition, translation bears the deep vein of heterogeneous phantoms attesting not only to transmission but also to the lasting gaps, divisions, and folds distinguishing cultural histories and representations of otherness.[26] As Florio aptly puts it: "let confession make halfe amends, that every language hath it's *Genius* and inseparable forme; without *Pythagoras* his *Metempsychosis* it can not rightly be translated. The Tuscan altiloquence, the *Venus* of the French, the sharpe state of the Spanish, the strong significancy of the Dutch cannot from heere be drawne to life" (A5r).

Keeping in mind Florio's figuration of French genius, I might mention his admission in the 1603 folio that his translation of Montaigne is admittedly a "defective edition (since all translations are reputed femalle, delivered at second hand)" (A2r). I want to emphasize this cryptic reference to Florio's ambiguous gendering of translation not only to follow the thread of Montaigne's female incorporation of his "virile part" but also to align my reading of this gendered site with recent rethinkings of the fold, "le pli," in philosophy and psychoanalysis. In this context the fluid "folds" of translation and reading call to mind something other than the pulsating vein of the writing instrument of Montaigne. While Gilles Deleuze and Hubert Damisch (although to a lesser extent) theorize the variation and inflexion of the monadic "pli" of Leibniz, one figuring the Baroque monad as "a book or dark cabinet of reading," Christine Buci-Glucksmann links Lacan with Merleau-Ponty to read "le pli" as the figure of Baroque *jouissance,* that is, "feminine *jouissance,* supplementary *jouissance* beyond the phallus."[27] Ultimately, such a foregrounding of Baroque *jouissance* brings my melancholic trajectory to Abraham and Torok's stress on the mother as guarantor of linguistic signification, especially when considered in relation to the feminist project of Luce Irigaray for whom "le pli," or rather "les plis," is the liminal figure of "the *Venus* of the French," the fluid crypt of woman's relation to her language as "contiguous," as "touching upon," as containing the enigmatic fluids and stories produced by Medusa and her sisters.[28]

Altarbiography

Such a theoretically heterogeneous "pli" is, I want to suggest, what pervasively marks the cryptic writing projects of Montaigne and his first English translator. Indeed, the textual apparati of the first three editions of Florio's translation could be said to engage in the struggle described by Montaigne between the "weake bending, and faint stopping bodie" ("le corps, courbe et plié") and the soul which "must bee rouzed and raised gainst the violence and force of this adversarie" (36). I am referring to the metamorphosis undergone by the translation's front matter over the course of the three editions. The first edition is introduced by a title page dedicated to three pairs of female patrons. This gesture of titular praise of these women is folded over stategically into the *Essayes* proper. Florio opens each book of the *Essayes* with lengthy dedicatory epistles to these women, thus grafting or introjecting "le corps, courbe et plié" of these feminine epistles onto the phallologocentric soul of the Frenchman's text. In the second edition of 1613, Florio replaces these dedications and epistles with briefer dedicatory texts denoting in different ways the intertextual folds of multiple editions. Here an unremarkable dedication to Queen Anne of Denmark competes with a frontispiece portrait not of Montaigne but of the translator himself.[29] Similarly, the title page flaunts references to Florio's aristocratic position: "DONE INTO ENGLISH, according to the last French edition, by IOHN FLORIO. Reader of the Italian tongue unto the Soveraigne Maiestie of Anna, Queene of England, Scotland, France, and Ireland. &c. And one of the Gentlemen of hir Royall Privie Chamber." Finally, as if to rub dirt in the eyes of readers taunted by conflicting multitextual frames, the front matter of this second edition includes a long dedicatory poem by Samuel Daniel who decries the perils of printing which oppresses the public with "Books, like superfluous humors bred with ease" (A3^r).

The second edition's front matter of dedicatory poems and

Figure 1. Title Page, third edition of Florio's translation, *The Essayes* (1632). Courtesy of Cornell University Library, Ithaca, New York.

To the Beholder of this Title.

WHen first this portlike *Frontispeece* was wrought,
To raise a *Pile* compleat, it was our thought,
Whose *Roomes* and *Galleries* should have been trim'd
With *Emblemes*, and with *Pictures*, fairly lim'd,
And drawne from those neat *Peeces*, which do lurke
Within the *Closets* of this *Authors* worke:
So placing them, and them contriving so,
That ev'ry *Reader* (passing to and fro)
By casting thereupon a glauncing eye,
Might in that *Model* or *Epitomie*,
(Ev'n at the first aspect) inform'd have beene,
Of ev'ry *Raritie* contain'd within.
But walking through that *Plaace* of *Invention*,
(The better to accomplish our intention)
Wee found unlookt for, scattred here and there,
Such *Profits*, and such pleasures, ev'ry where,
In such *Variety*, that, to but name
Each one, would make a *Volume* of the same.
For, in those *Angles*, and among those *Leaves*
Whereon the rash *Beholders* eye perceives
No shewes or promises, of such choice things,
A diligent unfolder of them brings
Concealed *Fruits* to light: Ev'n thus did we
In such abundance, that they prove to bee
Beyond a briefe *expression*, and have stop't
Our purpose in presenting what wee hop'd.
In stead of *Emblemes* therefore, to explaine
The scope of this great *Volume*, we are faine
To fixe the *Authors Title*, on the *Gate*,
Annexed to his *Name*; presuming that
Will give this following *Treatise* much more praise
Then all the *Trophies* which our skill can raise.
For, he that hath not heard of *Mountaine* yet,
Is but a novice in the schooles of *wit*.
You that so please may enter: For, behold
The *Gate* stands open, and the *doores* unfold
Their leaves to entertaine you. That French *ward*
Which lately kept you forth, is now unbard,
And you may passe at pleasure ev'ry way
If you are furnish'd with an *English-key*.
That, wee suppose you want not: If you do,
Wee are not they, whom *this* was meant unto:
Pray passe along, and stare no more on that
Which is the *Picture* of *you know not what*.
Yet, if it please you *Spell it*, And if than
You understand not, *Give them roome that can*.

Figure 2. "To the Beholder of this Title," third edition of Florio's translation, *The Essayes* (1632). Courtesy of Cornell University Library, Ithaca, New York.

prefaces to the reader, as hysterical as it is heroical, is then preceded in the third edition of 1632 by a dauntingly baroque frontispiece (Figure 1) which replaces the portrait of Florio and his place of distinction on the 1613 title page. The cryptic folds and crooked passages of this triumphal arch are the subject of an explanatory verse printed on the page facing it (Figure 2). A few selected passages reveal the gist of the message:

> When first this portlike *Frontispeece* was wrought,
> To raise a *Pile* compleat, it was our thought,
> Whose *Roomes* and *Galleries* should have been trim'd
> With *Emblemes,* and with *Pictures,* fairly lim'd,
> . . . .
> But walking through that *Plaace* of *Invention,*
> (The better to accomplish our intention)
> Wee found unlookt for, scattered here and there,
> Such *Profits,* and such pleasures, ev'ry where,
> In such *Variety,* that, to but name
> Each one, would make a *Volume* of the same.
> For, in those *Angles,* and among those *Leaves*
> Whereon the rash *Beholders* eye perceives
> No shew of promises, of such choice things,
> A diligent unfolder of them brings
> Concealed *Fruits* to light: Ev'n thus did we
> In such abundance, that they prove to bee
> Beyond a briefe *expression,* and have stop't
> Our purpose in presenting what wee hop'd.
> Instead of *Emblemes* therefore, to explaine
> The scope of this great *Volume,* we are faine
> To fixe the *Authors Title,* on the *Gate,*
> . . . .
> If you are furnish'd with an *English-key.*
> That, wee suppose you want not: If you do,
> Wee are not they, whom *this* was meant unto:
> *Pray passe along,* and stare no more on that
> Which is the *Picture* of *you know not what.*
> Yet, if it please you *Spell it,* And if than
> You understand not, *Give them roome that can.*

Especially fascinating is how this passage invests translation in a hyperbolic economy of the lack. Florio offers his readers access to his native tongue, English, only in relation to suppositions about its want or undoing: "That, wee suppose you *want* not: If you do . . . stare no more on that which is the *Picture* of *you know not what.*" The image highlighted here by italics, the *"Picture"* of *"you know not what,"* further positions the reader in relation to the same threatening specter of the French Venus or *je ne sais quoi* which petrified both the translator himself and the many philosophers preceding him. Even when the poetic key to the title page appears to lend itself to English spelling, it provides little more than a supplement to the lacking supplement of translation. For the titular coda recounts how the limitless profits and pleasures within prohibited the designer from drafting the kind of allegorical frontispiece which might "raise a *Pile* compleat." The specter of the untold pleasures of the text has the same destabilizing effect on the cunning designer as it has on the more "rash *Beholders* eye." So even in lieu of staring at the disquieting figure of *"you know not what,"* the English readers, both rash and diligent, come to recognize phallogocentric truth to be piled only as high as pleasure's wound cuts deep.

Still, this condition says less about antimetaphor, the linguistic literalization and materialization of the buried textual phantom, than it does about allegory, about how, in Paul de Man's words, the "emphatic clarity of representation does not stand in the service of something that can be represented."[30] The *je ne sais quoi*, in this context, stands for little more than the loss, or better, the deferral of the text's phallic presence. But were the French Venus to be thought to figure a phantom literalization of some forgotten crime or clandestine pleasure, it might be grasped through a more careful look at the first English edition.

The edition of 1603 flaunts a two-page iconographic frontispiece (Figures 3, 4) unusual in its representation not merely of title, author, and translator but especially of the six female patrons to whom Florio dedicates the book: "First written by him in French. And now done into English by him that hath inviolably vowed his labors to the AEternitie of their Honors, whose names he hath severally inscribed on these his consecrated Altares." This dedicatory tableau reads literally as the materialized allegory of consecration promised by Florio. In the parlance of Renaissance poetics, an "altar" is "a metrical address or dedication, fancifully written or printed in the form of an altar" *(OED)*. As such, the ornamental altar is the perfect iconographic match of the rhetorical emblem described in Florio's 1603 dedicatory epistle prefacing the third book of the *Essayes*.[31] This is where Florio equates the limitlessness of woman with the Baroque figure of the dark cabinet:

> Be you (as he there scoffeth) *capsula totae*, All hid, all cabinets (which I the rather heere expound, because I there omit) but so hidde, as much more good is in you than knowne of you; such Cabinets of Natures treasures, Vertues jewelles, learnings modelles, as all the Muses and Graces can scarce shew the like. What neede you to enquire but what

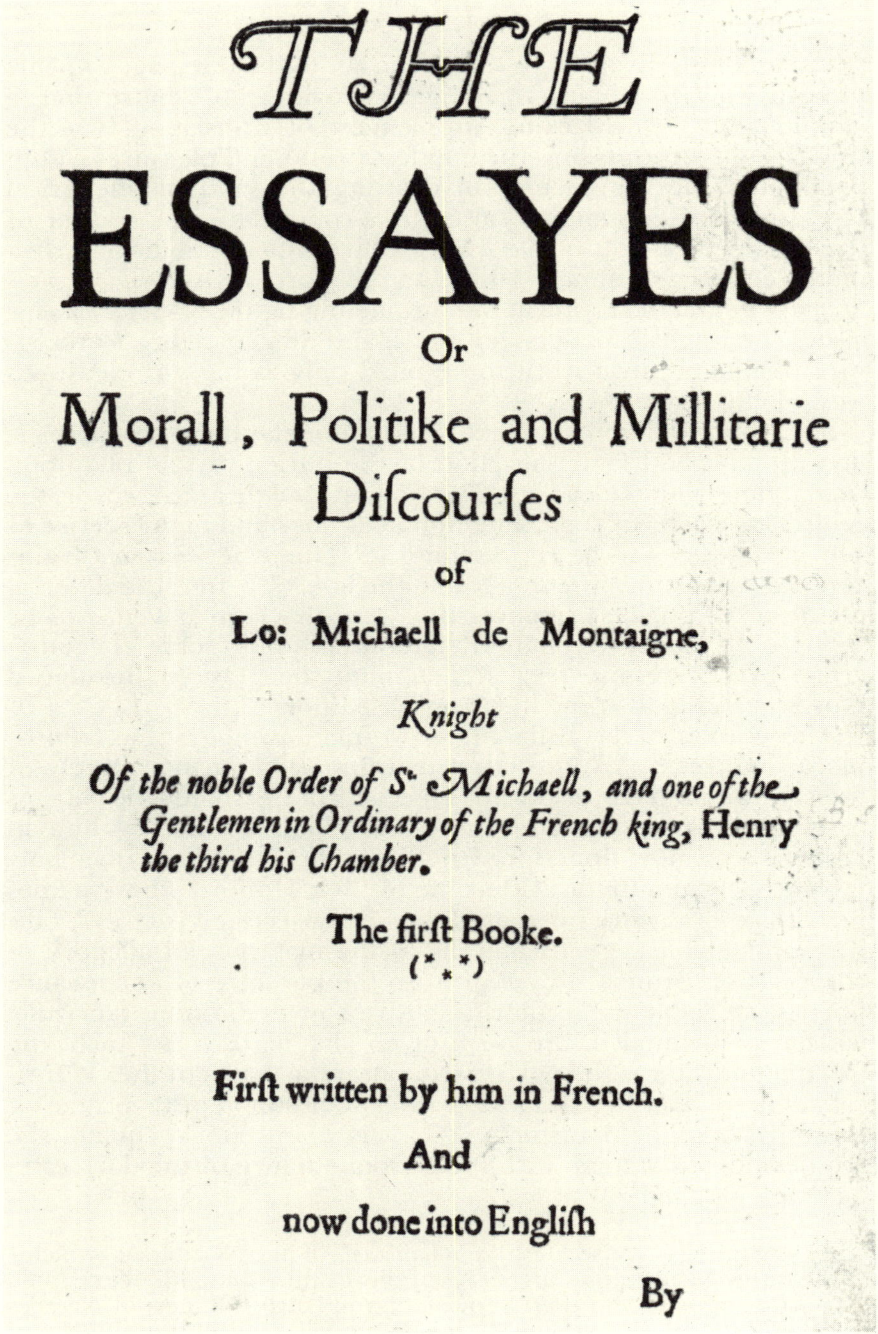

THE
ESSAYES

Or

Morall, Politike and Millitarie
Difcourfes

of

Lo: Michaell de Montaigne,

Knight

Of the noble Order of S: Michaell, *and one of the Gentlemen in Ordinary of the French king,* Henry *the third his Chamber.*

The firft Booke.
(***)

Firft written by him in French.

And

now done into Englifh

By

Figure 3. Title Page of the first edition of Florio's translation, *The Essayes* (1603). Courtesy of Cornell University Library, Ithaca, New York.

By him that hath inviolably vowed his labors to the Æternitie of their Honors, whose names he hath severally inscribed on these his consecrated Altares.

The first Booke.

> TO THE RIGHT HONORABLE
> LVCIE CO: OF BEDFORD:
> AND
> LADIE ANNE HARRINGTON
> HER HO: MOTHER.

The second Booke.

> TO THE RIGHT HONORABLE
> ELIZABETH CO: OF RVTLAND,
> AND
> LADIE PENELOPE RICHE.

The third Booke.

> TO THE RIGHT HONORABLE
> LADIE ELIZABETH GREY,
> AND
> LADIE MARIE NEVILL.

IOHN FLORIO.

¶ Printed at London by Val. Sims for Edward Blount dwelling in Paules churchyard. 1603.

Figure 4. Verso of the Title Page of the first edition of Florio's translation, *The Essayes* (1603). Courtesy of Cornell University Library, Ithaca, New York.

you neede? You are rich, and may require such ornaments as fitte your state. (Rr2ᵛ)

Florio's nomination of his dedicatees in the form of an altar surely provides a fitting metaphorical ornament of their state. And still, it is curious, is it not, that the visual presentation of this metaphor works so well to evoke the literalization of a different kind of dark cabinet: a crypt, bier, or casket. Might it be, then, that these three caskets function not merely as signs of patronage but also as something more like a screen image of a phantom life extending beyond the material relation of Florio to his patrons? Readers of Freud's essay "The Theme of the Three Caskets" might note the coincidence of the casket's multiplication by three—as happens literally in *The Merchant of Venice* (S.R. 1598; published 1600) and figuratively in the rich folklore tradition which Freud aligns with *King Lear* (S.R. 1607; published 1608). These readers might be tempted to cite the conclusion of Freud's essay as a means of interpreting the psychoanalytical status of these caskets—as figures, say, of the liminality of the philosopher's life and death:

> We might argue that what is represented here are the three inevitable relations that a man has with a woman—the woman who bears him, the woman who is his mate and the woman who destroys him [all common themes in Montaigne]; or that they are the three forms taken by the figure of the mother in the course of a man's life—the mother herself, the beloved who is chosen after her pattern, and lastly the Mother Earth who receives him once more. But it is in vain that an old man yearns for the love of woman as he had it first from his mother; the third of the Fates alone, the silent Goddess of Death, will take him into her arms.[32]

In so positioning the epic task of man in relation to his agonistic dependence on the figure of woman, Freud could be said to provide a methodological update to Montaigne's autobiographical project: that to psychoanalyze is to learn how to die. And whether the dedicatory caskets denote the project of autobiography or that of its translation, the reader of Freud should have no difficulty taking them as ornaments of the life and death of the castrated writer.

Yet, this reading seems credible only because it depends on a philo-psychoanalytical economy whose transformational syntax necessarily positions crypts as decipherable symbols of phallologocentric loss or introjection. But what this trajectory can't account for, indeed what it won't allow to be considered, is the possibility that these crypts might denote a phantom life of clandestine pleasure, of *jouissance,* unknown to the phallic condition of autobiography.³³ In coming closer to my end, I would like to propose that a "differend" strain of graphics lies marble bound in the front matter, "les plis," of Florio's translation.³⁴ In bringing together a few previously unmentioned citations, I hope to touch upon the possibility that these texts are the carriers of a feminine relation to literary representation, one which might be called *altarbiography*. To do so, I wish to place together two passages from Florio's first and third dedicatory epistles of 1603, the first opening book 1, the third opening book 3: two texts, then, held apart from themselves by the temporal apparatus of pagination and two folds which rub together only in the fluid procedures of . . . reading.

Florio's dedicatory epistle prefacing book 3 makes a pointed reference to the site of altarbiography by alluding to the three caskets of the title page. Concluding his dedication to Ladies Elizabeth Grey and Marie Nevill, Florio writes, "Wherefore to both your Honors (renowned GREY and NEVILL) as to *Iuno* in *Greece*, or *Vesta* in new *Rome* on the Altare of your vertues, I consecrate without idolatrie, prophanenesse, or blasphemie, both the incense of Praise and Thankes, and the never-failing fire of an ever-faithfull affection, which the Vestall Virgins of pure thoughts shall still-still keepe alive" (Rr3). This passage here transmutes the triple caskets of the Freudian death drive into celebratory altars of the primal history of Occidental woman. As sketched by Page Dubois, in *Sowing the Body: Psychoanalysis and Ancient Representations of Women*, some of this forgotten history has been encapsulated in the two figures with which Florio compares Ladies Grey and Nevill. A text dedicated to Hera, the Greek Juno, could be said to be inscribed in the narrative account of her double deification as the goddess of marriage and of the life, especially the sexual life, of women. To recognize how the deity of marriage has functioned historically as the phantom carrier of female sexuality *(jouissance)*, one need merely cite the brief justification of her marriage to Zeus provided by Robertson and Rose in *The Oxford Classical Dictionary*: "Her connection with Zeus is perhaps best explained by supposing that the Greeks on arrival found her cult too strong to be suppressed or ignored, supposing that they wished to do so, and made room for her by making her the wife (and sister) of their principal god. It seems conceivable that the persistent stories of the quarrels of the divine pair (eg. *Il.* 1.540ff.) reflect a faint memory of a time when the two cults were not fully reconciled. That in pre-Hellenic belief she has no male partner or none of any importance is quite in accord with what is known of early religion."³⁵ It could be argued that the other dedicatory figure, the Roman Vesta, kin of the Greek Vestia, symbolizes the contrary example of the equitable consolidation of these two irreconcilable traditions. This is because Vesta is the loyal guardian of the hearth and fire at the center of the polis. Yet DuBois argues that the Greek virgins, who serve as treasurers for the city, should be aligned not only with the legacy of female thesaurization but also, and perhaps most significantly in view of Florio's altars, with the earlier tradition of autochthony. It is this other legacy, preferably ignored by patriarchy, which allows DuBois to describe the Athenian caryatids who uphold and guard the temples as not "abject, not humiliated, not led in triumph," but as "stable, balanced, and proud . . . as the contented guardians, as the support for sacred space, for a 'treasury' of the most ancient and precious of the city's objects. Their billowing robes conceal their rounded bellies, emblematic of the hidden interiority of their bodies."[36]

So it is, returning to Florio, that the Vestal virgins, being "guardians, treasuring and protecting that inner space, that potentiality,"[37] preserve something of their own while figuring for patriarchy the keepers of "the never-failing fire of an ever-faithfull affection." I might add, in stressing this comparison of the dedicatees to the Vestal virgins, that the organization of Florio's dedicatory altars in three sets, each with two inhabitants, even bears numerical significance. Mythological accounts report that there were initially two Vestals, before their number was increased to six—in increments of two.

In elaborating on the implications of ancient signs of such an altarbiography, DuBois argues that the Greek female legacy of sexual plenitude and *jouissance* dispels the universality of castration anxiety built, as it is, on the myth of woman's sexual lack. I do not mean to suggest, however, that Florio intentionally set out to undermine this weak prop of male authority. If one were to insist on establishing a phallic strategy, Florio's epistles could provide evidence suggesting such a thing. In the previous epistle introducing book 2, for example, Florio presents his six dedicatees as living disputation of Montaigne's claim that "onely a bare trinity" of good women exist "at any time in one place"(R2ᵛ). An interesting fact about Montaigne's argument is that the measure of female goodness lies in her faithfulness to her husband's biography. "I have heere made choice of three women, who have also imployed the utmost endevor of their goodnes and affection, about their husbands deaths" (2.35, 379). But in tendering the counterexample of six dedicatees, Florio aligns their goodness with a different sort of loyalty in the face of death, that praised by Montaigne in "Of Vertue," of "this custome highly reputed in the new discovered East Indiaes, where not only the wives are buried with their husbands, but also such slaves as he hath enjoyed" (2.29, 360). In this curious elaboration of his allusion to the Vestal virgins and his six ever-faithful women, Florio unveils more strands of the extensive fabric of altarbiography. His reference to this "contemporary" Indian tradition echoes the ancient Occidental custom in which "all Greek wives were meant to guard and hoard and protect the stores of their husbands' houses."[38] But if we consider the untold tales of female plenitude empowering such thesaurization, we should be able to acknowledge that figures of female goodness (as well as those of slavery)[39] remain encrypted in this literature not only by the long history of woman's forced loyalty to patriarchy but also by the kind of counterrevolutionary logic which I discussed at the outset as Montaigne's periphrasis. My previous suggestion that cryptation would turn the periphrasis "he hath lived" into "he lives buried," could be said, in Montaigne's words, "to allay and dilate" the unpleasant sound of a "differend" reality which figures so prominently in the work of DuBois and others: "she lives buried."

What is significant about such a cryptonymic altarbiography, I wish to emphasize, is the complex way in which Renaissance representations of the "goodness and affection" of women are kept alive, if not also generated, as phantoms of the same textual apparati entombing them and their voicings of the patriarchal crimes committed against them. Scattered here and there in the various burial grounds of early printed historical accounts, fictions, and dedicatory matter lie heterogeneous traces of female actors and textual *jouissance* which male authors and translators denied ever having lost or silenced. Through such phantom voices can be heard a vibrant literary tradition of altarbiography which has been systemically foreclosed, but therefore not, in the words of Freud, "totally impoverished," by the misogynistic principles of early traditions of authorship and printing.[40]

The staying power of this phantom tradition (perhaps this is the meaning of Montaigne's incorporated virile parts) is made further evident by a final example taken from Florio's epistle prefacing book 1. This epistle includes a complex autobiographical account which provides a fitting way to conclude this discussion. In directing his words to Lady Anne Harrington, Florio describes her ability to ease the burden of his passionate undertaking:

> when I with one Chapter found my selfe over-charged . . . your Honor having dayned to read it, without pitty of my failing, my

fainting, my labouring, my languishing, my gasping for some breath (O could so Honorable, be so pitty-lesse? Madame, now doe I flatter you?) Yet commaunded me on: (and let me die outright, ere I do not that commaund.) I say not you tooke pleasure at shore (as those in this Author) to see me sea-tosst, wether-beaten, shippe-wrackt, almost drowned. Nor say I like this mans Indian King, you checkt with a sower-sterne countenance the yerneful complaint of your drooping, neere-dying subject. Nor say I (as he alleadgeth out of others) like an ironically modest Virgin, you enduced, yea commaunded, yea delighted to see mee strive for life, yea fall out of breath. Unmercifull you were, but not so cruell. (Madame, now doe I flatter you?) Yet this I may and must say, like in this French-mans report, our third in name, but first and chiefe in fame, K. *Edward*, you would not succour your blacke, not sonne, but servaunt, but bade him fight and conquere, or die: Like the Spartan imperious Mother, a shield you gave me, but with this Word. *Aut cum hoc, aut in hoc.* (A2ᵛ-A3ʳ)

Following a familiar logic, Florio produces yet another allegory of the wounded autobiographical subject who droops near death from the crushing weight of labor and the breathless deprivation of conquest. Neither the Madame patron, the ironically modest Virgin, nor the Spartan imperious Mother (more traces of the triple Freudian mother) are said to bear the burden of the writing project. But while the cherished signs of black bile and melancholic genius grace the servant-son of culture, a curious, if not disturbing, mastery falls to the figure of the patronness. Some of this deference must be attributed to the ideology of the epistle. This is the genre, after all, that stages the master/slave nexus of patron and scribe while ironizing mastery with hyperbole and apostrophe—both made doubly flippant in this case by alliteration ("Madame, now doe I flatter you?").[41] Still, exceeding the historical relations of author and patron, this passage concludes with a cryptic reference to a tool which empowers the representation of altarbiography.

The figure privileged here is not the stylus of autobiography but the shield of the Spartan imperious Mother which, like the crypt of the East Indies or the Venus of the French, can harbor contradictory readings. The motto, "aut cum hoc, aut in hoc," most likely refers to the (castrating) warning with which Spartan mothers are reported to have sent their sons off to battle: "come home with your shield or on it."[42] Analogously, the shield of patronage and what lies *on* it may be said to encrypt an entirely different and antimetaphorical account of what lies *in* it. Looking back to Athens instead of Sparta, I am thinking of what is figured on/*in* the armor of Perseus, given to him by the imperious mother, Athena, as well as the historical dispute over its interpretation.

This tradition, which is the one embraced by Freud, reads the shield as the empowering emblem of patriarchy. It has come to represent not only the castration of Medusa and her sisters but also the subsequent virility of the sons of Perseus. While Freudian psychoanalysis appropriates the apotropaic effect as the essence of male sexuality, ancient medicine similarly derived its fiction of the self-sufficiency of the male seed from the origin myth of Athena, who was not of woman born.[43] Still, this same shield has begun to shine forth only recently in feminist theory and historiography as the phantom of "differend" accounts of its subject, Medusa.

Discounting Freud's equation, "to decapitate = to castrate," DuBois stresses accounts of the Gorgons in which the male phallic snake is subordinate to the female body: "Hesiod does not mention the petrifying power of the Medusa's look. . . . She mated with Poseidon in a meadow and gave birth from her severed head."[44] This is only one of the accounts of the Medusa's head as a source of birth rather than death which DuBois cites to support her claim that "the whole culture is concerned with this image of the mother who is parthenogenetic, like the earth, or who is androgynous, equipped with a snake/phallus. This mother is omnipotent, adequate in herself, not needing the male."[45] Feminist literary and film theorists no doubt will embrace DuBois's historical research in support of a different reading of Medusa brought back from the dead by Hélène Cixous, Teresa DeLauretis, and Christine Buci-Glucksmann. Albeit in differing ways, they have read the Medusa shield as preserving the memory of those contiguous but not univocal traces of a Medusa still smiling parodically at the silly notion of her castration. In Cixous's words, "You only have to look at the Medusa straight on to see her. And she's not deadly. She's beautiful and she's laughing."[46] If perceived straight on in the texts of Montaigne and Florio, the mocking phantom of the Medusa image can be seen glancing back in denial of Montaigne's motto of autobiothanatography, "the deadest deaths are best." As if celebrating heterogeneous, Baroque *jouissance*, the visual and textual matter of altarbiography confirms that "the best deaths live buried."

Notes

1. Michel de Certeau, "Montaigne's 'Of Cannibals,'" *Heterologies: Discourse on the Other*, trans. Brian Massumi (Minneapolis: University of Minnesota Press, 1986), 79.

2. Michel de Montaigne, *The Essayes or, Morall, Politike, and Militarie Discourses*, trans.

John Florio (London: Royston, 1632), 35. Unless otherwise noted, all subsequent citations of *The Essayes* will be from this, the third, edition of Florio's translation and will be cited in the text.

3. In "Mourning and Melancholia," *The Standard Edition of the Complete Psychological Works of Sigmund Freud*, ed. and trans. James Strachey (London: Hogarth Press, 1953–74), 14:245, Freud identifies the patient's inability to distinguish *what* has been lost as a significant feature of the ideal loss of melancholia: "one cannot see clearly what it is that has been lost, and it is all the more reasonable to suppose that the patient cannot consciously perceive what he has lost either. This, indeed, might be so even if the patient is aware of the loss which has given rise to his melancholia, but only in the sense that he knows *whom* he has lost but not *what* he has lost in him."

4. Ibid., 253.

5. For accounts of Baroque perspectival architectonics, see Walter Benjamin, *The Origin of German Tragic Drama*, trans. John Osborne (London: NLB, 1977); Jacques Lacan, "Du baroque," *Encore, le seminaire XX* (Paris: Seuil, 1975), 95–106; Louis Marin, *Le Portrait du Roi* (Paris: Minuit, 1981); Christine Buci-Glucksmann, *La Folie du voir: De l'ésthétique baroque* (Paris: Galilée, 1986); Hubert Damisch, *L'Origine de la perspective* (Paris: Flammarion, 1987); Gilles Deleuze, *Le Pli: Leibniz et le baroque* (Paris: Minuit, 1988); Timothy Murray, *Theatrical Legitimation: Allegories of Genius in Seventeenth-Century England and France* (New York: Oxford University Press, 1987); Christopher Pye, *The Regal Phantasm: Shakespeare and the Politics of Spectacle* (London: Routledge, 1990).

6. Louis Marin, "Montaigne's Tomb, or Autobiographical Discourse," trans. Geoff Bennington, *The Oxford Literary Review* 4, no. 3 (1981):46.

7. For superb readings of the relation of this passage to Montaigne's autobiographical project, see Marin, "Montaigne's Tomb," and Georges Van Den Abbeele, "Equestrian Montaigne," *Critical Displacements: The Economy of Travel in Early Modern French Philosophy*, forthcoming from the University of Minnesota Press.

8. Benjamin, *The Origin of German Tragic Drama*, 139.

9. In addition to Benjamin's *The Origin of German Tragic Drama* and Buci-Glucksmann's *La Folie du voir*, see Marie-Claude Lambotte's *Ésthétique de la mélancolie* (Paris: Aubier, 1984) for an interesting analysis of death and Baroque aesthetics. In *Detours of Desire: Readings in the French Baroque* (Columbus: Ohio State University Press, 1984), Mitchell Greenberg describes the extent to which death forces itself on Montaigne's writing: "In Montaigne's text Death, that nefarious Other, is incorporated into the structure of writing, into the living corpus of the text" (56). For other provocative readings of death in Montaigne, see Terence Cave, *The Cornucopian Text: Problems of Writing in the French Renaissance* (Oxford: Clarendon Press, 1979), 303–16; J. M. Blanchard, "Of Cannibalism and Autobiography," *Modern Language Notes* 93, no. 4 (May 1978):654–76; Antoine Campagnon, *Nous, Michel de Montaigne* (Paris: Seuil, 1980), 120–216; John O'Neill, *Essaying Montaigne: A Study of the Renaissance Institution of Writing and Reading* (London: Routledge & Kegan Paul, 1982), 100–38; Stephen Rendall, "The Weave of Voices," an unpublished chapter on "Que philosopher, c'est apprendre à mourir," in his book in progress on Montaigne.

10. Freud, "Mourning and Melancholia," 249–51.

11. See also Van Den Abbeele; Greenberg; and Irma S. Majer, "Montaigne's Cure: Stones and Roman Ruins," *Modern Language Notes* 97, no. 4 (May 1982).

12. On autobiography and phallologocentric loss in Montaigne, see Marin; Greenberg; Campagnon; Van Den Abbeele; Majer; Philippe Lacoue-Labarthe, "L'Écho du sujet," in *Le Sujet de la philosophie, typographies I* (Paris: Aubier-Flammarion, 1979), 217–303; Anthony Wilden, "Par divers moyens on arrive à pareille fin: A Reading of Montaigne," *Modern Language Notes* 83, no. 4 (May 1968): 577–97; and Tom Conley, "*De Capsula Totae*: Lecture de Montaigne, "De trois commerces," *L'Esprit Créateur* 38, no. 1 (Spring 1988).

13. Montaigne, *The Essayes or Morall, Politike and Millitarie Discourses,* trans. John Florio (London: Blount, 1603), A3r.
14. For helpful readings of Freud's analysis of the Medusa Head (decapitation = castration), see Louis Marin, *Détruire la peinture* (Paris: Galilée, 1977), 117–99; Neil Hertz, "Medusa's Head: Male Hysteria under Political Pressure," *The End of the Line* (New York: Columbia University Press, 1985), 161–92.
15. See Hélène Cixous, "The Laugh of the Medusa," trans. Keith and Paula Cohen, in Elaine Marks and Isabelle de Courtivron, eds., *New French Feminisms* (New York: Schocken Books, 1981), 245–64; Cixous, "Castration or Decapitation?" trans. Annette Kuhn, *Signs* 7, no. 1 (Autumn 1981): 41–55; Luce Irigaray, *Ce sexe qui n'en est pas un* (Paris: Minuit, 1977); Teresa de Lauretis, "Desire in Narrative," *Alice Doesn't: Feminism, Semiotics, Cinema* (Bloomington: Indiana University Press, 1984), 103–57; Page DuBois, *Sowing the Body: Psychoanalysis and Ancient Representations of Women* (Chicago: University of Chicago Press, 1988), 86–109.
16. Irigaray, "Le Marché des femmes," *Ce sexe qui n'en est pas un,* 167–85. For Julia Kristeva, "abjection" is woman's (only) symbolic condition: *Pouvoirs de l'horreur: Essai sur l'abjection* (Paris: Seuil, 1980) and *Soleil noir: Dépression et mélancholie* (Paris: Gallimard, 1987).
17. Nicolas Abraham and Maria Torok, *L'Écorce et le noyau* (Paris: Flammarion, 1987), 229–75, 393–433; Abraham and Torok, *Cryptonymie: Le verbier de l'homme aux loups* (Paris: Flammarion, 1976); Abraham, "The Shell and the Kernal," trans. Nicholas Rand, *Diacritics* 9, no. 1 (Spring 1979): 16–28; Abraham, "Notes on the Phantom: A Complement to Freud's Metapsychology," trans. Nicholas Rand, in Françoise Meltzer, ed., *The Trials of Psychoanalysis* (Chicago: University of Chicago Press, 1988), 75–80. Excellent overviews of Abraham and Torok are provided by Esther Rashkin, "Tools for a New Literary Criticism: The Work of Abraham and Torok," *Diacritics* 18, no. 4 (Winter 1988): 31–52, and Peggy Kamuf, "Abraham's Wake," *Diacritics* 9, no. 1 (March 1979): 32–43.
18. Abraham and Torok, "Deuil *ou* mélancolie: introjecter-incorporer," *L'Écorce et le noyau,* 266.
19. Ibid.
20. Ibid., 268.
21. In *"De Capsula Totae"* Conley provides a lead for a polysemic reading of "veines" as the writing marble, matter, of his textual monument: "Montaigne recèle et s'exhibe dans l'essai: Il creuse, façonne, et orne son tombeau" (18). I wish to add that I follow the lead, in this section, of Maria Torok, who discusses penis envy as the camouflaging *capsula totae* of *jouissance.* See Torok, "La Signification de 'l'envie du pénis' chez la femme," *L'Écorce et le noyau,* 132–71.
22. Montaigne, *Essays Written in French,* trans. John Florio (London: Blount and Barret, 1613), A3v.
23. Jacques Derrida, "Me—Psychoanalysis: An Introduction to the Translation of 'The Shell and the Kernel' by Nicolas Abraham," trans. Richard Klein, *Diacritics* 9, no. 1 (March 1979): 10–11. Nicholas Rand provides a theoretical discussion of translation and cryptonymy in "Lectures de la traduction: La drama baroque et les voies secrètes de l'histoire des lettres (Walter Benjamin)," *Le Cryptage et la vie des oeuvres* (Paris: Aubier, 1989), 51–73.
24. Tom Conley, "Institutionalizing Translation: On Florio's Montaigne," in Samuel Weber, ed., *Demarcating the Disciplines: Philosophy, Literature, Art,* Glyph Textual Studies 1 (Minneapolis: University of Minnesota Press, 1986), 48.
25. A very similar claim can be made, of course, for the texts of Montaigne (indeed for "écriture" per se). In *The Matter of My Book: Montaigne's "Essais" as the Book of the Self* (Berkeley: University of California Press, 1977), Richard L. Regosin, among others, stresses that "we must emphasize as well the many elements that undermine, postpone, and

make presence problematic [in the *Essais*]. Rather than being fully realized, it is continually deferred" (206). One of Montaigne's favorite staging grounds of deferral, self-conscious intertextuality, provides the focus for Steven Rendall's many rich studies of the *Essais*. See "The Weave of Voices"; "Reading Montaigne," *Diacritics* 15, no. 2 (Summer 1985):44–53; "Reading Faces (Montaigne)," in Manfred Frank and Anselm Haverkamp, eds., *Sonderdruck aus Individualität: Poetic und Hermeutik XIII* (Munich: Fink, 1988), 325–36; "The Portrait of the Author," *French Forum* 13, no. 2 (May 1988):143–51.

26. Of Montaigne, Greenberg, *Detours of Desire*, writes that "the act of translating, of moving from Latin to French, is a (failed) ritual passage for Montaigne. . . . As he writes Montaigne reproduces the echo of masculine alterity in various registers throughout the *Essais*. All the surrogate fathers whom he incorporates into his text—Seneca, Plutarch, Vergil, La Boétie—are metaphoric substitutes for that undefinable object of virility (perfection) that Montaigne pursues" (43).

27. Buci-Glucksmann, *La Folie du voir*, 95.

28. Irigaray, *Ce sexe qui n'en est pas un*, 15.

29. I should mention that, as is common with the plates of early printed books, the location of Florio's portrait varies from copy to copy. In a Cornell University Library copy, said to have belonged to King James, Florio's portrait does not appear until A6^v.

30. Paul de Man, "Pascal's Allegory of Persuasion," in Stephen J. Greenblatt, ed., *Allegory and Representation* (Baltimore: Johns Hopkins University Press, 1981), 1–25.

31. I am grateful to Ian Donaldson for suggesting that I emphasize the poetic convention of the "altar."

32. Sigmund Freud, "The Theme of the Three Caskets," *Complete Works*, 12:301.

33. Writing of the unresolved dichotomy in Montaigne between identity and difference, Wilden, "Par divers moyens," proposes that "Montaigne's melancholia is dependent upon the *jouissance* of something lost" (590).

34. Reflecting on the incommensurability of certain political discourses, Jean-François Lyotard, in *The Differend: Phrases in Dispute*, trans. Georges Van Den Abbeele (Minneapolis: University of Minnesota Press, 1988), chooses the word *différend* to signify "the case wherein the plaintiff is divested of the means to argue and becomes for that reason a victim. . . . A case of differend between two parties takes place when the 'regulation' of the conflict that opposes them is done in the idiom of one of the parties while the wrong suffered by the other is not signified in that idiom" (9).

35. Charles Martin Robertson and Herbert Jennings Rose, "Hera," in N. G. L. Hammond and H. H. Scullard, eds., *The Oxford Classical Dictionary* (Oxford: Clarendon Press, 1970), 497.

36. DuBois, *Sowing the Body*, 104.

37. Ibid., 107.

38. Ibid.

39. DuBois establishes a clear link between the historical representation of wives and slaves in *Centaurs and Amazons: Women and the Pre-History of the Great Chain of Being* (Ann Arbor: University of Michigan Press, 1982).

40. Complicating the argument of Cecile Insdorf, *Montaigne and Feminism* (Chapel Hill: North Carolina Studies in the Romance Language and Literatures, 1977), that Montaigne's texts assert the author's unequivocal misogyny, two interesting readings of Montaigne suggest how altarbiography might be scripted in the *Essais* themselves. In "Montaigne's Cure," Majer proposes that Montaigne's male journey to Rome figures as the vibrant substitute for a return to the womb and for the refiguration of "that person who is so conspicuously absent from Montaigne's life and works, his mother" (972). On a more general level, Greenberg, *Detours of Desire*, writes that "as 'feminine' textuality, Death inheres in Montaigne's writing in such a way as to shift the limits that define and order the

text on a thematic level and thus allows the *Essais* to exist both within and without those limits, which are no longer stable, taut, rigid, but become fluctuating and undulating textual margins" (56).

41. I discuss various aspects of seventeenth-century English and French epistolary and dedicatory literature in my book *Theatrical Legitimation*.

42. I wish to thank Gordon Teskey for calling this to my attention.

43. See Freud's essay, "Medusa's Head," *Complete Works*, 18:273–74. John Pinsent, in *Greek Mythology* (London: Hamlyn, 1969), explicitly links the birth of Athena to the development of the physiological theory of the self-sufficiency of the male seed (32). It is also important to note that the phrase "not of woman born" designates not only the ancient primacy given to the sperm but also the medieval and Renaissance tradition of Cesarean section. See Renate Blumenfeld-Kosinski, *Not of Woman Born: Representations of Caesarean Birth in Medieval and Renaissance Culture* (Ithaca: Cornell University Press, 1990).

44. DuBois, *Sowing the Body*, 89.

45. Ibid., 91.

46. Cixous, "The Laugh of the Medusa," 255.

Saints and Lovers: Mary Magdalene and the Ovidian Evangel

Debora Kuller Shuger
University of California, Los Angeles

I

THIS study will examine a long-forgotten strand of devotional literature, one originating in the late Middle Ages and retaining its widespread popularity through the early seventeenth century: the dramatization (or, alternatively, prosopopoeia) of the twentieth chapter of the Gospel according to John—the scene of Mary Magdalene at the tomb of Christ. Although this episode figures in patristic biography, the cycle plays, and saints' lives, only two versions—both dating from the late Middle Ages—and their subsequent permutations survive into the Renaissance. We may label these versions the "Chaucerian" and the "Origenist," since the former appears as part of the Chaucerian canon in every edition from 1532 through the early seventeenth century and the second is based on a sermon wrongly but consistently attributed to Origen.[1] There may have been some contamination between the two versions, since Chaucer himself, in the *Legend of Good Women*, mentions that he translated "Orygenes upon the Maudeleyne,"[2] evidence that the sermon was available in England by the late fourteenth century. The Chaucerian variant is composed in macaronic verse and has Mary herself speaking alone; these texts end before Mary's encounter with the risen Christ. The Origenist starts out as a sermon that slips into a dialogue among Mary Magdalene, the narrator-preacher, the angels, and Christ; that is, the narrator begins simply as an exegete but quickly becomes a character, interrogating Mary, expostulating with Christ, asking questions, and offering (often useless) advice; these generally use a rhythmic and schematic prose, although some late versions are written in doggerel.

The Chaucerian and Origenist texts, as well as the sermons,

poems, and commentaries based on these, continue to be published up through the first quarter of the seventeenth century. Thus the Chaucerian *Lamentation of Mary Magdalene* is reprinted seven times (as part of Thynne's edition of Chaucer) between 1532 and 1602. The anonymous *Complaynte of the Louer of Cryst Mary Magdaleyn* of 1620 seems virtually identical to this text. Origen's sermon has at least three English editions between 1504 and 1604, two in Latin and one (or perhaps two) in the vernacular. There are also several Continental translations of this piece. In addition, the pseudo-Origen is the basis for Southwell's *Marie Magdalens Funeral Teares,* which went through nine editions between 1591 and 1624, as well as for Cornelius à Lapide's *The Great Commentary* (the standard Tridentine compendium of biblical exegesis), Lancelot Andrewes's fourteenth Easter sermon, and Gervase Markham's *Marie Magdalens Lamentations* (1601).[3] What all these versions and variants are, however, is a recasting of the biblical narrative on the model of Ovid's *Heroides*—probably the most popular Ovidian work in the late Middle Ages.[4] The *Heroides,* in turn, constitute a female version of the rhetorical *suasoria,* an imaginary speech (letter) urging someone to do something—in this case, women who have been forsaken by their lovers, writing to them, pleading with them to come back. Along with the *Aeneid* (to which it is closely related), the *Heroides* are probably the most influential classical representations of female voice: of female desire and subjectivity articulated in contrast to and in competition with the male arena of heroic and tragic action (all their lovers are epic/mythological heros: Theseus, Achilles, Aeneas, and so forth). The Mary Magdalene narratives emerge out of the fusion of this highly eroticized Ovidian representation of abandoned females with the Song of Songs and the hagiographic tradition, producing a curious rapproachment of abandoned women and religious subjectivity.[5]

The influence of the *Heroides* drastically reshapes the medieval hagiographic accounts of the Magdalene. Her initial harlotry and repentance, which figure prominently in the cycle dramas and hagiographies, are barely mentioned in the Chaucerian and Origenist narratives; similarly, her subsequent miracles and evangelism, detailed in most medieval versions of her life, disappear in these accounts. Instead both the Chaucerian and Origenist versions deal exclusively with Mary's desolation at the tomb of Christ. In these, she exhibits the characteristic features of the abandoned women familiar from Vergil's Dido and Ovid's forsaken heroines. Unlike the masculine hero (Aeneas, Achilles, Jason) who acts, all she can do is weep: passive, frozen—in a word, maudlin. So Andrewes describes her: "Whose presence she wished for, *His* misse she wept for; whom she dearly loved, while she had *Him,* she bitterly bewailed, when she lost *Him. Amor amare flens,* Love running downe the cheekes."[6] In all the versions she simply stands at the tomb and decides to remain until she dies, when she hopes some bystander will wrap her in Christ's now-empty winding sheet.[7] She is, in fact, almost hysterical with grief: "dread and amazement have dulled her senses, distempered her thoughts, discouraged her hopes, awaked her passions, and left her no other liberty but onely to weepe."[8] She often exhibits a pathological obsessiveness, refusing to eat, sleep, move, talk. In Markham and Southwell she begins to hallucinate, imagining that Christ is before her, that she is embracing him and folding his feet in her arms.[9] She is frequently suicidal. This grief quite clearly is not religious despair in any theological sense but explicitly erotic; she is miserable because the man she loves is dead and even his body has disappeared. Her language borrows heavily from the vocabulary of romance heroines. In the *Complaynte,* for example, Mary refers to Christ as her "derlynge," her "peramoure," and she is his "lover";[10] the Latin version of the pseudo-Origen refers to her as his *amatrix* and *dilectrix.*[11] In Markham, she speaks of her "hearts hot desire," "deepest passion of true burning love," and "love-sicke heart."[12] The grief, passion, longing, confusion all come out in the pseudo-Origen's reweaving of Canticles. This is Mary thinking:

> But what may I do to finde him? whither shall I turne me? to whom shall I go? . . . who shall shew me whom my soul loveth, where he is bestowed, where he lieth at noontide? where he resteth? I beseche you tel him how I pyne with love and consume with sorowe . . . Turne againe my beloved, turn again my hartes desire and dearling.[13]

Repeatedly she pleads to touch him: to "amplect" his body, to die in the arms of his corpse, to wrap her body in his gravecloth.[14] Southwell thus imagines Mary carrying the body of Jesus "naked in thy armes" and the Resurrection as a sort of Venus and Adonis scene; the narrator thus addresses her: "if lying in thy lap, thou mightest have seene him revived, and his disfigured and dead body beautified in thy armes with a divine majesty."[15] Over and over she emphasizes her need for physical contact. In Markham she thus asserts:

> To see him therefore, doth not me suffice,
> To heare him doth not quiet whole my mind,

> To speake with him in so familiar wise,
> Is not ynough my loose-let soule to bind:
> No, nothing can my vehement love appease,
> Least by his touch my wo-worne heart I please.[16]

There is something macabre in the insistent physicality of her longing for the dead body, for the corpse. Again, the feelings expressed are not "religious"—she has no notion of the Resurrection; what she wants is at least the dead body of the man she loves. Moreover, like all abandoned women, she refuses to resolve eroticism into some sort of transcendence, whether of duty (Aeneas) or devotion (Dante). This refusal is made clear in Markham and Southwell: when Christ finally does come and tell her to announce the Resurrection to his disciples, this responsibility throws her into renewed hysterics. She is not particularly interested in being part of salvation history; she wants to stay with Jesus and touch him. Instead of moderating or sublimating either desire or grief, she insists upon the rightness of both. More surprisingly, she (and, in the Origenist texts, the narrator) comes very close to blaming Christ for her suffering. He, that is, assumes the lineaments of the faithless male—the necessary narrative counterpart to the abandoned woman—even though this is narratively incoherent since he is presumably dead and therefore not responsible for the disappearance of his body. Thus in the *Complaynte,* Mary cries: "Why suffrest thou me than to stonde alone, / Thou has I trowe my wepynge in dysdeyne"; so in Southwell, the narrator reproaches Christ: "why art thou so hard a Judge to so soft a creature, requiting her love with thy losse"; likewise in pseudo-Origen:

> O moste gentle Master, what hath this disciple since offended the? and wherein hath this thy dere lover displeased the kyndenes of thy heart, in that thou goest so from her? . . . If truly thou lovedst her after thy wonted manner, what meanest thou to prolonge her desire?[17]

Both the narrator and Mary try to understand what she might have done wrong, how she might be responsible for her own abandonment, yet both tend to shift the blame from Mary to Christ: he seems indifferent to her pain for no reason. In the conclusion of the Origenist narratives the story deviates from Ovid: Christ comes and with him abundant recompense. In the Chaucerian versions, he does not come—but we will get to this later.

The probable strategy of the learned reader at this point will be to defuse these narratives by attempting to read them allegorically, further insisting that to take the erotic situation here literally is to evince either historical ignorance or spiritual vulgarity. There is no question but that the Mary Magdalene narratives draw on the traditional allegorization of Canticles, but with a crucial difference. Allegories of Canticles resolve the surface eroticism into relationships between the soul or the Church and the glorified Christ; that is, into relations between incorporeal or abstract persons. Hence, the *locus classicus* of sacred eroticism, Bernard of Clairvaux's commentary on the Song of Songs, explicates the love between the bridegroom (Christ) and bride (soul/Church) in a way that radically differentiates spiritual desire from ordinary erotic relationships.

> But the bride—in what form or exterior loveliness, in what guise did St John see her coming down? . . . It is more accurate to say that he saw the bride when he looked on the Word made flesh, and acknowledged two natures in the one flesh. For . . . when we came to know the visible image and radiant comeliness of that supernal Jerusalem, our mother, revealed to us in Christ and by his means, what did we behold if not the bride in the Bridegroom?[18]

There is no possible literal/romantic reading of a relationship where the woman is the flesh of the man, as well as in some sense a city and a mother. Bernard consistently spiritualizes his erotic terminology, carefully distancing supernatural from romantic desire. At one point he thus imagines Christ speaking to the bride, who at this moment has coalesced with "the woman . . . [who was] forbidden to touch the risen flesh of the Word"—that is, Mary Magdalene:

> Become beautiful and then touch me; live by faith and you are beautiful. In your beauty you will touch my beauty all the more worthily, with greater felicity. You will touch me with the hand of faith, the finger of desire, the embrace of love; you will touch me with the mind's eye.[19]

This overt allegorization is not found in the exegeses of John 20 considered here. These depict a woman alone, waiting almost hopelessly for her dead and absent lover; their mode is not allegory but rhetorical romance, and thus susceptible of literal/erotic interpretation. Thus Calvin, who violently rejects the whole Ovidian exegesis of this passage, conflates it with the parallel scene in Luke, in which Mary comes to the tomb accompanied by two other women—apparently precisely to preclude any private encounter between this heterosexual couple in their early thirties.[20]

The eroticism resists allegorization and can only be removed by erasure. In both the Chaucerian and Origenist texts, Mary is a real woman interested in a conspicuously physical man. This realism does not divest the scene of spiritual implications, but it does thwart efforts to efface the letter under the proprieties of allegory. Instead, the generic conventions adopted in both versions accentuate the literal sense. Unlike the medieval exegesis of Canticles, which employs the conventional system of verse by verse commentaries, these versions of John 20 are either soliloquies or dialogues—that is, dramatic modes. There is, for example, a wonderful scene in Southwell where the narrator tries to convince Mary that she is behaving foolishly, and she just devastates him in reply. The exegete here becomes a character, the voice which traditionally read the allegory being subsumed into the letter of the fiction.

Moreover, especially in the Origenist texts, it is quite clear that a purely spiritualized reading is impossible. These works make explicit the epistemological basis of their eroticism, and this, put simply, is identical to the phantasmic psychology spelled out by Aristotle and thereafter characteristic of virtually all premodern epistemologies. According to this paradigm, desire and thought depend upon a process of imaging, for "the words of the soul's language are phantasms," and thus *"the phantasm has absolute primacy over the word."*[21] But if love requires images, then the physical/corporeal is a sine qua non of desire. As Mary says, Christ's image has been sculpted in her soul, and she needs his body to renew the image, enabling her love to endure; she is afraid of falling out of love if she cannot see and touch him.[22] Her grief is likewise a product of this phantasmatic psychology: her soul/image has been literally sucked into his body: "for the spirit of Mary was rather in thy body, then in her owne body, and when she eaftsones soughte for thy body, she did then also seeke for her own spirit: and when she lost thy body, she lost with it her own spirit."[23] She is in his corpse not in herself, and thus experiences the obsessive suffering and anxiety Culiano details in *Eros and Magic* where one is deprived of one's state as a subject, tortured by the absence of the Other who contains one's very self, desperately needing the Other—the body—to keep from collapsing into nothingness.[24] Christ's body therefore is not a metaphor or allegorical sign but essential to the opposition of presence and absence that governs these texts. She wants, as Southwell puts it, to have him "within her."[25]

One can see the link between eroticism and epistemology by

contrasting the pseudo-Origen with Calvin's commentary on John 20. Knowledge in Calvin is based on textuality rather than phantasms/images, on reading rather than seeing. This "inner iconoclasm," which becomes explicit in Ramus, replaces the "phantasmic essence of intellect" with a verbal/textual account of cognition. The earlier valorization of the tangible over the verbal is set in sharp relief in à Lapide's conservative Catholic commentary; when Mary hears Christ call her name, she interrupts him with "Rabboni," for, à Lapide notes, "she thought that having found the 'Word' she did not require a single *word* more, and she deemed it more profitable to touch the 'Word' than to hear any words whatever."[26] In Reformed theology, however, this preference for the body over the text is reversed. Since, according to Calvin, Mary and the other disciples had "abundantly clear testimonies" from Scripture for the Resurrection, they have no excuse for their grief and confusion. He thus brushes away Mary's weeping as "idle and useless." In this juridic, textualized epistemology, Mary's interest in "the dead body of Christ" is beside the point; it "leaves out the most important matter, the elevation of her mind to the divine power of his resurrection." She has "grovelling views" and an "earthly," "carnal" mind.[27] The risen Christ forbids her to touch him precisely because the lesson of this verse is that "all who endeavour to go to [Christ] must rid themselves of the earthly affections of the flesh."[28] As the text displaces Christ's body as the epistemic center, Mary's affection for the dead Christ becomes evidence of her carnality. That is, the shift from a phantasmic to a text-based epistemology accompanies and authorizes the familiar dualist oppositions of earthliness and elevation, carnality and spirituality. What seems surprising is the absence of such dualism in the Mary Magdalene narratives. In these there is no movement toward rising above the body, no transcendence. She desires nothing except this man, this body. She rejects heaven—or is totally indifferent to it. So in the pseudo-Chaucer she confesses:

> The joy excellent of blissed paradise,
> May me, alas! in no wise comforte,
> Song of angel nothing may me suffise
> As in min harte now to make disporte.[29]

In all the versions, she refuses even to speak to the angels when they show up at the tomb, despite the horrified urgings of the narrator. Her love undergoes no Platonic ascent—no moment when she realizes that her desires are misdirected or guilty or sinful; the erotic impulse is never spiritualized. She wants only Christ. Her (to use Calvin's phrase) carnal feelings should be seen in contrast not only to Protestant logocentrism but also, more generally, to narratives of male desire, which, as mentioned above, almost always either finally etherealize or abandon the object of erotic pursuit. In male narratives, one has the sense that the transformation or annihilation of eros forms the terrible yet liberating essence of the hero's *Bildung*. For this trajectory, female narratives (secular as well as Christian) substitute the stasis of passion—a *passio amoris* with strange affinities to the *passio crucis*.

II

In order to grasp that affinity, we need to investigate the implications of erotic abandonment as represented in these texts—trying to get at the significance both of the eroticism and the abandonment. The question of sacred eroticism seems particularly important because, lacking an adequate understanding of this, it might be hard to avoid the assumption that the language of religious desire merely articulates an imperfect sublimation of frustrated sexuality, even though it seems unlikely that the dominant metaphor for affective spirituality from Plato up to the early modern period would be a curiously overt admission of libidinal difficulties. In order to theorize such desire, however, we need to broaden our inquiry from the Magdalene narratives to the problem of sacred eroticism in general.

To ask why these texts represent spirituality in terms of sexual desire may be a misleading question, since it seems to assume that the forms of sexual desire are prior to and largely untouched by their cultural inflections, an assumption rendered dubious by much recent criticism.[30] With respect to sacred eroticism, such an assumption entails the problematic conclusion that religious persons somehow did not notice that their habitual imagery implicated their spirituality in the urges and impulses of the lower reaches of the body. This conclusion can be avoided by noting that the representation of sexual desire in the Middle Ages itself emerges from a theological matrix—the affective spirituality of Augustine and the twelfth-century Cistercians. That is, medieval secular eroticism (courtly love) is itself modeled on the analysis of spiritual longing, so that the latter is theoretically anterior to the former, rather than the reverse. Thus the medieval historian Nicholas Perella observes that

> The whole matter of yearning for the beloved, the restless longing for something superior to and beyond the immediate grasp of mortality, accompanied by the belief that it would, if possessed, bring an untold bliss and solace—this is at the very heart of troubadour love poetry; but all this was first at the very heart of Christian spirituality.[31]

To the extent that medieval sexuality is constructed out of the secularized materials of religious discourse, it need not be viewed as the repressed origin of sacred eroticism.

But this may not be an adequate answer. Even if Cistercian spirituality precedes troubadour poetry, insofar as the former uses erotic imagery it would seem still to bear the marks of only very partially repressed libidinal urges. In order to "get at" the significance of sacred eroticism it is helpful to begin at the other end and examine not the origins of the link between religious subjectivity and erotic desire but the reasons for its occlusion. In England, this has taken place by the early eighteenth century, as Pope's attempt at Christian Ovidianism makes evident. "Eloisa to Abelard" (1717) is, in fact, about the "pious fraud of am'rous charity" (l. 150),[32] about the *contamination* of religious devotion by erotic longing, where "erotic" has now become identical to "sexual." Eloisa's love for Abelard manifests itself in orgasmic swooning (ll. 271–76) and sexual phantasies (ll. 223–40). Whereas in the Mary Magdalene narratives, the saint's desire to see and touch her beloved remains undifferentiated from supernatural love, for Eloisa "all is not Heav'n's while *Abelard* has part" (l. 25). Eroticism, only half-concealed by her attempts at sublimation, muddies and corrupts the spiritual. That is, Pope's heroic epistle differs from the Mary Magdalene narratives because, by disclosing the bodily desires that filter up through the "pious fraud" of religious sublimation, it uncovers the mechanisms of repression that structure and subvert sacred eroticism.

The difference between Pope's epistle and earlier accounts of the relation between the erotic and the religious points to a major shift in the cultural history of the body, occurring sometime during the later seventeenth century. Put very simply, what happened was the discovery of genital sexuality—not that people learned how to make babies sometime around 1660, but for the first time one finds the assertion that sexual drives constitute the authentic substance of the erotic, other manifestations of desire (including religious ones) being sublimations of repressed genital urges. Before this, what Culiano observes of the Greeks seems generally applicable, namely, that "physical desire, aroused by the irrational soul and appeased by means of the body, only represents, in the phenomenology of love, an obscure and secondary aspect."[33] In the Middle Ages and Renaissance, physical desire generally provides the matter of bawdy or, interestingly, signifies *per synecdochen* the effects of Original Sin.[34] The identification of the erotic with physical desire, already apparent in Pope, emerges sometime after 1650.

The primary evidence for this shift is found in works on erotic and religious pathology but is supported by other cultural evidence as well. Before 1650, erotic desire is represented as a process originating in the desirable object (especially the eyes), which enters the erotic subject through his own eyes, traveling thence to the imagination or phantasy and finally dwelling in the heart. In romantic love, which is generally sexual, the trajectory is the same: from object to eye to imagination to heart, but finally in this case to the bowels or liver.[35] For Plato, love is an ocular disorder *(ophthalmia)*, or as Southwell puts it: "In true lovers every part is an eie, and every thought a looke."[36] For Burton, whose *Anatomy of Melancholy* conveniently summarizes two millennia of erotic speculation, love-melancholy "is a passion of the brain, as all other melancholy, by reason of corrupt imagination," most commonly originating in "sight, which conveys those admirable rays of beauty and pleasing graces to the heart."[37] The same model of what we may call "ocular eroticism" informs secular literature as well: one thinks of Wyatt's "Through mine eye the stroke from her did slide, / Directly down unto my heart it ran," or perhaps an even more pointed privileging of ocular over genital eroticism: "And if an eye may save or slay, / And strike more deep than weapon long."[38] The same psychology occurs in both Neoplatonic and Petrarchan contexts: in the "eye-sonnets" of Spenser and Sidney, in Bembo's peroration in *The Courtier,* in Shakespeare's "Tell me where is fancy bred" from *The Merchant of Venice.* It is perhaps needless to multiply examples, since the same ocular eroticism is presupposed by virtually every Renaissance writer. The movement of eros is always inward and down so that sexual desire is an inflection of erotic longing not its origin or essence; whereas in the model which privileges genital sexuality, movement takes place outward and up, via cathexis and sublimation.[39] Nor is there any reason to claim that a model which locates eros in the head and chest is merely a disguise or periphrasis for a libidinal one, since the bodily experience of eros, especially unhappy eros, has more to do with a constricted heart and upset stomach than any form of genital arousal.[40]

The ocular model entails that there is no inherent connection between genital and spiritual desire, nor is such a connection found in Renaissance treatments of religious pathology, where, if the libidinal-repression hypothesis were available, one would expect to find it. This is particularly noticeable in Burton, where the section on religious melancholy comes immediately after that on love melancholy, yet no relation (besides both being forms of melancholy) is established between the two. The only place where Burton does discuss sacred eroticism is in the opening of the chapters on religious melancholy where he lays out the nature of a *nonpathological* love of God. Here the language is suffused with erotic imagery drawn from Canticles and the Platonism of the church fathers: the "divine form" which is "the essence of all beauty . . . ravish[es] our souls"; Christ "woos us by His beauty, gifts, promises, to come unto Him; 'the whole Scripture is a message, an exhortation, a love-letter' "; his is " 'a divine beauty, an immortal love, and indefatigable love and beauty,' with sight of which we shall never be tired nor wearied, but still the more we see the more we shall covet Him."[41] The perversions of religion, however, do not emerge from this psychological matrix but rather—and this is wholly traditional—from diabolic malice, priestly greed, ignorance, fear, pride, ambition, and the Pope.[42] Interestingly, when Burton does turn to the physiological causes of spiritual pathologies, he never mentions celibacy but rather focuses on immoderate fasting and solitude.[43]

The shift from ocular to genital eroticism does not belong to the history of the secular/sexual body but rather to that of ecclesiastical politics. It originates as a form of ideological demystification (both demystifying sectarian ideologies and itself an ideology whose fundamental trope is demystification) in the Restoration critique of religious enthusiasm; it thus originates simultaneously with the disappearance of sacred eroticism from English religious discourse. The relocation of the erotic in the genitals and the link between sexual desire and spiritual excitement emerge together in the Cambridge Platonist, Henry More's, *Enthusiasmus triumphatus*, first published in 1656 and frequently thereafter. Like Burton, More diagnoses religious enthusiasm as a form of melancholy but relocates its seat from the brain to regions below the waist. Bodily fluids (and gasses) thus reverse the path of the ocular *species*, surging upward from the loins to the heart and finally the imagination, so that "the *Enthusiast* . . . being as it were drunk with new wine drawn from that Cellar of his own that lies in the lowest section of his Body, though he be not aware of it, but takes it to be pure *Nectar,* and those waters of life that spring from above."⁴⁴ Sacred eroticism is thus reconstructed as libidinal sublimation, for

> *Religious heat* in men, as it arises merely from Nature, is like *Aurum fulminans,* which though it flie upward somewhat, the greatest force when it is fired is found to goe downward.⁴⁵

Hence *"Enthusiastical Love"* arises from these "venereous fumes and vapours," from the "hidden and lurking fumes of *Lust.*"⁴⁶

The tendency to ground the erotic in genital sexuality manifests itself generally in the discourses of eroticism after the Restoration. That is, I take it, the point of Rochester's salacious lyricism or Pope's cave of spleen where "Maids turn'd Bottels, call aloud for Corks."⁴⁷ Of course, at least since *Astrophel and Stella,* the problematic relation of "Platonic" (or Petrarchan) eros to sexuality had been articulated but within the framework of the older ocular eroticism; Astrophel's surprise that "desire . . . so clingst" to his "pure love" only makes sense in a context where the erotic and sexual remain (conceptually) distinct.⁴⁸ The reconfiguration of the body first becomes explicit in More's *Enthusiasmus triumphatus,* precisely where it impinges on and problematizes sacred eroticism. This reconfiguration then circulates from the ecclesiological treatise to the literary satire in Swift's "Discourse Concerning the Mechanical Operation of the Spirit" and the sections on Aeolism in *A Tale of a Tub,* published together in 1704. These presuppose and extend More's thesis—that spiritual passions originate in scato-sexual vapors—for, as Swift puts it, "Persons of a Visionary Devotion, either Men or Women, are in their Complexion, of all others, the most amorous."⁴⁹ As in More, religious desire is a sexual pathology grounded in the physiology of libidinal ascent, that is, the reversion of sperm from the loins upward. Thus when, in *A Tale of a Tub,* Henry IV finds his intended mistress out of reach, "the collected part of the *Semen,* raised and enflamed, became adust, converted to Choler, turned head upon the spinal Duct, and ascended to the Brain."⁵⁰ The discourse of sacred eroticism is likewise anatomized, privileging, as it were, the phallic signifier, as in the case of the *"Saint* [who] felt his *Vessel* full *extended* in every Part (a very natural Effect of strong *Inspiration*)."⁵¹ Similarly, the "*Orgasmus* of their Spiritual exercise" culminates in its sexual correlative.⁵² For Swift, as for More, the critique of religious enthusiasm rests on the exposure of the libidinal origins of sacred eroticism, for "however Spiritual Intrigues begin, they generally conclude like all others; they may branch upward toward Heaven, but the Root is in the Earth."[53]

This mapping of the erotic body pathologized religious longing, since the incongruity between erotic desire and spirituality depends upon the location of the former in the genitals. This construct has become so familiar that it takes an effort to remember that it was virtually unavailable before 1660, but that unavailability constitutes the precondition for sacred eroticism. On the model of ocular eroticism, there exists no necessary physiological or affective difference between sacred and secular desire; each engenders the same sense of lack, the same longing, constriction of the heart, excited apprehension of beauty, alternations of joy and desolation, desire for presence, and lachrymose pain. Hence the language of romantic passion can articulate religious desires because the bodily/emotional experience of such desires are *like* those felt by, as it were, women in love. Furthermore, and this is Perella's point, this likeness at least in part results from the fact that the medieval representation of romantic passion is patterned after the discourse of spiritual longing in much the same way that the romantic "Platonism" of the Renaissance evolves from Plato's analysis of eros as a transcendent appetite for the permanent possession of the Good. It follows from this, it would seem, that identifying the eroticism of the Mary Magdalene narratives with some sort of displaced sexuality is as fallacious (from a historical point of view) as its scholarly erasure—and furthermore both strategies derive from the modern definition of the body as the sexual body.

Yet to note that before the middle of the seventeenth century (and much later in some milieus and genres) sexual and religious desire remain equally manifestations of erotic longing is too general an observation to account for the peculiar fusion of Ovidian and Canticles material characteristic of the Mary Magdalene narratives. In particular, it does not explain the significance of abandoned women for sacred eroticism or what cultural work may have been carried out by these texts, for although they are not, strictly speaking, allegorical, they are (like most cultural artifacts) symbolic.

III

In his recent *Abandoned Women and the Poetic Tradition*, Lawrence Lipking distinguishes two senses of abandonment: 1) forsaken by one's lover, but also 2) outside norms, conventions, respectability. Curiously (since these are "orthodox" religious works), both senses of abandonment characterize Mary Magdalene. That is, although her grief is passive, a sort of paralyzed weeping that finds no vent in action—and is therefore typically feminine—it also has a subversive edge, especially but not exclusively in Southwell's version. In all the variants, the intensity of Mary's love and grief pushes her toward disregard of hierarchy and authority, especially in the scene where the angels address her, and she refuses to answer them. In Origen she reflects, "Do they therefore question with mee, to let me from wepinge? I beseche them, not to swade me to that.... What needes mo wordes? I will not obey them."[54] The narrator in Origen is shocked by her defiance, by the fact that she is not honored or pleased by the angels' attention. Yet the paternalist narrator who tries to normalize her response fades and shrinks beside her passion. The exchanges between the conservative male narrator and the transgressive female disciple are particularly vivid in Southwell, who, as a Jesuit in Elizabethan England, may have had more sympathy with transgression than most. The narrator tries to dissuade Mary from attempting to find the body by accusing her of stepping outside the norms of morality and decency; if she tries to reclaim the body she will become a thief. To this she responds with indignation that she would be happy to be a thief or anything else for her lover's sake, and furthermore that her love justifies her transgression of moral rules.

> And if no other meane would serve to recover him but force, I see no reason why it might not very well become me.... O Judith lend me thy prowesse for I am bound to regard it.... But suppose that my force were unable to winne him by an open enterprise, what scruple should keepe mee from seeking him by secret meanes: yea and by plaine stealth[.] It wil be thought a sinne, and condemned for a theft. O sweete sinne why was not I the first that did commit thee? ... If this be so great a sinne, and so heinous a theft, let others make choice of what titles they will: but for my part I would refuse to be an Angel, I would not wishe to be a Saint ... if I might both live and die such a sinner, and be condemned for such a theft.[55]

She accepts abandonment—her own lawlessness and freedom. And her passion silences the narrator. The "male" voice of reason, hierarchy, decorum, and law is mocked and silenced by Mary Magdalene's anguish.

Lipking identified two senses of abandonment, as mentioned above. But there is also a third sense or connotation: the association of abandonment with Christ's lonely suffering on the Cross. And to the extent that the text allows this meaning to emerge, it implicitly associates the figures of the abandoned woman and dying savior, erotic passion and Christ's passion. And this is in fact what happens. Both the Origenist and Chaucerian variants identify the sufferings of Mary and Jesus by the same typological maneuver, although the Chaucerian versions develop the equation much more fully. The connection is always made by putting in Mary's mouth biblical phrases associated with the crucifixion. In all the versions Mary thus claims that "there is no dolor as is my dolor," or in the Latin, "nec est dolor sicut dolor meus"[56]—a quotation of the christological passage in Lamentations. The allusion thus claims a parity of suffering. It also seems to suggest that the sorrows of abandoned women are not of less weight than the adventures of the men who leave them. Mary and Jesus enact the same passion play.

This linkage is spelled out in the Chaucerian *Lamentation* and its poetic offspring, the anonymous *Complaynte*. Both of these end *before* Mary identifies the gardener; they conclude rather with a long, elegiac and pathetic farewell song addressed to her absent lover, which ends:

> My soule for anguysshe is now full thrysty
> I faynt ryght sore for hevynesse
> My lorde, my spouse Cur me derelinquisti
> Syth I for the suffer all this dystresse
> What causeth the to se me thus mercylesse
> Syth the it pleseth of me to make an ende
> In manus tuas My spyrtye I commende.[57]

Mary Magdalene and Christ here coalesce. This kind of identification involves rather more than the conventional *imitatio Christi*. By appropriating these words and gestures—this time a woman addressing her lover rather than the Son pleading with his Father—she makes her own desolation equal to Christ's, at the same time casting Christ in the role of the now distant and indifferent lover and herself as the voice of exiled and suffering humanity. Not only does human pain parallel Christ's passion, it seems to supplant it. Even in the versions where Christ does come, and all Mary's pain is soothed, the suspicion always remains that the man is being thoughtless or insensitive by staying away for so long; it is the woman left behind who bears the helpless pain of longing and forsakenness. In other words, the theological "solution" of the Augustinian-Calvinist tradition, which justifies God by blaming man, is here problematized.[58] This time, it is not the lady who is culpable but—at least hypothetically—her Lord. The texts will not allow the metamorphosis of human pain into guilt and punishment. The narrator tries to blame Mary for her dereliction but fails; she likewise attempts to locate her pain in some fault of her own but finally denies her guilt. She becomes, instead, simply an abandoned woman, or as the narrator in the pseudo-Origen tells her, "he whom thou sekest semeth to set nought by thy sorowinge, he semeth not to regarde thy teares. Thou calleste him, and he heareth not."[59] She is the one who has been forsaken, not Christ—and so the narrative focus and authorial sympathy shift from the Lord to the lady. This is sentimental and subversive realism.

The term *subversive* implies some notion of the authorship, audience, and function of a text, and here we have to be careful. Since the primary texts are anonymous, one cannot absolutely rule out female authorship. Yet, since they are all addressed to men, it seems unlikely, despite Skeat's comment on the *Lamentation* that "this lugubrious piece was probably the wail of a nun, who had no book but a Vulgate version of the Bible."[60] For example, Origen concludes by remarking that "sinfull man" should learn of a "sinfull woman"; similarly Southwell: "Learne O sinfull man of this once a sinfull woman."[61] These are stories about forsaken women for male use. They exemplify the "deeply ingrained tendency of all men in the ancient [and Renaissance] world, to use women 'to think with.'"[62] It is important to note, however, that the explicit "function" of Mary Magdalene in these texts is rather different from that of most female symbols, who are almost always objects, even if infinitely valuable objects—whether abstractions (Dame Nature, Lady Philosophy) or ideals (Beatrice, Stella, Laura). Mary Magdalene is an exemplary figure but in a curious way: she is not the goal of the quest but lost in the forest along with everyone else. That is, she supplies a model of suffering, solitary, forsaken humanity. She is neither Madonna nor Whore but a figure for all that is marginalized, powerless, solitary, unhappy; as she says in Southwell: "poore I [am] left alone to supplie the teares of all creatures."[63] This should not be surprising since most societies symbolize forsakenness and loss of love as female; to be abandoned means to be female, and therefore when a man wishes to write about his own abandonment, he writes as a woman or about a woman.[64] "*Madame Bovary, c'est moi.*"

But what sort of abandoment? The Mary Magdalene texts are popular devotional works articulating the fundamental spiritual anxiety of the Reformation period—anxieties centering on desolation and the absence of God.[65] But "Reformation period" is too vague. Although both the Chaucerian and Origenist versions are late medieval works, after the Reformation they seem specifically connected to Catholic and Anglo-Catholic piety: Cornelius à Lapide, Southwell, Lancelot Andrewes. Protestant writers like Calvin, Lewis Wager, Thomas Robinson, and Henry Smith (the latter three of whom wrote, respectively, a play, poem, and sermon on the Magdalene) reject or ignore this material. This confessional difference points to the specific theological function of the Magdalene texts considered here. Mary does not believe in the Resurrection; she thinks Christ is dead. Nevertheless, because she loves him, she is made first witness to the risen Christ and apostle to the apostles. She is justified despite her lack of faith. That is, these texts critique the Protestant doctrine of justification by faith and the concomitant fear that disbelief implies reprobation. They are pastoral works, designed to relieve such fears by affirming that love, even without faith, is sufficient. This undercurrent is, not surprisingly, most explicit in the versions written after the Reformation. Andrewes's sermon thus begins, "She loved much: we cannot say, Shee beleeved much. For . . . it seemes, shee beleeved no more, than just as much as the High Priests would have had the world beleeve, that *He was taken away by night*." But he concludes quoting Saint Bernard: "*Domine, amor quem habebat in Te, et dolor quem habebat de Te, excuset eam apud Te, si forte erravit circa Te:* That the love she bare to Him, the sorrow shee had for Him, may excuse her with Him, if she were in any error concerning Him."[66] So Southwell's narrator, after repeatedly attempting to pinpoint what Mary has done wrong, confesses (somewhat grudgingly):

> I cannot say thou art faultlesse, sith thou art so lame in thy beliefe: but thy fault deserveth favor, because thy charity is so great, and therefore O mercifull Jesu, give me leave to excuse whom thou art minded to forgive.

In the end, even he admits to her that "the Angels must still bathe themselves in the pure streams of thy eies."[67]

In addition, the Magdalene narratives concern the *body* of Christ, that is, the real presence. Their emphasis on Christ's body is eucharistic as well as erotic—or rather both at once. This is particularly clear in Southwell; his narrator thus addresses Christ:

> Doe not sweet Lord any longer delay her. Behold shee hath attended thee these three daies, and shee hath not what to eate, nor wherewith to foster her famished soule, unlesse thou by discovering thy selfe doest minister unto her the bread of thy body, & feede her with the foode, that hath in it all taste of sweetnesse.[68]

The analogy, one notes, works both ways: the longing for the real presence of Christ discovers itself as erotic desire and simultaneously this desire for corporeal touch tropes sacramental theology.

These theological readings seem consistent with Stephen Greenblatt's Althusserian treatment of subversion and containment, since the Magdalene texts indicate that (just as carnivals and stage plays were liscenced by the authorities) doubt, female desire, and transgressive excess may be "contained" and authorized within the dominant culture that prohibits them. In his prefatory epistle, Southwell states that the purpose of the Magdalene narratives is to teach men to "draw this floud of [erotic] affections into the righte chanel." Passion, that is, rather than being repressed is to be redirected on to religious objects. Religion functions as a sanctioned locus for certain needs which cannot be met within the social realm, particularly erotic and masochistic desires. Hence rather than reduplicating the sociopolitical disciplines of civility, religion supplements (in the Derridean sense) them, simultaneously providing a "safe house" for women and keeping them off the streets. But furthermore, this containment is not merely negative, merely the depoliticization and mystification of female desire, but also implicated in the structuring of subjectivity in the early modern period—that is, in the discursive formation of inwardness as erotic, transgressive, abandoned, and female: the inwardness of Donne's *Holy Sonnets* as well as *Clarissa*. (Molly Bloom, *c'est moi*.) To the extent that Renaissance ideology installs subversive impulses in the center of religious subjectivity, the practices of piety are central—as central, let us say, as courtesy manuals or penal disciplines—to the economy and organization of Renaissance selfhood.

Lisa Jardine is therefore mistaken in her claim that "female sexuality (personified in Mary Magdalene, the anti-type of Mary, mother of Christ) negates all those attributes which bring women closer to the ideal model."[69] The sacred eroticism of Mary Magdalene suggests that female sexuality, like female transgression, although proscribed as cultural praxis, inhabits an "ideal model" of religious subjectivity, which leads one to suspect that there exists an inverse relation between the interior gendering of the subject and the gendering of social codes, rules specifying sex-typed behaviors being more rigid as the interior sexing of the self remains ambiguous/androgynous. Although this formula may be oversimplified, it still points to a real need to account for the work done by religion in the cultural economy of the Renaissance, which in part involves complicating the relations between the cultural and the social. "That women might not be objects but subjects, not the other but the self"—what Stephen Orgel has called the age's "greatest anxiety" seems nevertheless implicit in a strain of late medieval piety that remains in circulation through the middle of the seventeenth century, for the specter of female desire is also the structure of religious (and male) subjectivity. Even up to the middle of the eighteenth century—and I am thinking of Bach's cantatas now—the voice of the soul is always soprano.

Notes

1. A fourteenth-century manuscript version is probably more accurate in crediting it to Bonaventure. Its realism, sentimentality, and proto-Euphuistic Latin suggest a Franciscan source. Cf. Pierre Janelle, *Robert Southwell: The Writer* (New York: Sheed & Ward, 1935), 184.

2. Geoffrey Chaucer, *The Legend of Good Women*, Text G, 1.418, in *The Works of Geoffrey Chaucer*, ed. F. N. Robinson, 2d ed. (Boston: Houghton Mifflin, 1957), 493.

3. General surveys of Magdalene material can be found in Helen Meredith Garth's *Saint Mary Magdalene in Medieval Literature* (Baltimore: Johns Hopkins University Press, 1950) and John James McDermott's "Mary Magdalene in English Literature from 1500 to 1650" (Ph.D. diss., University of California, Los Angeles, 1964).

4. Lawrence Lipking, *Abandoned Women and Poetic Tradition* (Chicago: University of Chicago Press, 1988), 35; Heinrich Dörrie, "L'Épitre héroïque dans les littératures moderns," *Revue de Littérature Comparée* 40 (1966):48–64.

5. On the fusion of Ovid and Canticles in the Middle Ages, see Nicholas James Perella, *The Kiss Sacred and Profane: An Interpretative History of Kiss Symbolism and Related Religio-Erotic Themes* (Berkeley: University of California Press, 1969), 115.

6. Lancelot Andrewes, *Sermons*, ed. G. M. Story (Oxford: Clarendon Press, 1967), 198.

7. In pseudo-Chaucer, however, at one point she decides to flee into the wilderness and become a hermit—the basis of the most familiar visual representations of the Magdalene, i.e., the penitent Magdalene. This pictorial genre (based on medieval legend) tends to incorporate the same combination of sensuality and devotion characteristic of the Chaucerian and Origenist narratives.

8. Robert Southwell, *Mary Magdalens Funeral Teares (1591)* (Delmar, N.Y.: Scholars' Facsimiles, 1975), 8; cf. Gervase Markham, *Marie Magdalens Lamentations* (1601), C4r. Hereafter cited as Southwell or Markham. I have modernized the i/j and u/v orthography of the quotations throughout.

9. Markham, G3r; Southwell, 64.

10. *The Complaynte of the Louer of Cryst Mary Magdaleyn* (ca. 1620), 8, 18–19.

11. *Omelia origenis de beata Maria Magdalena* (London, 1504), n.p.
12. Markham, B2ᵛ, C3ʳ.
13. *An Homilie of Marye Magdalene, declaring her fervent loue and zele towards CHRIST: written by that famous clerke ORIGENE* (1565), B6ʳ.
14. Markham, B2ʳ; Southwell, 17–18; pseudo-Chaucer, *The Lamentation of Mary Magdalene*, in *Poetical Works of Geoffrey Chaucer*, ed. Robert Bell, 4 vols., rev. ed. (London: Bell, 1886), 4:413.
15. Southwell, 54. The two narratives may be connected. One of Titan's Mary Magdalene's also derives for a bas-relief of Venus and Adonis.
16. Markham, Gᵛ; cf. Southwell, 61.
17. *Complaynte*, 17; Southwell, 11; pseudo-Origen (1565), A8ʳ–B1ʳ; cf. pseudo-Chaucer, 4:398, 410.
18. Bernard of Clairvaux, *On the Song of Songs II*, trans. Kilian Walsh OSCO, 4 vols., (Kalamazoo, Mich.: Cistercian Publications, 1976), 3:80, sermon 27,7.
19. Bernard, 3:95–96, sermon 28, 9–10.
20. John Calvin, *Commentary on the Gospel according to John*, trans. William Pringle, 2 vols. (Grand Rapids, Mich.: Eerdmans, 1956), 2:254.
21. Ioan P. Culiano, *Eros and Magic in the Renaissance*, trans. Margaret Cook (Chicago: University of Chicago Press, 1987), 4–5, 39–40.
22. Southwell, 3; Markham, C3ᵛ, C4ᵛ; pseudo-Origen (1565), A4ʳ.
23. Pseudo-Origin (1565), C2v; Markham, C4r; Southwell, 6; Cornelius à Lapide, *The Great Commentary*, trans. Thomas Mossman, 10 vols., 3d ed. (London: Hodges, 1892), 8:261.
24. Culiano, *Eros*, 31–32.
25. Southwell, 13.
26. à Lapide, 8:262.
27. Calvin, *Commentary*, 2:253–60. But Calvin's criticism of Mary's disbelief in the Word, evinced by her desire to see and touch her Lord, has been anticipated in Bernard, 3:95, sermon 28, 8; see also Ambrose, cited in à Lapide, 8:259.
28. Calvin, *Commentary*, 2:259.
29. Pseudo-Chaucer, 4:404.
30. See, for example, Thomas Laqueur, "Orgasm, Generation, and the Politics of Reproductive Biology," *Representations* 14 (1986):1–41; Caroline Bynum, "The Body of Christ in the Later Middle Ages: A Reply to Leo Steinberg," *Renaissance Quarterly* 39 (1986):399–439.
31. Perella, *The Kiss*, 85. For the purposes of this argument, it does not much matter whether the theological origins of courtly love be traced to Christian, Gnostic, or Arabic mysticism, the latter two positions being held by Denis de Rougemont, *Love in the Western World*, trans. Montgomery Belgion (New York: Pantheon, 1956) and Culiano, *Eros*, 16–18, respectively. What is significant in each case is the conceptual priority granted to the representation of spiritual experience in the formation of discourses of secular eroticism.
32. *The Poems of Alexander Pope*, ed. John Butt (London: Methuen, 1963). Line numbers will be cited in the text.
33. Culiano, *Eros*, 4.
34. Shakespeare's sonnets to the young man are thus, by and large, about eros/love/longing; his dark lady sonnets, in contrast, concern sexuality, guilt, and carnality.
35. Robert Burton, *The Anatomy of Melancholy*, ed. Holbrook Jackson (New York: Dutton, 1977), 2.86.
36. Culiano, *Eros*, 30; Southwell, 12.
37. Burton, *Anatomy*, 2.58, 65.
38. Sir Thomas Wyatt, in *Silver Poets of the Sixteenth Century*, ed. Gerald Bullett (London: Dent, 1947), 25, 37.

39. Although the alternative may not have been strictly an "unthinkable thought" in the Renaissance—a notion intelligently criticized by Richard Levin, "Unthinkable Thoughts in the New Historicizing of English Renaissance Drama," *New Literary History* 21 (1990):433–47. Burton thus cites someone's opinion that love melancholy may be due to excess semen, but he also dismisses it. The question is not whether some thoughts were "thinkable" or not, but their cultural functions and structural position within a conceptual system.

40. The identification of the bodily with the sexual organs seems problematically implicit in some feminist attempts to link gender and writing, which assume that gendered selfhood originates in and is modeled on the secretions and tumescences of genitals.

41. Burton, *Anatomy*, 2.314–15.

42. Ibid., 2.325–40.

43. Ibid., 2.343, 397. The same basic analysis reappears in Meric Casaubon's digressive hodgepodge, *A Treatise Concerning Enthusiasme* (1655) (Gainesville: Scholars' Facsimiles, 1970), which diagnoses its subject as a form of melancholy or "depravation of the Understanding, as well as of the Imagination," caused perhaps by the devil or ambition (52, 114–17, 130).

44. Henry More, *Enthusiasmus triumphatus*, The Augustan Reprint Society 118 (Berkeley: University of California Press, 1966), 12. Note that the path of this "new wine" traces that of semen (thought to originate in the brain, descending down the spinal column) in reverse.

45. Ibid., 17.

46. Ibid., 28, 37. The discovery of genital eroticism seems related to the simultaneous substitution of sexual wrongdoing for ambition and pride in the representation of evil; as desire is traced to its sexual origin, Lovelace replaces Faustus and Iago.

47. Alexander Pope, *The Rape of the Lock*, 4.54, in *Poems of Alexander Pope*.

48. Sir Philip Sidney, *Astrophel and Stella*, 1. 72; cited from *Silver Poets of the Sixteenth Century*, 199.

49. Jonathan Swift, *A Tale of a Tub to which Is Added The Battle of the Books and The Mechanical Operation of the Spirit*, ed. A. C. Guthkelch and D. Nichol Smith, 2d ed. (Oxford: Clarendon Press, 1958), 287.

50. Ibid., 164–65.

51. Ibid., 281.

52. Ibid., 288.

53. Ibid.

54. Pseudo-Origen (1565), B6^v–B6^r; cf. Andrewes, 205.

55. Southwell, 41–42.

56. Pseudo-Origen (1565), B6^r, pseudo-Origen (1504), n.p.; pseudo-Chaucer, 4:412.

57. *Complaynte*, 24; cf. pseudo-Chaucer, 4:415.

58. Hans Blumenberg, *The Legitimacy of the Modern Age*, trans. Robert M. Wallace (Cambridge: MIT Press, 1983), 133–35. Note the curious similarity to Chaucer's treatment of the Griselda story, where the original allegory in which Walter figures God and Griselda stands for humankind (or Christian obedience) is suddenly rejected because the narrative justifies Griselda at the expense of Walter, who becomes the cruel and tormenting male.

59. Pseudo-Origen (1565), A7^r. So in Southwell the narrator tells Mary, "Thou hast hitherto sought in vaine, as one either unseene, or unknown, or at the least unregarded, sith the party thou seekest, neither tendereth thy teares, nor aunswereth thy cries, nor relenteth with thy lamentings. Either he doth not heare, or he will not helpe, he hath peradventure left to love thee, and is loath to yeelde thee reliefe" (8–9).

60. Walter W. Skeat, ed., *Chaucerian and Other Pieces* (Oxford, 1897), xi.

61. Pseudo-Origen (1565), C6^r; Southwell, 67; cf. Markham, H2^v.

62. Peter Brown, *The Body and Society: Men, Women, and Sexual Renunciation in Early Christianity* (New York: Columbia University Press, 1988), 153.

63. Southwell, 22.
64. See Lipking, *Abandoned Women*, passim.
65. This sense of desolation is movingly articulated by Southwell's Mary: "Alas O my onely desire, why hast thou left me wavering in these uncertainties, and in how wilde a maze wander my doubtfull and perplexed thoughts?" (16).
66. Andrewes, *Sermons*, 196, 211; cf. à Lapide, 8:259.
67. Southwell, 48, 57. Southwell makes this motif explicit in his dedicatory epistle, commenting "and if her weaknes of faith, (an infirmity then common to all Christes disciples) did suffer her understanding to be deceived, yet was her will so setled in a most sincere and perfect love, that it ledde all her passions with the same bias, recompensing the want of beliefe, with the strange effectes of an excellent charity."
68. Ibid., 55–56.
69. Lisa Jardine, *Still Harping on Daughters: Women and Drama in the Age of Shakespeare* (Sussex: Harvester Press, 1983), 77.